PRAEGER LIBRARY OF U.S. GOVERNMENT DEPARTMENTS
AND AGENCIES

The Atomic Energy Commission

PRAEGER LIBRARY OF U.S. GOVERNMENT DEPARTMENTS
AND AGENCIES

Consulting Editors

ERNEST S. GRIFFITH

Former University Professor and Dean Emeritus, School of International Service, American University; former Director, Legislative Reference Service, Library of Congress; and author of *The American System of Government; The Modern Government in Action;* and two volumes in *A History of American City Government: The Conspicuous Failure, 1870–1900;* and *The Progressive Years and Their Aftermath, 1900–1920*

HUGH LANGDON ELSBREE

Former Chairman, Department of Political Science, Dartmouth College; former Managing Editor, *American Political Science Review;* former Director, Legislative Reference Service, Library of Congress

THE U.S. GOVERNMENT today is a maze of departments and agencies engaged in a worldwide range of programs and activities. Some departments are as old as the government itself; others are newly created or have been expanded or redirected by recent legislation. The books in this series describe the origin, development, function, methods, and structure of specific departments or agencies and explain how far their activities extend and how they relate to other branches of the government and to the public. All are written by authors with firsthand knowledge of their subjects.

The *Praeger Library of U.S. Government Departments and Agencies* is the only comprehensive, detailed source of such information. A list of those titles already published appears at the back of this volume.

—THE EDITORS

The Atomic Energy Commission

Corbin Allardice
and
Edward R. Trapnell

PRAEGER PUBLISHERS
New York · Washington

Published in the United States of America in 1974
by Praeger Publishers, Inc.
111 Fourth Avenue, New York, N.Y. 10003

© 1974 by Praeger Publishers, Inc.

Library of Congress Cataloging in Publication Data

Allardice, Corbin.
  The Atomic Energy Commission.

  (Praeger library of U.S. Government departments and agencies,
no. 42)
  Bibliography: p. 227.
  1. United States. Atomic Energy Commission. I. Trapnell, Edward
R., joint author. II. Title.
HD9698.U52A63   353.008'55   76-122088
ISBN 0-275-55460-1

This book is No. 42 in the series
Praeger Library of U.S. Government Departments and Agencies

Printed in the United States of America

To
Henry DeWolf Smyth

One Author's Note

By Edward R. Trapnell

This prefatory note is in response to the publisher's interest in the background of our qualifications for saying some of the things we have said in this book. It will also serve to flag for the reader the unusual nature of our writing partnership, particularly the difficulty under which Corbin Allardice works.

Completion of this manuscript late in 1972 marks another job that Corb, as he is known to friends, and I have worked on together in the field of atomic energy over a period of more than a quarter century, the last five years of which involved the writing of this book on the U.S. Atomic Energy Commission. Our association in behalf of public understanding and support of nuclear development predates the Commission by half a year.

In the spring of 1946, when we joined the staff of Major General L. R. Groves, commanding the Manhattan Project, we were Johnny-come-latelies to the organization, which, behind a barrier of wartime secrecy, had carried out the unprecedented $2 billion research, development, engineering, construction, manufacturing, test, and military deployment effort that produced the atomic bomb. The paths by which we came by our still unsatisfied interest in things nuclear were quite different, but it now seems foreordained that our paths should cross. We had traversed the common ground of technical education, Corb's in mathematics at

New Jersey's Seton Hall and mine in electrical engineering at the Virginia Military Institute.

Entering college a decade later than I, Corb had the advantage of texts covering the advances in physics through the 1930's, but he really learned his nuclear physics from the Smyth Report—the official account of the wartime project—which he mastered on his wedding trip. His wife Kay, then an NBC audience measurement specialist, has often reminded him with good effect and good humor of the hours he spent studying Smyth on his honeymoon. Corb, a Coast Guard pilot with hundreds of hours on Atlantic submarine patrol, had been steered into the Manhattan Project by one of General Groves's legal and intelligence advisers, Colonel William A. Consodine, who before the war had taught Corb journalism. Corb had been managing editor and columnist of the student newspaper at Seton and had shown a deep interest in the physical sciences.

My own introductory lesson in modern nuclear physics— aboard the S.S. *Marina* in a World War II convoy across the Atlantic—was by Dr. Arthur Vance of RCA Laboratories, designer of a new piece of antiaircraft fire control equipment, which I, as an Army Ordnance officer, was taking to the European Theater of Operations for combat tests. The lesson was by way of explanation for a month's delay in our originally scheduled departure. The Manhattan Project, with a higher priority, had preempted some critical electronic components ordered for our equipment. The original explanation of the Manhattan Project given me was a cover story by my brother, Holmes, a Du Pont engineer, who had told me when we met in Chicago in November, 1942, that he was there in connection with a research project at the Metallurgical Laboratory of the University of Chicago on a process for making nylon out of natural gas. The story satisfied me until I heard Dr. Vance's explanation. Our European combat tests were completed in the spring of 1945, but tests planned for the Pacific theater were canceled after the atomic bomb had been used in Japan.

Arthur Vance was one of many scientists who knew of the nuclear weapon development effort, not despite wartime secrecy but because of it. He had to be told the secret so he could protect it. Nonscientists were told too. One of these was Jack Lockhart, assistant deputy director of the U.S. Office of Censorship, who had been my competitor in the news business in Memphis. After the war, Lockhart was a consultant to the War Department Bureau of Public Relations and recommended me for a position as General Groves's civilian public relations adviser. That was in May, 1946, and Allardice joined me within a month.

Corb and I quickly fell into harness as a writing team. We worked closely with Dr. Walter H. Zinn on the public documentation for postwar conversion of the Metallurgical Laboratory to Argonne National Laboratory, and similarly helped Dr. Norris Bradbury with the changeover of the Los Alamos weapons center to the Los Alamos Scientific Laboratory. We persuaded General Groves to ban the use of industrial contractors' names on government-owned facilities. We did a report for General Groves on the first postwar year of his custody of the atomic energy project. On the basis of the Smyth Report and Allardice's interviews with the scientists who took part in the first chain reaction experiment, we wrote the "First Pile" story, which William L. Laurence, later science editor of the *New York Times,* said was the first government press release ever used verbatim by his paper.

These small successes were damped by difficulties stemming from General Groves's role in the fight over civilian control of the atom. When transferred to the newly formed civilian Atomic Energy Commission in November, 1946, we were looked upon with some suspicion by certain of Lilienthal's early staffers, who took a dim view of anybody who had worked closely with General Groves during the period of debate on the Atomic Energy Act. The General later tried to dissuade me from staying with AEC.

With one competent helper, Mrs. Jane Woods, an experienced reporter-turned-secretary, we worked through the rough months of Lilienthal's confirmation and the planning and organization of the AEC information activities. In 1948, Corb moved to the New York Operations Office of AEC and later became Special Assistant to the Manager. We were in weekly if not daily communication until January, 1952, when I was detailed to the National Security Council, returning to AEC in the fall to a new job as special assistant to the general manager for congressional liaison. In January, 1953, the Republicans organized Congress and, on the recommendation of Admiral Lewis L. Strauss, Chairman

Sterling Cole of the Congressional Joint Committee on Atomic Energy brought Allardice from New York to be director of the committee staff. When we were "introduced" at the first meeting of the newly organized Joint Committee and the AEC Commissioners, the vice-chairman, Senator Bourke B. Hickenlooper, said in a jocular aside to Cole, "These two guys have been committing liaison together for years."

Corb's work on the drafting and passage of the Atomic Energy Act of 1954 is one of the outstanding contributions to nuclear power development. Broadbased support for unprecedented legislation, built up on the basis of language carefully chiseled out to take into account a wide spectrum of legislative views, was almost lost in the Senate, however, due to Democratic objection to the Dixon-Yates contract (see Chapter V). It was Allardice who finally worked out with the staff of Senator Hubert Humphrey, the Democratic Whip, the compromise language that permitted the bill to pass.

Since my opposition to the Dixon-Yates arrangement had impaired my relationships with the AEC Chairman and General Manager, I left at the end of 1954 to become Director of the Nuclear Energy Division of Bozell and Jacobs, a public relations firm representing power companies. When the International Atomic Energy Agency was established in the fall of 1957, I joined the staff in Vienna. Corb left the Joint Committee on Atomic Energy in the summer of 1955 to become nuclear power adviser on the staff of the World Bank. We next "committed liaison" in Rome in 1958 when Allardice was putting together the so-called SENN nuclear power project for the Italian Government and the World Bank, and I was representing IAEA.

We were to do no work together again until 1967 when the opportunity came to write this book, a job we took on with the double-barreled aim of occupational therapy and revenue-producing for Corb. In February, 1961, he had been stricken with what the doctors have been able to identify only as viral encephalitis, leaving quadriplegia and dysarthria. Our aim has been diverted somewhat by the time it took to get Corb's "cablese" into a form agreeable to us and the publisher, and by external interference in the form of weddings, grandchildren, floods, job changes, and a heart attack. We would never have made it without the continuing encouragement and good-humored patience of Lois O'Neill, the publisher's Washington representative.

Despite Corb's admonitions against alibis or apologies, I have to make some record of the conditions under which this book was written. It is mostly Corb's, certainly as far as meat and bones are concerned, mine as to fat and complexion. My job was research and development, in this case, checking facts and extending the language. For the first three years, we worked during Corb's alternate three-month periods at home (for what the doctors called maintenance therapy) from the New York Institute of Physical Medicine, known to many as the Rusk Clinic. Since Christmas, 1970, he has been at the Veterans Ac.ninistration Center at Martinsburg, West Virginia, with holiday visits at home. The staff at Rusk Clinic worked with Corb for nearly eight years in a never-ending struggle to rebuild and restore muscular control and communication capabilities. They had built a frame to hold a roll of paper on his typewriter carriage (he couldn't change paper), and the original manuscript for this book is on long strips which he calls papyrus. A sample is reproduced on the following page.

With his elbow suspended in a sling or supported by a cantilevered arm on his wheelchair, Corb can hit the keys of an electric typewriter with the stiff middle finger of his left hand from five to seven times a minute. Such imposed economy of writing led him to develop a form of cablese which, while varying with subject matter, generally dispensed with capitals, vowels, and punctuation. His abbreviations were innovative compactions. Once, in the middle of a sentence about the peaceful uses of atomic energy, separated by a few extra spaces, he stumped me with ". . . c gtsbg. . . ." He meant, "See Glenn T. Seaborg," former AEC Chairman. Kay Allardice has served as Corb's interpreter, has provided loving care and encouragement, has run copy on her weekly trips to Martinsburg, has run a house and worked on a liberal arts degree, and has guided three sons through their teens.

Over the twelve years of Corb's illness, we have kept up with the atomic energy program from the outside. During that period, and particularly during the time it has taken us to write this book, the Atomic Energy Commission has had an eventful history of its own. It is no longer the success-conscious island of bureaucracy it was before it became engulfed in a sea of public concern folder 1...no.12

    ned...i forgot jcae when descrbng aeact46 !!

    T aeact46 also estblshd a jnt cmmtt of wxkcngrss
to deal w/ all aspcts of ae (xcpt apprprtns) , to be
"fully and currently informed" by t aec, to hold
meetings and hearngs whnvr it wshd, and w/ all t
othr powers of a cmmtt of cngrss. Nine mmbrs
were to cm frm each house, five from majority, four
frm minrty. T chrmn was to be from t majority.
Altho t act didn't so specfy, until 1953 when t jcae
itself dcdd t chrmnshp wld altrnt btwn t houses
each ssn, t chrmn was a sntr. Frm jan47 thru dec49
t chrmn was repblcn sen. b. b. hcknlpr of iowa. From
jan 51 thru dec ...oops, abv shld be dec 48...dec52,
it was sen. b. j. mcmhn of cnntctt.Whn bjm died on
kuming, t dpty chrmn, reprsnt c. l. drhm of nrth
crlna, assmd fnctns, but not t title???

    Sm stdnts of gvrnmnt see this uniquely
powrfl jnt cmmtt as an encrhmnt of t exctv
brnch's powers, or at very least, its
prvcy, by cngrss. A few writers hv seen t jnt
cmmtt as ,in embryonic form, a sort
of cngrssnl brd of directors. Be tht as it may,
all agree tht t jnt cmmtt, as an insttn, hs
srvd a highly useful function (see Chptr 00).

    NED...NOW BACK TO AEC JAN 47.

    T mmbrs, and terms of offc of each,
tht prestruman apptd were: XYZ (5 year term),
Chrmn;ZYX (4 year term); YXZ (3); ABC (2);
MNO (1). (See appndx 00 for chrt of names
and tenure of all cmmssnrs.)

    T first 5 cmmssnrs (and all sbsqnt cmmssnrs)
were sbjct to Snt cnfrmtn. Bcs t Snt was not in
ssn when they were appointed, t 5 cld assume office
and serve w/ all powers, until t Snt acted. This
is normal practise.Bcds, t rpttn and calibre of
t appntees made each confident of easy hearings
and quick confirmation./

about the environment and the national energy crisis, lashed by waves of earned—and unearned—public criticism. The nation's critical need for nuclear fuel as a source of energy is not less important, only more visible and more pressing, than it was when we started writing this book. We have worried about keeping up to date but decided that was immaterial. We have neglected the regulatory side of AEC, but that is another book. What we have tried to do is paint a portrait of an agency and to convey an impression of the determination—necessarily bureaucratic—of the people in AEC to push the development of nuclear energy within the framework of adversary proceedings. We hope our report encourages valid criticism of AEC specifics and deters blanket condemnation of the agency as a whole.

Some critics seem to feel that the AEC and its constituency—the power companies (public and private), the nuclear engineer-constructors, and the equipment suppliers—run over the public interest like a pack of nuclear wolves. The real problem is that they may not be able to meet the demand for power. The pack can be restrained. One little-mentioned factor that may create a less manageable deterrent to progress is an actual shortage of capital to finance construction of the scores of costly nuclear power plants. Some restraint on the use of electric energy within this decade is almost inevitable, despite AEC efforts. The nation faces serious energy problems, and the Atomic Energy Commission is at the forefront of the attack on those problems. AEC as a government agency and the atomic energy field as a whole offer every kind of challenge to the young, every kind of opportunity for public service.

The list of people to whom we are indebted is very long. Among those near the top are Richard G. Hewlett, Norman Hilberry, Edward L. Heller, Wayne P. Brobeck, John Harris and all his staff, Edward J. Brunnenkant, Jean O'Leary, Jeanne Hopkins, and—for essential backup—May Trapnell.

Arlington, Virginia
January, 1973

Contents

A section of photographs follows page 112.

The Atomic Energy Commission

I

Challenge to Democracy

In the beginning, three men met to write a letter. They wrote it, and set in motion a branching chain of events that would link all men and all of man's days from that day on. Each day is a new link. Some strands of chain lead to promising new horizons. One strand leads over a precipice—there is no horizon.

The three were Eugene Wigner and Leo Szilard, both Hungarians, and Albert Einstein, a German—all refugees from the Europe of the 1930's. The letter was to the President of the United States. They weren't sure how they were going to get it to him, but they had friends who they thought could find a way.

It was the summer of 1939. The three men were nervous, but their words were calm. They wrote with care and deliberation, but at the same time they wrote out of desperation. They had already decided that only the President of the United States could respond effectively to their grim message. They strove to define for him the then dimly perceivable (even for such farseeing scientists as those three) outlines of a new weapon of war of such destructive power as to test man's credulity if not his imagination. They warned that Adolf Hitler's Nazi scientists were investigating the feasibility of such a weapon. The first inkling of the awesome possibility of an atomic chain reaction had come from work done by German scientists.

3

"Look into This"

The three letter writers could describe this weapon only in terms of its probable effect. They could not say what it would look like or how, or even whether, it might be made to work. But six years to the week from the time they wrote (August, 1939), such a weapon would wipe out a city, killing 100,000 people at Hiroshima, and presenting mankind ultimately—and our democratic republic immediately—with a challenge to survival.

The letter, almost casual in tone, cited the accomplishments of Enrico Fermi, Szilard himself, and others, indicating that uranium might become a source of unimaginable explosive energy. At that time uranium was a little-used, little-known, very heavy metal, widely distributed in the earth's crust but known to exist in only a few concentrations worth mining. Only one such concentration, the dimly defined deposit in Canada's Great Slave Lake region, is in the Western Hemisphere.

The letter mentioned the possibility of constructing a bomb, referred to the shortage of uranium in the United States, and suggested to President Franklin D. Roosevelt that he name someone in whom he had confidence to oversee the government effort and speed up the experimental work in several universities.

Leo Szilard had prompted the meeting. He understood the potentials of a uranium-source explosion and feared the potentials of its accomplishment by the Nazis. He was feverish in his determination to bring about a test of the possibilities of a chain reaction in uranium. The idea had been in gestation since the fall before when two German scientists, Otto Hahn and Fritz Strassman of the Kaiser Wilhelm Institute at Berlin, had found barium in the residue material from an experiment in which they had bombarded uranium with neutrons from a radium-beryllium source.

Unable to account for it—or willing not to in Hitler's Germany—they passed their data to their former colleague, Lise Meitner, who had fled Nazi Jewish persecution and was then working with Niels Bohr at Copenhagen. It was the beginning of a string of ironies that helped tie together the strange and varied events of the early days of the atomic era. Meitner deduced that the uranium atom had been split with a loss in the total mass of material and an equivalent release of energy in accordance with the 1905 theory of Albert Einstein that there is an equivalence between mass and energy that can be stated in the formula $E = Mc^2$. Bohr brought the data and Meitner's conclusions to America in January of 1939, when he came to see Einstein, another refugee, like Meitner, from Nazi madness. Bohr also conferred with Enrico Fermi, an Italian physicist working at Columbia University who had fled Mussolini's Italy after winning the Nobel Prize in 1938 for his own work in search of the transuranic elements. While Bohr was in the United States, confirmation of Meitner's thesis that the uranium atom could be fissioned, or split, by neutron bombardment came practically simultaneously from four laboratories. The word came from the Carnegie Institution of Washington, Columbia University in New York, Johns Hopkins University in Baltimore, and the University of California at Berkeley. And within a month, Frédéric Joliot-Curie reported similar results from France.

By spring, scientists working at Columbia with the understanding support of their dean of graduate faculties, Dr. George B. Pegram, took more steps toward the chain reaction. Two teams— Walter H. Zinn and Szilard working together, and Fermi working with H. B. Hanstein and Herbert L. Anderson, the latter a graduate student—found that on the average more than two neutrons were emitted with each fission of a uranium atom. The chain reaction was therefore theoretically possible. Both the Fermi and the Zinn teams observed something in addition: that all of the neutrons were not emitted the same instant. Some were delayed. This was vital to control of the reaction. The significance of the discovery was emphasized after allied victory over Nazi Germany in 1945.

The frenzied wartime race for atomic weapons was really terribly one-sided, since the Germans never achieved a chain reaction, partly because they never detected the delayed neutrons.

With the theoretical possibility of a chain reaction established, the practical demonstration of the theory called for an experiment far beyond the resources of any of the groups working in the field. They had to construct an arrangement of uranium-bearing materials in which the neutrons emitted by the fissioning of one uranium nucleus would find other uranium atoms to split, thus setting up a self-sustaining chain reaction. The prospect of causing billions of fissions in millionths of a second was a sobering one. The indicated energy release was almost beyond imagination. It excited the mercurial Szilard so that he could not rest until somebody in the government did something. He succeeded in stirring the President.

Fermi was excited just as much as Szilard but followed a different line. With the backing of Columbia's prestigious Pegram, he had taken the matter up with ordnance specialists of the Army and Navy. There was interest but no money. Nor would anyone else take on the job. German scientists had experienced similar frustrations. Their military was too preoccupied with immediate demands of war. Probably more important, the German academic community was lacking in Pegrams and its bureaucracy could hardly tolerate a Szilard. Pegram, Fermi, and Szilard kept on, trying one strategem after another. Bothersome and persistent, Szilard hounded the Naval Research Laboratory, where he received sympathetic understanding but no support. He then sought guidance from his esteemed countryman Eugene P. Wigner, a soft-spoken, modest, and brilliant physicist at Princeton. It would be hard to find two more dissimilar personalities, but they found themselves in full and prompt agreement. They decided word had to be gotten directly to President Roosevelt. Through friends of friends, they interested Alexander Sachs, an investment banker who could both understand the problem and communicate with the President. Sachs suggested that they have a letter signed by the biggest name in science, Albert Einstein.

Einstein worked at the Institute for Advanced Study at Princeton, but had gone to Long Island for the summer. This was how the three men got together that Wednesday afternoon in August, 1939, on the porch of a cottage at Nassau Point. With the scholarly Wigner suggesting the words and Einstein nodding approval, Szilard typed the letter on a portable typewriter on an unsteady cardtable. Einstein signed the letter. Szilard took it a few days later to Sachs, who wanted supporting scientific papers in addition, probably as much for himself as for the President and the staff people who would have to follow through on the President's response.

Before the papers could be made ready and a date arranged at the White House, war broke out in Europe. Sachs, knowing the situation in Washington, bided his time. Despite the pressures of the first month of war, he had to talk to the President personally about a distant future possibility. He was not able to get a face-to-face meeting with Roosevelt until October 11, 1939. Before seeing the chief executive that day, he went over the story with the President's secretary, Major General Edwin M. "Pa" Watson, and two ordnance officers called in by Watson, Colonel Keith F. Adamson of the Army and Commander Gilbert C. Hoover of the Navy.

Sachs, who had an unusual understanding of the potentials of such early-stage scientific knowledge, read the letter aloud to the President. The two men were well acquainted, and Roosevelt was impressed with his friend's earnestness as well as the indorsement of the world's most outstanding scientist, Einstein, whose homeland was now America's accepted, if not formally declared, enemy.

"Alex, what you are after is to see that the Nazis don't blow us up" was the President's response reported later by Sachs. Then FDR called in Watson and said, "Pa, look into this. It requires action."

FROM INTEREST TO INVESTMENT

There were many weeks of "looking," first by a few, then many, before there could be much action. But there was never anything but a continuing increase in momentum. The community of American science was never to be the same again. Nor was the federal government in terms of its relationship to the scientific community and its dependence upon research. Science attained full recognition as a national resource.

Up to that time, there was no real machinery for mobilizing the nation's research resources for a national effort. The only organization remotely approaching the need was the National Academy of Sciences, chartered by Congress during the Civil War for exactly this purpose, but by its very nature, the Academy could not respond quickly enough. Nor could it ever command the resources for the action program Roosevelt foresaw, much less that envisioned by the frenzied Szilard.

President Roosevelt's laconic order to Pa Watson to "look into this," set in motion an effort unprecedented in scope, complexity, and cost. Never had so much scientific and engineering brainpower been mobilized in a single-purposed organization as when the atomic bomb project went into full swing. Soon hundreds, then thousands, then tens of thousands of scientists, engineers, technicians, and craftsmen were looking and working. It was a desperate search. They began to spend hundreds of thousands, then hundreds of millions of dollars to find what they were looking for before Hitler's scientists found it first. Many technologists thought America was already seriously behind in the search.

First, as usual, there were committees. Study panels gave way to action groups and review boards. A succession of emergency government agencies directed the effort, first the NDRC (National Defense Research Council), then the OSRD (Office of Scientific Research and Development), and finally the army's enigmatically named Manhattan Engineer District, also known as the Manhattan Project, formed in September, 1942. With the guidance of such men as Dr. Vannevar Bush, who headed OSRD and stayed close to the program throughout World War II, FDR's order led to a national investment of $2 billion by the end of 1946 and twenty times that amount twenty years later.

The definitive account of the work for the period through the end of World War II was written as an official Manhattan Project accounting by Dr. Henry DeWolf Smyth of Princeton in order to inform the public. It stands out among the official documents of all governments of all time as a straightforward account of a history-making government program. Familiarly known as the Smyth Report, it was published immediately after the end of the war. Officially titled *A General Account of the Development of Atomic Energy for Military Purposes,* it is still available from the Superintendent of Documents, Washington, for $2.00. It became a classic in its first year. It is the starting point for public education and understanding of the potentials of nuclear energy. The fact that it was prepared during the war and promptly released at war's end reflects the conviction of nuclear scientists that an understanding of the technical aspects of atomic energy is a part of the foundation for an understanding of the political aspects of atomic energy.

The significance of the Smyth Report has been submerged by the tumultuous tides of political argument that followed its publication and out of which came the first organic atomic energy law of the country. The argument over who should control the atom, military or civilian managers, could hardly have taken place, or at least it could not have led to a constructive settlement, had it not been for the Smyth Report. The War Department authorized release of the report within a week after the bombing of Nagasaki on grounds that it provided the only basis by which to control the release of information. That semitechnical account was to be · the secrecy defense line. Smyth didn't object to the War Department reasoning. He had his own reasons, clearly stated. The people of the country, he wrote, "must be informed if they are to discharge their responsibilities wisely." Men of science, Smyth hoped, would use his report to explain the potentialities of atomic energy to their fellow citizens and help them reach wise decisions.

The technical details, particularly in the production activities, were kept under tight security by the Manhattan Project. The basic principles involved—and the fact that the energy of the atom's nucleus could be used at all—were covered in the Smyth Report. It made clear that Einstein's formula is truly one of the most important bits of knowledge man has acquired up to now. $E=Mc^2$ tells us very briefly and precisely that one gram of mass has the energy equivalent of 25 million kilowatt-hrs. of electricity. The "conversion" of mass into explosive energy for military purposes was the single objective of the U.S. wartime atomic energy development effort. In the course of the work, however, the foundation was also laid, in terms of technology, facilities, and organization, for the peaceful uses of atomic energy.

The real birth of the atomic era coincides with the accomplishment of the big experiment that Fermi and Zinn and Szilard knew had to be performed, the actual demonstration of a chain reaction.

They believed it was possible. They felt it would be the keystone in the foundation of a great peacetime atomic structure, but they knew at the same time it was the essential first step in one of the two indicated methods of obtaining an explosive for military purposes. One method was to use plutonium-239 as the explosive. It could be produced only by a chain reaction in uranium, in which the more plentiful U-238 (99.3 per cent of naturally occurring uranium) is transformed into plutonium-239 by absorption of neutrons from the fissionable U-235 atoms (0.7 of 1 per cent of normal uranium). The other possible military explosive was U-235 itself, but the separation of this fissionable isotope from the U-238, while attainable by known and demonstrated laboratory techniques, presented unprecedented production engineering problems. Uranium has another fissionable isotope, U-233, formed from neutron bombardment of thorium, but this possibility wasn't pursued during World War II.

The plutonium experiment proving the chain reaction theory was completed December 2, 1942, under the west stands of Stagg Field, the University of Chicago Stadium and monument to the school's former football glory. That was the day Enrico Fermi and his crew, which included Szilard, Zinn, Hanstein, Anderson, and thirty-eight others, first released the energy of the atom's nucleus and controlled it. Arthur H. Compton, in over-all charge of the plutonium project, was present. The first self-sustaining nuclear chain reaction was the single most significant scientific accomplishment of the wartime atomic development effort.

This is a good place at which to put the nuclear chain reaction into some kind of perspective for the lay reader and to indicate its place in the energy picture. Think of a nuclear reactor as a kind of furnace, with uranium-235, plutonium-239, or uranium-233 as fuel. It produces ashes in the form of highly radioactive fission debris and produces lethal radiation, which must be contained by thick shielding. Most importantly, it produces heat. That heat has to be removed—and fast. The coolant can be pressurized water or steam, as in most nuclear power plants operating today; it can be liquid metal, as in the developmental breeder reactors, or gas, as in two power plants now in operation. Gas coolant probably has the most potential for the future. One can understand the motivation and excitement of the group that performed the December 2, 1942, experiment when it is realized that 1 gram of nuclear fuel releases the same energy as 2.5 tons of coal.

Nearly a quarter of a century later, AEC reproduced as a booklet in its "Understanding the Atom" series, the War Department press release, titled "The First Pile," drafted (by the authors of the present volume) for publication on December 2, 1946. The Atomic Energy Commission's introduction to subsequent issues of the booklet stated:

Throughout history, only a few single events have materially altered the course of civilization. Among these was the completion and successful operation of the first nuclear reactor, an accomplishment that has been compared to the invention of the steam engine or the manufacture of the first automobile in its impact on the future and its significance for social change.

The first pile crew (reactors were then called "piles" because they were just that, piles of uranium and graphite) acknowledged the significance of their accomplishment and briefly celebrated the occasion by a toast with Chianti wine, which Wigner had brought. They drained the bottle and signed the label. Compton then slipped out to call Dr. James B. Conant at Harvard to report on the experiment. Their code was improvised, not prearranged.

"The Italian navigator has landed in the New World," said Compton.

"How were the natives?" asked Conant.

"Very friendly."

To Make a Weapon Before the Enemy Can

It was to get enough U-235 or Pu-239—and we got both—and produce a deliverable weapon that the Manhattan Project under Lieutenant General Leslie R. Groves of the United States Army Corps of Engineers spent $2 billion in less than three years. This wartime spending rate has actually increased under subsequent civilian management of the atom.

To be sure, the direction of the effort was determined by the work of the scientists prior to the establishment of the Manhattan Project in September, 1942. Indeed, the accomplishments of the loose and highly personalized organizations of scientists in Britain and the United States in the 1939–42 period could have few parallels in the history of science. The full story is covered in constructive and interesting detail in *The New World,* by Richard G. Hewlett and Oscar E. Anderson, Jr. This is Volume I of the official history of the Atomic Energy Commission, published in 1962, and brings atomic energy development up to 1946.

The research accomplishments of the scientific community, first on its own, then under the leadership of "Van" (for Vannevar) Bush, starting in the National Defense Research Committee (NDRC) and gaining real momentum under the Office of Scientific Research and Development (OSRD), formed the foundation for the record-shattering development and production plant built later under the Manhattan Project. The work and facilities were organized in the contractor-operated management structure that became the house in which AEC has lived and worked for more than a quarter of a century, with slight remodeling and continuing additions.

Following is a list of the main things the scientists had learned, or in which they had sufficient confidence to justify President Roosevelt's decision in the late summer of 1942 to form a new War Department agency to take over the job of trying to make an atomic weapon before Hitler's scientists could:

- An explosion could be created in at least two fissionable materials, uranium-235 and plutonium-239.
- The essential mechanism could be assembled in a weapon deliverable by an aircraft then in early stages of development.
- The plutonium could be produced in a uranium chain-reacting mass or pile, still to be demonstrated, and separated by a chemical process that had to be carried from microscopic to mammoth proportions in one great leap.

Four processes offered means for separation of the 0.7 of 1 per cent of fissionable U-235 present in normal uranium from the nonfissionable isotope. Each process was supported and recommended by scientific proponents in a climate of intense differences of opinion as to which would work best when laboratory capabilities were scaled up a thousand times. These processes were:

1. Gaseous diffusion, by converting the metal into uranium hexafluoride, the only known gaseous form at normal temperatures, and passing it through literally hundreds of thousands of filter barriers so that the lighter atoms were concentrated at the end of the cascade;
2. Centrifuging, whereby the gas is whirled in a huge machine like a cream separator at such speeds as to separate the lighter from the heavier atoms;
3. Electromagnetic separation, in a series of great cyclotron-type machines in which separation was effected through the different responses of the heavy and light atoms to an intense magnetic field; and
4. Thermal diffusion, in double-walled tubular columns in which temperature differentials caused separation of the lighter from the heavier atoms.

Work along all of these lines was under way when Secretary of War Henry L. Stimson put then (1942) Brigadier General

Groves in charge of all Army activities relating to the development, manufacture, and employment of atomic bombs. Groves thus became the chief architect of the house into which a civilian successor-management was to move nearly a year and a half after A-bombs were used to end the war.

Groves, a heavy-set, surprisingly lightfooted, hard-driving, self-confident (to the point of arrogance, his detractors said) Corps of Engineers officer, with a penchant for rich chocolate turtles and ice cream sundaes at tea-time, who liked fast tennis and fast responses from his staff, was known to "think big" and welcome innovations in doing a job. As a colonel in the Corps of Engineers, he had been in charge of bringing the vast and novel, but very functional, Pentagon building into being on an around-the-clock construction schedule, shorn of many of the delaying impedimenta of conventional construction practices. The atomic bomb project was a complex and massive construction job, with unprecedented specifications of delicacy and precision. It called for a decisiveness that was almost reckless in terms of management precedents, governmental commitment, and the making of decisions as to the investment of resources. Throughout the war, Groves carried the ultimate management responsibility for coordinating the whole atomic effort—from raw materials acquisition to target selection—and keeping it directed toward its single military objective.

Smyth, writing in the summer of 1945, having had more direct personal contact and communication with more leaders of the project than anybody else except perhaps Groves himself—and Smyth's communication was quite different—said of the general:

> It has been his duty to keep the various parts of the project in step, to see that raw materials were available for the various plants, to determine production schedules, to make sure that the development of bomb design kept up with production schedules, to arrange for use of the bombs when the time came, and to maintain an adequate system of security. In discharging these duties, General Groves has had the help of his tremendous organization made up of civilian scientists and engineers and Engineer officers and enlisted men.

Two of the military people mentioned by Smyth were civilians in uniform. Groves's deputy, Brigadier General Thomas F. Farrell, was chief public works engineer for the state of New York. Colonel Stafford L. Warren, medical chief of the project, was one of the nation's top radiological specialists, later Dean of the Medical School of the University of California at Los Angeles. Groves also used two of the nation's top scientists as civilian advisers, James B. Conant and Richard C. Tolman. His project leaders included Arthur H. Compton for the plutonium work, Ernest O. Lawrence for the electromagnetic separations work, and J. Robert Oppenheimer for the weapons work.

During the first six to nine months after the war, many of these men lent their great prestige and experience to Groves to lay the groundwork for a continuing program. Dr. Tolman, for example, headed a committee that set the policy for release of technical information. Postwar research objectives were established by an advisory committee on which Tolman also served and which included Robert F. Bacher (later an AEC Commissioner), Arthur H. Compton, Warren K. Lewis, John R. Ruhoff, Charles A. Thomas, and John A. Wheeler.

Since the program was still under military control, however, the first year after the war was also the time for the surfacing of resentments and criticisms that had lain submerged under wartime secrecy and urgency. In wartime, Groves had to make decisions that constituted endorsements (by a military man, no less) of one side or the other in justifiable scientific arguments that the scientists couldn't settle for themselves. On one important decision, he simply overruled a Nobel Prize winner who concluded that a certain laboratory-tested process couldn't be performed on a production scale. On top of these came daily management and security policies and decisions not discussed with those affected. This was quite unlike the practice in the academic community from which many of the "victims" came. In these circumstances, Groves demonstrated consistently good technical and managerial judgment, but the manner in which he dealt with people raised more hackles than doubts.

Not surprisingly, Groves acquired an articulate coterie of critics, particularly among the junior scientists who had their say during the 1945–46 argument over civilian-versus-military control of the atom. Criticism of Groves, aimed not unjustly at his over-zealous support of the concept of continued military direction of the scientific research effort, reached a crescendo of volume and bitterness just before passage of the McMahon Act establishing

civilian control of atomic energy. Since then, review of what he did during the war credits him with a remarkable demonstration of managerial leadership, salted with sound technical judgment and unusual insight in the selection of people.

GETTING INTO PRODUCTION

Groves and his prestigious scientific advisers decided immediately after his appointment in September, 1942, that both the plutonium and U-235 routes should be followed. He wanted the dual assurance, even though this meant two major production centers. On the recommendation of a then little-known physicist selected by himself from the University of California at Berkeley, Groves decided on a third major center for the ordnance phase. The young physicist was J. Robert Oppenheimer, and the center was the Los Alamos Scientific Laboratory, to be headed for the next twenty-five years by another of Groves's selections, Dr. Norris Bradbury.

Back in the winter of 1941–42, Arthur Compton had moved the plutonium work to the University of Chicago where it was carried out under the cryptic name of the Metallurgical Laboratory. Within a month of the historic demonstration of a nuclear chain reaction on December 2, 1942, a site was chosen for the production facility that would employ the chain reaction process to manufacture plutonium. Production commitments had been made before the team of scientists under Fermi had demonstrated that the idea would work at all.

Unusual requirements determined the selection. These included a huge area isolated from population centers for both security and safety, geological formations able to support skyscraper-weight masses of concrete and metal, immense amounts of water for cooling, and tremendous amounts of electric power. Such a site was found along the west bank of the Columbia River, a few miles north of the confluence of the Yakima in south central Washington. Within the area was a small town that disappeared in the process but gave its name to the Hanford Works. The Army acquired 450,000 acres of land on which to build the huge plutonium production complex. There was enough space to place the reactors along the river so as to use the Columbia's snowmelt waters for cooling. A small mountain separated the reactors from the chemical processing plant. Before the job was completed, $350 million was invested in facilities and another $50 million in the first year and a half of operation. The Du Pont Company was in charge of engineering design, construction, and operation. The company took the job under the condition that it be relieved of the assignment immediately upon the cessation of hostilities. Old Du Ponters said the company still smarted from the "merchants of death" label which post-World War I critics tried to stick on it.

Power requirements were the dominant criteria for selection of the other site—for the isotope separation plants. Things like isolation, water supply, and topography, which provided natural protective separation of several plants, were also important. Space and water temperature were not critical as they were at Hanford. The thinly populated area around Oak Ridge, Tennessee, on the Clinch River, with high hills and wide valleys into which the Tennessee Valley Authority (TVA) could pour power from several points on its system, was selected for the isotope separation facilities.

Oak Ridge became the field headquarters of the Manhattan Project. Colonel K. D. Nichols, the District Engineer, directed from here the construction activities and, in accord with Corps of Engineers practice, supervised the sprawling administrative management functions, including paying the bills. He would have been in the hot seat if things had gone wrong in a way that invited congressional investigation. One of the first projects started at Oak Ridge was a scaled-up model of the Chicago pile, built to provide design data for the production piles at Hanford. The developmental complex (pile, irradiated plutonium handling system, and associated chemical separation test facilities) was aptly called a "semi-works" by Du Pont. It was more than a model but not a full-scale production plant. This reactor (a postwar term, more generic if less graphic than "pile") became the centerpiece of the world-renowned Oak Ridge National Laboratory, successor to the wartime Clinton Engineer Laboratory.

It wasn't for any reason related to the romantic appeal of the Tennessee hill country, with its remnants of Elizabethan speech and quaint Appalachian ways, that Oak Ridge gained its fame. It was because of the vast array of technical facilities built there that the name Oak Ridge became synonymous throughout the world with atomic energy—with secret military production activities and promises of unlimited peacetime benefits.

Besides the headquarters, the laboratory, and the semi-works for the Hanford operations, the Manhattan Engineer District built the following production facilities at Oak Ridge:

- An electromagnetic separations plant, which cost $300 million to build and $177 million to operate until it was closed in the fall of 1945. It produced the first shipment of weapon-grade U-235 for the Los Alamos weapons center.
- A thermal diffusion plant, which cost only $10 million to build and $5 million to operate. It was the first atomic plant to be closed at the end of the war, but it hastened initial production from Oak Ridge by providing feed for another plant. It had offered an alternative route at the beginning and the possibility of fitting into a tandem operation.
- A gaseous diffusion plant, which turned out to be the most efficient, dependable, and productive of the three. It cost $460 million to build and, while the warbuilt sections are no longer operable, the gaseous diffusion system at Oak Ridge is still operating under its wartime contract operator, Carbide and Carbon Chemicals Company, which continues to improve the efficiency of the process. This is the plant Groves was advised wouldn't work.

The Atomic Energy Commission later built two more gaseous diffusion plants, one near Paducah, Kentucky, to use TVA power from the other end of the system (from Oak Ridge), and one near Portsmouth, Ohio, taking its electric power from two huge, new, especially built electric generating plants—among the largest ever built up to that time—operated by a private utility group formed for the purpose by American Electric Power Company. AEC had to get statutory authority for the long-term contracts for this power. The Paducah and Portsmouth gaseous diffusion plants, the former operated by Carbide and Carbon (operator of the Oak Ridge plant), the latter by Goodyear Atomic Corporation, were added to the AEC production system to meet greatly expanded military demands in the early 1950's. But that is getting ahead of the story.

The third major center of the Manhattan Project was Los Alamos, 7,400 feet above sea level on a mesa in the Jemez Mountains of northern New Mexico. The site was chosen largely for its isolation and inaccessibility. It was the site of a boys' school, which contributed the first building to the weapons research and development complex. About $75 million was spent here during the war, mostly on temporary facilities. It proved to be a sound investment. Despite isolation, frontier living, and wartime inconvenience, many of the staff liked the place. After the war, AEC spent more than $100 million converting it into the modern Los Alamos Scientific Laboratory. When the renewal program was announced, the word-conscious first Chairman of AEC, David E. Lilienthal, came close to "blowing his stack" over a reference in the draft of a press announcement to "permanentizing" Los Alamos.

A second weapons center was established about five years after the war to concentrate on the H-bomb and fusion technology. It was built on the site of a former naval air station near Livermore, California. Like Los Alamos, it is operated by the University of California under contract with the AEC. The University was nudged into this strange role from its initial key position as operator of its own Radiation Laboratory at Berkeley, whence came the brains and hardware for electromagnetic separation. This was the scientific home of the cyclotron and of its inventor Ernest O. Lawrence.

In addition to the wartime fissionable material production centers at Oak Ridge and Hanford and the weapons center at Los Alamos, there was a large number of smaller and highly specialized supporting facilities. One of these, of course, was the Metallurgical Laboratory at the University of Chicago where the critically important plutonium experiment had been performed. Another was the Radiation Laboratory of the University of California at Berkeley, mentioned above, long the world center for the development of electromagnetic machines. This was the laboratory where Glenn T. Seaborg (later chairman of AEC) isolated and identified plutonium and found it to be fissionable. The Rad-Lab, as it was known, also provided the brains, the pattern, and even some of the materials for the electromagnetic separation plant at Oak Ridge. It is now the Lawrence Radiation Laboratory. The Met-Lab at Chicago became the Argonne National Laboratory and has been the center for reactor development. Both of these laboratories and the third research facility built in wartime, now the Oak Ridge National Laboratory, have continued to grow and carry the heaviest burden of government research in the nuclear field. Two other critically important but little known facilities were the Iowa State University chemistry laboratories at Ames, Iowa, where the initial stocks of high-grade uranium oxide were produced under Dr. Frank Spedding, and the Monsanto Chemical Company research facilities at Dayton, Ohio, where weapon components were produced during the war in emergency quarters converted from a greenhouse and a summer theater. The Dayton work, managed by Monsanto, was later consolidated at the Mound Laboratory at Miamisburg, Ohio, in unique underground facilities, where the highest concentrations of hazardous materials were handled remotely in operating spaces of reduced pressure so that any leakage would always be toward the inside.

The mix of tough-minded industrial builders and the academicians was not without its ironies. The AEC's first General Manager, thirty-six-year-old Carroll Wilson who had gone into the Office of Scientific Research and Development direct from M.I.T., inspected the Miamisburg plant just before the production line enclosures—for lethally radioactive operations—were buttoned up. The engineer pointed with pride to the standard automobile grease-fittings used on the long shafts of the remote-control mechanism ("You can lubricate 'em with an ordinary grease gun"). Wilson, his head poked through one of the openings for a two-inch-thick lead-glass window, squinted behind his professorial hornrimmed glasses and asked, "How is a man supposed to get the grease gun to the fittings once this space is radioactive?" The lubrication system was redesigned.

One aspect of Manhattan Project management philosophy has had as great an influence upon AEC's operations as the concrete and steel structures it inherited. All of the wartime work, that is, the production and development operations, was done under contract with academic or industrial organizations. Only the over-all policy guidance and direction, the maintenance of security, and the acquisition and handling of special nuclear materials were kept directly in government hands. Many of the academic and industrial contractors are still on the job. The University of Chicago still operates Argonne, although in a kind of partnership with an association of Midwest universities. The University of California has always operated Los Alamos, in addition to the Lawrence Radiation Laboratory, and in the 1950's was employed to operate Livermore. The Du Pont Company, which designed and built Hanford and operated it until relieved by General Electric in 1946, was called back to do the same job at Savannah River, which it still operates for the production of plutonium and H-bomb materials, utilizing reactors of postwar design. The Oak Ridge gaseous diffusion plant is still operated by a Union Carbide subsidiary, Union Carbide Corporation Nuclear Division, which also now operates the Oak Ridge National Laboratory and its electromagnetic facilities. One of the nation's greatest general research institutions, the Brookhaven National Laboratory on Long Island, was built after the war, but it was planned in 1946 and committed to a nonmilitary program by the Manhattan Project, which also named the operator, Associated Universities, Inc. The same year, a specialized developmental laboratory, the Knolls Atomic Power Laboratory, was committed for location and operation within the General Electric sphere of influence at Schenectady, New York. The assignment was related to the responsibilities that General Electric agreed to take over from Du Pont at about the same time.

Thus, the physical plant and equipment of the Atomic Energy Commission, as well as its managerial approach, stem from the pressures of the wartime race for atomic weapons. The story of AEC thus starts nearly five years before the agency itself was created.

Truman's Fateful Decision

During the bureaucratic gestative period there was another area of government activity that shaped AEC and has influenced the continuing national atomic energy effort. This influence starts with the actual wartime use of the atomic bomb. It involves the political policy decisions and the military response in the months immediately preceding and following the end of the war, and extends well into the era of civilian responsibility for the atom.

President Franklin Roosevelt did not live to see the awesome result of the train of events triggered by his response to Albert Einstein's letter. On April 12, 1945, while sitting for a portrait at Warm Springs, Georgia, he succumbed to a massive stroke. Within a few hours, the Vice-President, Harry S. Truman, the man from Independence, Missouri, with thick lenses but with a 20/20 vision of American democracy, was sworn in as President.

A day later, after his first Cabinet meeting, the new President was given his first official briefing on the atomic bomb project by Secretary of War Stimson, the Grand Old Man of bipartisan wartime government. It was not the first exchange between the two on the subject. While in the Senate and serving as chairman of an investigating committee that earned national respect and acclaim, the aides of then Senator Truman had become suspicious of the funds pouring into the Knoxville, Tennessee, area. Committee staff members had gotten wind of the supersecret facility at Oak Ridge. At the request of Secretary Stimson, Chairman Truman called off his investigators, taking on faith the personal assurances of the venerable Stimson that everything was on the up-and-up and that the national interest was being served. As Vice-President, Truman had received no more information on the work than as senator.

Not many weeks after Truman's takeover, the war in Europe ended. Truman, Winston Churchill, and Joseph Stalin met at Potsdam in East Germany to set postwar policies for Europe and plan a concerted final effort against Japan. At Potsdam, Truman received word of the successful Alamogordo test of an atomic weapon precursor. Designated Project Trinity, the test had been successful beyond all expectations. The cryptic message to Secretary Stimson from his office in Washington was a bit more wordy than Compton's report on the friendly natives but it too made the point without benefit of a formal code. The message said:

> Operated on this morning. Diagnosis not yet complete but results seem satisfactory and already exceed expectations. Local press release necessary as interest extends great distance. Dr. Groves pleased. He returns tomorrow. I will keep you posted.

A subsequent message revealed the details—an energy release equivalent to 15,000–20,000 tons of TNT, "the brightness of several suns at midday," the steel tower supporting the atomic device turned to gas, and windows shattered 125 miles away. A jubilant Churchill immediately gave the consent of the British Government, as required by the Quebec agreement of two years before, to use the atomic bomb against Japan. When Truman told Stalin of the atomic explosion and its potential as a weapon in the

Pacific war, he (or the translator) may not have been specific enough—either that, or Stalin had foreknowledge of the outcome based on espionage or the work of Soviet scientists, for the poker-faced Georgian received the portentous news without a visible sign of emotion.

The ultimatum to Japan that came out of the Potsdam Conference made no reference to the atomic weapon.

The news of Alamogordo, however, had special significance for President Truman and Army Chief-of-Staff George C. Marshall, who accompanied him to Potsdam. The atomic weapon meant that the costly invasion of the Japanese home islands would not be necessary, and the frightening loss of life could be avoided. This was the basis for Marshall's recommendation to use the A-bomb. Months before, he had started the planning for that invasion, including arrangements for the transfer of the commander and key headquarters elements of First Army from the European Theater of Operations to the Pacific. The man Churchill called the true "organizer of victory" had already started measuring the cost of an invasion of Japan. The Potsdam Ultimatum threatened devastation of the home islands unless Japan surrendered. The Japanese premier publicly rejected it scornfully, although feelers as to possible terms of surrender had already been put out to the Russians.

Truman was left with little choice but to go with the military recommendation. He had the benefit of months of discussion within his own government. The military position was opposed by the strongly expressed views of the scientists led by the Met-Lab group, that a demonstration should be made before the weapon was actually used. At the top, Truman's close military, scientific, and political advisers—Vannevar Bush, James B. Conant, Henry L. Stimson, James Byrnes, and others—could not predict the subsequent steps if the demonstration failed to cause the Japanese to give up the fight. George Marshall could foresee only invasion. Truman decided he wanted one more consultation. He called in Arthur Compton, whom he had known before the war when Truman was senator from Missouri and Compton was president of Washington University at St. Louis.

"Arthur," said Truman, "you are a Christian man, a scientist, and an educator. In your personal view, all political and military views aside, what should I do?" Compton asked how much time he had. One week. Compton considered the problem for a week, then advised the President to use the bomb. Years later, he told friends he would not change the decision, but he was still not sure he was right.

The Presidential order to the B-29 unit on Tinian would be the second of two historic decisions—as Secretary of War Patterson pointed out in 1946—made in the course of the wartime atomic energy program. The first was President Roosevelt's decision to make the bomb. The second, Truman's decision to order its use, was far more difficult and would have tremendous and lasting impact. The main U.S. air and sea forces in the Pacific had established a blockade of Japan, with a focus on the island of Honshu, where the principal landing would be made in case of invasion. Estimates of the cost were as high as a million casualties. Truman had a harsh and terrible choice. His decision was undeserving of the bitterly cruel criticism registered later.

Great care had gone into the selection of targets. Kyoto had been first choice of the military planners because it was Japan's most important production center. The city was ruled out by Secretary of War Stimson and General Henry "Hap" Arnold, commanding general of the U.S. Army Air Forces, because the destruction of the religious shrines of such importance to the Japanese might have created resentment that would have interfered with any constructive cooperation or negotiation. Hiroshima was also a preferred target and had actually been spared in the terrible fire raids of the spring months. Five other cities were on the approved list. Two were hit: Hiroshima on August 6 and Nagasaki on August 9. On the tenth, the war was over, although it was not until four days later, August 14, 1945, that the President of the United States announced the surrender of the Japanese forces.

The atomic bomb, about which Albert Einstein had written President Roosevelt six Augusts before, had cut the war short. By how much is an unanswerable question. By how much the loss of life was cut is also unanswerable. There is good reason to believe that the number of lives saved by avoidance of continuing fire raids and a head-on invasion would far exceed the number killed at Hiroshima and Nagasaki. But the fact that these questions are not answerable is not the only reason for shelving them. The questions that have to be answered, and even some that still have to be asked, are more important. Military writers and historians said war would never be the same again after the energy of the atom's nucleus was made available for exploitation as a military explosive. But it wasn't very long before people everywhere began to realize that neither peace nor war would ever be the same again. The technical and industrial, the managerial and logistic effort that went into the making of the atomic bomb was unprecedented. It would seem that a people who could do such a job could effectively apply such talents to the constructive exploitation of the newly gained knowledge. The destructive potential of atomic energy presented a challenge to survival. But its benign promise presented an equivalent challenge to man's ingenuity, his determination, and his humanistic stamina in searching for a way to prevent nuclear war and avoid the hazards of radioactivity.

The initial burden of responsibility was on the Americans for obvious reasons. They had to harness this new force without harnessing themselves. Here was an immediate challenge to democracy.

II

Democracy's Response

If, as Will and Ariel Durant say, democracy is the most difficult of all forms of government because it requires the widest spread of intelligence, U.S. democracy was confronted with a critical test in trying to reap the benefits of nuclear energy without distorting the political and economic structure that had served the country since its beginnings. No such challenge had ever confronted any self-governing people, or any other people for that matter, as the awesome responsibility that settled upon the American government as a result of its two decisions to make an atomic bomb and to use it in war. Strangely enough, the government got help from a quarter not previously identified as a source of political guidance and influence.

The scientists had been thinking about the problem of the bomb while engaged in making it, and, even before the bomb was used, they decided they were going to have something to say about how the fruits of their studies were used. The spread of intelligence may have had something to do with the fact that the noisy, hastily organized, often naïve postwar effort of the scientists in the new (for them) political arena withstood the massive and experienced presentation of the military bureaucracy on the subject of direction and control of the atomic enterprise in peacetime. The key to the outcome was a man in the White House, who was neither scientific nor military but who understood the American people and the workings of their system of government.

At the end of the war, Congress was faced with the problem of what to do about atomic energy. All at once, it seemed, the government had acquired an industrial empire more complex and costly than any other conglomeration of research, development, and production facilities in the world. The American people had invested $2 billion in five pressured years in a business hardly heard of a few years before. Congress didn't think the government ought to be in business this way and yet didn't know how to get out. For more than a year, the business struggled along almost without policy direction. Instead of the managerial backup from a board of directors traditional in American industry, there was a policy vacuum. There was no identifiable line of policy direction to guide General Leslie R. Groves, who continued to head the sprawling atomic program. There was no vacuum, however, in the area of the public interest in policy development. Discussion of what should be done about the atom probably filled as much space in the printed media and as much news and public affairs time of the electronic press as any nonelection issue in American history. There was much confusion and there were antagonists— the young scientists considered General Groves the villain of the piece, the symbol of the evils of military control—but there was an undercurrent of common sense in the public discussion of the problem.

The design of a peacetime control mechanism for atomic energy had to meet five general specifications. These were the objectives of the American people, even though they may have had a hard time defining them at the time:

1. Prevent the use of atomic energy ever again in war.
2. But keep it available and ready for America's defense if necessary.
3. Provide protection against the hazards of explosion and ionizing radiation.
4. Develop to the fullest the constructive applications of atomic energy and its allied sciences, free of monopolistic influence.
5. Assure an equitable and public-interest-serving distribution of the benefits of atomic energy.

Typically, within the military bureaucracy, work on postwar legislation had been started months before, mostly by General

Groves's planners. They would not have quarreled with the above objectives, if anybody could have stated them as clearly as hindsight permits. The military planners simply had a different approach as to how to attain them. This initial approach to the problem was the obvious and superficially appealing one of legislating a peacetime agency along the lines of the successful wartime mechanism. Indeed, the identification of "atomic" with things military was so general that the cognizant committees in the House and Senate were the military affairs committees. A bill to establish an effective management system for the atom, drafted with the help of the War Department, was introduced by the respective committee chairmen, Representative Andrew Jackson May of Kentucky and Senator Edwin C. Johnson of Colorado. It became known as the May-Johnson Bill. The need for security and authority in the atomic agency became mixed up with the need for haste in passage. An effort at quick passage in the House lit the fuse of pent-up emotions among working scientists who wanted full freedom for research. They wanted to be out from under military managers, and they wanted release from restraints of any kind in their work, especially those due to the very size and narrow vision of the bureaucracy in which they felt imbedded. While some of the scientific leaders, such as Vannevar Bush, James Conant, Arthur Compton, Ernest Lawrence, and others who had served on a scientific panel advising the War Department, attempted to smooth the issue, a host of their colleagues demanded to be heard. The strongest protests came out of the Chicago and Oak Ridge laboratories. By the end of October, 1945, less than a month after the introduction of the War Department bill, the chorus calling for extended public hearings approached a crescendo. The situation was a very serious one for Secretary of War Robert P. Patterson, one of the great public servants of the era. It was described with scholarly perspective by Richard G. Hewlett and Oscar E. Anderson, Jr., in the first volume of their AEC history, *The New World:*

> Secretary Patterson had reason to be discouraged. Despite the weeks of study and planning which the War Department had invested in the bill, his worst fears were coming true. One of the most critical issues to face the nation was becoming entangled in political controversy and irresponsible emotionalism. But where did the fault

lie? It took a man like Karl Compton, who had been on both sides of the issue, to see its full context. He was certain that "the bill was prepared and introduced with the wisest of motives and that back of it there is nothing of the sinister intent which some people, including a good many of our scientists, have suspected."

At the same time, there was no question that the bill was badly handled. The War Department had underestimated public interest in the measure and the sudden shift in attitude toward the military and leaders of the war effort. The same men who could command unquestioned support for a two-billion dollar secret project a few months earlier were now looked upon as power-hungry connivers. The decision to hasten the bill through the military affairs committees of Congress, the clumsy impatience of Andrew May, the badgering of witnesses, the indefinite powers which the bill granted to the commission were all elements of human shortsightedness, pettiness, and folly. No one person had set in motion this complex chain of events, and if anyone were to blame it was not Patterson. The Secretary of War, nonetheless, would bear the burden of the prolonged struggle. Indeed, new troubles were about to harass him.

The new troubles were to last almost a year. Regardless of the Hewlett-Anderson assessment of "shortsightedness, pettiness and folly," the furious debate that attended the writing of the first atomic energy legislation, which President Truman was to sign on August 1, 1946 (the seventh August since Einstein's letter), was a demonstration of the vigor of American democracy and the product was an indication of the spread of intelligence throughout the populace. Both the scientists and a majority of the politicians can take pride in the affair.

The story of what the atomic scientists did when they decided to make the political machinery respond constructively to the new situation should be an inspiration to later generations. During the course of writing this book, it occurred to the authors that there should be a monument to the effort carried on under the banner of the Federation of American Scientists. In a way there is. It is the science and public policy journal that has undergone a recent title change—*Science and Public Affairs: Bulletin of the Atomic Scientists*. One of the key contributors to the bomb project, William A. Higinbotham, became the Washington representative of the Federation and proved to be an effective lobbyist for the peacetime atom.

Senator Arthur Vandenberg of Michigan, the ranking Republican member of the Senate Foreign Relations Committee, seemed to have been aware of the ferment among the scientists, if not actually knowledgeable as to some of their suggestions about postwar control of the atom. A raft of bills were hastily introduced, reflecting one thing the scientists knew and feared—that nobody outside of the governmental atomic community, which was mostly subject to military order, knew enough about atomic energy to judge the proposals. One of those bills had been introduced in the Senate by Brien McMahon, the freshman senator from Connecticut. Vandenberg introduced a resolution to establish a joint Senate-House committee to go into the problem in depth. The maneuver later proved useful in his move to prevent assignment of the War Department bill to the Military Affairs Committee. There followed the creation of a special committee of the Senate to fully explore the issues. Young McMahon, with the help of the aged and blustery president pro tem of the Senate, Kenneth D. McKellar of Tennessee, was named chairman of a committee of members nearly all his seniors in experience and service but not in realization of the importance of the question. McMahon and the country were fortunate in obtaining the services of a lawyer and science historian then in government service, James R. Newman, as special counsel for the committee. It would be hard to overestimate the value of the work of this committee and Newman's contribution to it in bringing into the open for public review the real issues of atomic energy control and management in a free society.

UNCHARTED PATH TO A SOUND DECISION

The committee took to heart Professor Henry D. Smyth's lesson that the people had to be informed in order to make wise decisions. It found that the Smyth Report was not enough. In its effort to get from General Groves a whole lot more information than he thought they needed, the committee ran head on into what some considered the arch-military resistance to public participation in the business of government. The committee's information requests had to do with the essentials of the nation's military strength, even the numbers of weapons. This part of the request brought the first test of an area of security that even to this day is approached cautiously by legislators. President Truman talked McMahon out of the need for the most sensitive of the data and Groves was upheld. The President's support, however, did not change the committee's view that Groves was deliberately holding out on them in other areas. The experience may have led the committee to an historic policy position on the question of military participation in the management of the atomic energy agency. The policy, subsequently built into the McMahon Act as it came to be known, was to subordinate the military role to an operating or technical level. At the top policy level, the military participation was provided through a liaison committee with its own access to the President.

While Groves's position on secrecy and security in the fall of 1945 appeared to be either a dog-in-the-manger attitude or an outright distrust of civilian control, he was at the same time serving as the one-man fulcrum of a delicately balanced series of international agreements and arrangements involving the participation of diplomatic, legal, and technical experts in all parts of the world, especially in connection with the acquisition of raw materials, wherever they could be obtained. He was also victimized by what turned out to be unjustified confidence that no other nation could catch up with America and her allies in the atomic weapon field at least for a decade, unless, of course, the U.S. secrets were stolen. Very delicate relationships with wartime partners, principally the British, were involved.

There was another whole area of complication—cooperation with the Russians. The Truman Administration committed itself to international control of the atom, if humanly possible. International control seemed to offer the greatest promise of prevention of the use of the atomic bomb again in war. The United Nations offered the one possible forum for reaching agreement on truly international control. These views had to take precedence over the preservation of the wartime alliance with the British and Canadians. Groves never got across to the majority of the committee that he really feared the Russians more than he did the civilians. The military preoccupation with secrecy as the essence of security gave impetus to restrictive concepts among the noncommitted as well as among the military-oriented legislators on Capitol Hill. Some of these restrictive concepts were written into the McMahon Act, which was seven and a half months in the writing, partially in reaction to the practical exclusion of the military from the managing direction of the atomic energy program. About halfway through this legislative pregnancy occurred an event that, in terms of improving the congressional and public perspective on the issues of peacetime atomic development, was the most constructive foreign policy failure in history.

After having solicited and obtained Russian support for the creation of a United Nations Atomic Energy Commission to study the problem of control, the United States brought forth a proposal that was as imaginative and progressive in concept as it was technically and politically practical. It wasn't, it turned out, diplomatically realistic, and after six months of debate before the United Nations Atomic Energy Commission, there was head-on disagreement between the U.S. and the Russians on the plan, which had excited much of the free world and especially a good part of the U.S. This was the Dean Acheson–David Lilienthal proposal to overcome the negative threat of atomic energy by concentrating on the positive aspects. The idea, developed by a group of the country's top brains from the seed of an idea planted by the same J. Robert Oppenheimer who was chief architect of the atomic bomb, would have established a multinational corporation, chartered by the United Nations, and would have pushed development of the peacetime applications of atomic energy with production facilities and operations of such magnitude and extent as to discourage if not deter the build-up by individual nations of facilities for weapons purposes. As presented to the world by President Truman's representative to the United Nations Atomic Energy Commission (UNAEC), Bernard Baruch, a world-renowned financier and confidant of Presidents for four decades, the basic plan also included provision for punishing violators of the agreement, which was considered the stumbling point for the Soviets. It probably wasn't. The Russians apparently couldn't conceive that the U.S. really meant what it was saying. The Soviets certainly weren't going to join any international club except as equals. The point is that the proposal was an absolutely honest one in terms of relations between nations and was no more U.S.-serving than it was world-serving. Strangely enough, here was a case of developing domestic policy by first deciding on foreign policy.

Even before its final demise at the U.N., a basic feature of the plan proposed by Dean Acheson (then under secretary of state) and David Lilienthal (then chairman of the Tennessee Valley Authority) had been incorporated into the domestic atomic energy law. This was the combining of the development, production, and control activities under one management, under a statutory admonition to advance the technology as openly and rapidly as possible. Once these objectives were embodied in the declaration of foreign policy on the atomic front, they became acceptable for domestic application.

The acrimonious debate on the domestic legislation boiled along in the spring and summer of 1946, and finally terminated the last days of July in agreement on a bill that wasn't exactly what anyone really wanted but was probably the best possible compromise, given the differences of opinion and judgment arising from differences in the legislators' levels of understanding, depths of emotional involvement, and political and ideological orientations. President Truman's signing of the bill on August 1 marked the conclusion of the movement that the farsighted Bush and Conant had initiated two years before, behind General Groves's wall of secrecy. In form and objective, the McMahon Act was close to their original concept.

The Act provided for a 5-man, full-time civilian commission with a General Manager, all to be named by the President, and four operating divisions, one of which, called Military Applications, was to direct all the weapons work. The top-level defense concern was to be exercised by a Military Liaison Committee of six senior officers, three each from the Army and the Navy (later changed to two each from the Army, Navy, and Air Force). The law practically prohibited any kind of international cooperation, provided for FBI investigation of everybody who was to work for the commission and its contractors, established a new special category of information called Restricted Data,* and severely restricted the exploitation of patents owned by the government or

---

* Section 10(b)(1) of the 1946 Act defined Restricted Data as "all data concerning the manufacture or utilization of atomic weapons, the production of fissionable material, or the use of fissionable materials in the production of power, but shall not include any data which the Commission from time to time determines may be published without adversely affecting the common defense and security." Section 10(b)(4) provided the death penalty for anyone disclosing restricted data "with intent to injure the United States or secure an advantage to a foreign power."

developed in AEC-financed work. The Act established a complete government monopoly over the development and uses of atomic energy, including the ownership of materials and the facilities for producing or using them.

It took President Truman nearly two months to find the five men he wanted. He named four Republicans and an Independent. The chairman—and the Independent—was David E. Lilienthal, whom he took from the TVA, where Lilienthal had gained valuable experience in a pioneering public corporate effort. Lilienthal had also chaired the panel of specialists who advised the Secretary of State's committee, headed by Dean Acheson, whence came the Acheson-Lilienthal plan. But neither his professional accomplishments nor his self-applied label of Independent could save Lilienthal from one of the most scathing and brutal attacks ever made by a senator on a Presidential appointee appearing for senate confirmation. The eldest Democrat in the Senate, the same McKellar who had helped young McMahon, was permitted by senatorial courtesy to sit with the McMahon Committee passing on Lilienthal's fitness. The self-invited guest returned no courtesy but demeaned both the Senate and the process in an intemperate inquisition, which, some said, was an attempt to get revenge for Lilienthal's blocking of a proposal made years before by McKellar's Memphis supporters to name Pickwick Dam, the nearest TVA dam to McKellar's home, after the Senator. The prolonged hearings seriously interfered with the Commission's work during its first two months after taking over the Manhattan Project program and facilities on January 1, 1947. Lilienthal was confirmed of course and, with him, as high-caliber a group of public servants as ever served their country. The other members of the initial Commission were:

Sumner T. Pike, former member of the Securities and Exchange Commission, a Maine Republican with several successful business careers behind him, also a poker-playing crony of Speaker of the House Sam Rayburn and confidant of the President;

Lewis L. Strauss, one-time secretary to Herbert Hoover in the Belgian relief program at the close of World War I, partner in a major Wall Street brokerage firm, reserve admiral in the Navy, early supporter of E. O. Lawrence in the development of the cyclotron (probably proposed to Truman by Secretary of the Navy—later first Secretary of Defense—James Forrestal);

William W. Waymack, Pulitzer-Prizewinning editor of the *Des Moines Register-Tribune,* calm proponent of the McMahon Act during the hectic public discussion period, one of the nation's most respected journalists; and,

Dr. Robert F. Bacher, one of the key young physicists at Los Alamos, and surely the best-balanced and probably most knowledgeable bomb specialist, who had returned to his regular post at Cornell but was on loan to the Baruch staff.

The group had two months of work before the takeover of the Manhattan Project. Carroll Wilson, who had been special assistant to Vannevar Bush since the beginnings of the Office of Scientific Research and Development and so knew the atomic program as well as anybody, had been selected as General Manager. Lilienthal borrowed General Groves's legal expert, young Joseph Volpe, Jr., who had negotiated the uranium procurement contracts, and Herbert Marks, an ex-TVA lawyer who had been Dean Acheson's special assistant during development of the Acheson-Lilienthal plan, following wartime duty with the War Production Board. Lilienthal had met Volpe during the same period when Volpe was assigned as Groves's alternate to the panel of Acheson's consultants. These three carried a heavy burden during the organizing period of the AEC. Both Marks and Volpe subsequently served as general counsel of the AEC. Lilienthal and Groves had a hard time communicating, apparently due to bitterness over the civilian control issue, and Volpe was one of the few people who had the confidence of both. (Lilienthal and Groves never had anything but an arms-length relationship, and the latter sought to dissuade Volpe from joining the AEC.)

Volpe was named to review intelligence reports, intelligence being the only function of the Manhattan Project not transferred. It was retained by Groves in a new combined military agency called the Armed Forces Special Weapons Project (AFSWP), established to carry on the strictly military aspects of atomic energy. AFSWP eventually became the Defense Atomic Support Agency.

The early months, even the early years, of the Commission were rough, despite the constructive and competent stewardship of General Groves in that difficult period from August of 1945 to the end of 1946. Without direction from above, he laid much of the foundation on which AEC was to build. His custody of the program for nearly a year and a half between the war's end and its transfer to the new Commission was a competent managerial performance, as full of interference as it was free of policy guidance from anything like a board of directors. Not so with the new AEC. It had its share of interference but more than its share of policy advice. Among the many innovations of the McMahon Act was a permanent Joint Committee on Atomic Energy empowered to deal with every aspect of the national atomic energy program except appropriations. The Atomic Energy Commission was directed by statute to keep the Joint Committee "fully and currently informed." There were nine members from each house of Congress, five from the majority and four from the minority. The first two chairmen were senators, but the committee itself later decided to alternate the chairmanship between the two houses.

In 1946, the Republicans had won control of the Congress, so when the new Commission and the new Joint Committee became acquainted, the chairman was not the flamboyantly progressive McMahon but conservative Senator Bourke B. Hickenlooper of Iowa. He and most members of the Republican majority found little in common with the four progressive Republican members and the Independent Chairman of the AEC. Hickenlooper permitted the confirmation hearings to be prolonged by McKellar until well into the third month of the life of the new Commission.

CIVILIAN CONTROL BEGINS

The first year of the atom under civilian control was as busy a period as any during the war. The new Atomic Energy Commission had three tasks of overriding importance:

1. Rehabilitating production facilities hurriedly built and used during the war, and greatly expanding the wartime capacity for the production of fissionable materials
2. Organizing for the long haul and recruiting a staff of managers, scientific and technical people, and administrative help
3. Planning the permanent facilities required for the development of the peacetime uses of atomic energy, including power and expanded production and distribution of isotopes—started by the Manhattan Project in the late summer of 1946—for use in medicine, agriculture, and industry

In the meantime, Los Alamos had been busy under its new young director, Dr. Norris Bradbury, working on the new weapon designs. Late in that first year, the Commission began planning its first series of weapons tests, three shots in the spring of 1948, conducted by a Joint Task Force of Army, Navy, and Air Force units in support of a technical group from Los Alamos, establishing a pattern of close cooperation, which has continued.

During this period, reportedly at the suggestion of the British and with support, before the Joint Committee, by Bush and Secretary Forrestal and sharp prodding from within by Commissioner Lewis Strauss, AEC and the military started work on a remote atomic detection system. It first paid off in August of 1949, when one of the specially equipped long-range planes "sniffed" a radioactive cloud over the Pacific. The system went into high gear and confirmed that the Soviet Union had exploded an atomic weapon. It was only four years since the first U.S. nuclear explosion, less than half the time that it had been estimated it would take Russia to be capable of testing her first atomic weapon. The word shocked official Washington. AEC's first response, with full indorsement by both the President and the Joint Committee, was greatly to expand and speed up the production of fissionable materials and weapons on the grounds that a real and continuing superiority in weaponry was the only dependable defense. The AEC organization, Congress, and the rest of the government agreed to a man on intensive expansion in the field of fission weapons.

The second response was not so prompt and unanimous. It related to an entirely different line of weapons development. Even before the first fission bomb was tested at Alamogordo, some of the Los Alamos scientists, particularly Edward Teller, conceived the idea that a much more powerful bomb than the fission bomb could be made. This bomb, then graphically called the "super," would produce the equivalent of millions of tons of TNT blast from the fusion of the light elements into heavier ones. The yield of a fusion weapon, the H-bomb, would be in the megaton range as contrasted with the kiloton range yield of the fission bomb—or a thousand times more powerful. Work, except for some theoretical calculations, on the super was essentially nil during the war because achievement of a fission bomb at the earliest possible time was the absolute priority at Los Alamos. No talent, time, or facilities could be spared for anything that didn't contribute to that single goal.

After World War II, the pervasive belief that peace was really here to stay and the flight of talent from the laboratories diluted incentives to work on the fusion weapon. There was too much to be done on the existing mechanism, which not only seemed adequate for the nation's defense but was so overpowering that it might constitute a deterrent to war itself. After four fruitless years of trying to find some basis of understanding with the Soviets— starting with the abortive United Nations Atomic Energy Commission control concept and encompassing the disappearance of Poland, Czechoslovakia, Hungary, and Romania behind an iron curtain that prevented even normal communication with many of the people the war in Europe was supposed to have freed—the widespread confidence in peace began to contract. Soon after learning of the Soviet atomic bomb test, Commissioner Strauss urged that work on the H-bomb be restarted as a matter of high priority. After some discussion the matter was referred to the prestigious General Advisory Committee, the topside scientific advisers to the Commission provided for by law and appointed by the President. During the last weekend in October, 1949, after three days of deliberation, the views of the committee were conveyed to the Commission by Committee Chairman J. Robert Oppenheimer, who had left Los Alamos after the war to return to Berkeley but later became director of the Institute for Advanced Studies at Princeton. The General Advisory Committee's views added up to a recommendation against committing the vast resources required to develop an H-bomb, certainly not on a crash basis. While the substance of the communication did not become public until several years later (most of it in the Oppenheimer clearance hearings*), it was evident then that there was a heavy element of moral repugnance in the conclusions of some of the committee members. There was discussion later among the scientists and Commissioners of some kind of proclamation to be recommended for issuance by President Truman "renouncing" the H-bomb.

* See Chapter VIII for a discussion of AEC withdrawal of Oppenheimer's security clearance.

Unable to make up its collective mind, the Commission laid the problem in the President's lap. He had full reports on the great diversity of views, both technical and otherwise, and pressure from the chairman of the Joint Committee. All the while Strauss was growing stronger in his conviction that the super weapon had to be built pronto. His scientific backer was Edward Teller, who argued there was better than a 50 per cent chance of success. Gordon Dean, the newest Commissioner, had at first been hesitant, then joined Strauss. Senator McMahon was a relentless advocate of the "get on with fusion" position. The military said the situation of Soviet possession of a "super" weapon when the U.S. had none would be intolerable, but the Joint Chiefs of Staff didn't favor a crash program that would interfere with the flow of weapons already in production and readily at hand or the continued development and manufacture of those near at hand. Few on the AEC staff knew of the intensity of the debate or even of its existence. Among those who had reason to know, there seemed no choice. Although the military use of a super weapon couldn't really be evaluated, this untraveled avenue of nuclear weaponry had to be investigated. President Truman came to the same conclusion. After hearing all sides, he made a third critical decision. He told AEC to proceed full speed. That was on the last day of January, 1950.

With the decision to develop the fusion weapon, AEC entered a new high-gear phase. Within four years, investment in plant increased by nearly $2 billion, operating costs more than doubled. and manpower tripled. The biggest single construction job in history was the Savannah River production facility near Aiken, South Carolina, for which the Du Pont Company was called back to work by the President himself. New gaseous diffusion plants were built at Oak Ridge, at Paducah, Kentucky, and Portsmouth, Ohio. AEC power requirements were beyond anything even dreamed of before and were actually a sizable portion of the total demand for power.

What went on in the national atomic energy program in the 1950–53 period, for sheer mass effort, has probably never been equaled in peacetime. Easygoing, soft-spoken Gordon Dean, a former teacher and special assistant to the Attorney General, and a law partner of Senator McMahon when the senator was named to the Commission, was an effective chairman for this busy period. He was backed by a wise and quiet manager, Marion Boyer, "borrowed" from Standard Oil of New Jersey for three years to be General Manager of the Atomic Energy Commission. Dean and Boyer ran a job comparable in many ways to the wartime atomic effort. Raw material production was greatly expanded. Carefully planned and heavily pushed exploration brought vast new discoveries of uranium-bearing ores. The domestic uranium mining industry came into its own. New feed materials plants were constructed at Fernald, Ohio, and St. Louis. Hanford and Oak Ridge were greatly expanded. A new weapons component plant was built near Denver, and a new weapons laboratory was built at Livermore, California, to concentrate on fusion-type weapons, although it also worked on fission weapons. The Sandia Laboratory at Albuquerque, New Mexico, an ordnance facility operated by Western Electric for AEC—with technical backup from Bell Telephone Laboratories—was doubled. In terms of morale and accomplishment, this was a rare period for any bureaucracy and may have included the best years of AEC's life. The weapon specialists could not, of course, wait for the completion of facilities to develop a prototype H-bomb. The last day of October, 1952, thirty-three months after President Truman's order to go ahead, the first fusion explosive reaction took place at Eniwetok Atoll in the Pacific. It had a yield equivalent to 10 million tons of TNT and obliterated one of the islands. The U.S. margin of leadership in nuclear weaponry was short-lived. Ten months later, in August of 1953, the U.S.S.R. exploded a fusion device, apparently, in certain technological aspects, more advanced than the first AEC fusion device.

Throughout the stormy early years and despite the preoccupation with weapon development and related military application problems, the AEC made progress on many other fronts. The agency itself was an innovation in government, an extension of both powers and services compared with other agencies, past and present, and it had a strange new relationship with Congress. In the exercise of responsibilities on both sides, the executive and legislative, the record is one that provides a basis for confidence in the ability of our system of government to deal with complex problems of the atomic era. A case could probably be made that the influence of the Joint Committee on Atomic Energy on the operations of the AEC has at times distorted if not violated the theory of separation of powers.* Defenders of the arrangement usually don't argue that point. They just say it has been a good thing.

During the first seven years of civilian control of the atom, and by the time of the first change of Administrations in early 1953, the AEC had:

Discharged its defense responsibilities by building a nuclear ordnance capability fully responsive to continuing military demands;

Strengthened the nation's research and development capability by an order of magnitude with the establishment of new facilities and policies designed to support and extend the capabilities of both academic and industrial research communities;

Established a health and safety program that has permitted broad public exploitation of the peaceful atom;

Laid much of the technical foundation for the effective utilization of nuclear fuels to meet energy requirements;

Conducted a useful public information and education program, including a massive distribution of technical data, despite statutory restraints and secrecy-minded critics;

Encouraged and supported widespread use of radioisotopes in medicine, in industry, and in agriculture;

Managed the biggest "business enterprise" in history with clear regard for the public interest, the rights of individuals in a difficult security environment, and practical attention to the realities of our political system.

These are the observations of the authors with the advantage of nearly two decades of hindsight. At any one week during that period, the press might have given a different impression, but in light of the scope of AEC operations and its administration problems, the agency did a good job.

The record can also be cited in disagreement. On a Sunday in

* See Harold P. Green and Alan Rosenthal, *Government of the Atom,* Atherton Press, 1963, Chapter VII.

May, 1949, Senator Bourke B. Hickenlooper, then the senior Republican member of the Joint Committee on Atomic Energy, issued a statement criticizing the administration of the program, using the term, "incredible mismanagement." Chairman Lilienthal considered this an offense and a personal challenge that demanded full public inquiry. Staff writers for Senator Hickenlooper could hardly have anticipated the vigor of Lilienthal's response and the intensity of the dialogue over their ill-chosen words. For months, a good part of the Commission staff was kept busy digging up answers to questions about such things as the loss of a few grams of uranium oxide enriched in the fissionable isotope U-235, which was later found in the radioactive waste buried in steel vaults at Argonne National Laboratory. In October, the Joint Committee issued a report clearing the Commission of the charges. However, a minority report, while acknowledging program progress, criticized the Commission for making emergency clearances of personnel without prior FBI investigation, sending radioactive isotopes abroad, and "failing to maintain adequate supervision" over delegations of authority to field managers. This investigation had a chastening effect for years on both the Joint Committee and the AEC. Except for the period of the feud between AEC Chairman Strauss and the committee's Senator Clinton Anderson of New Mexico, consistent efforts have been made to handle congressional criticism of the AEC within the family. The Anderson-Strauss affair was a highly personal one and mutual friends could do little to mitigate it. It appeared to grow out of AEC's efforts to meet its power requirements and (in Anderson's thinking) strike a blow against public power at the same time (see the Dixon-Yates affair below). It carried through the second half of Strauss's five year term (1953–58) as Chairman and came to a climax a year after he had left the Commission when Anderson was able to mobilize enough support in the Senate to deny Strauss confirmation as Secretary of Commerce.

THE EARLY EISENHOWER YEARS

When General Dwight David Eisenhower was elected President in November, 1952, he brought the Republicans back to power in the Congress after four Truman years in minority status. Senator

Brien McMahon had died of cancer during the summer. His death was a loss to both the scene and the substance of national politics. When the Joint Committee organized in January, 1953, the House view that the chairmanship should alternate, not stay in the Senate, prevailed, and Representative Sterling Cole of New York became Chairman. It was a fortunate selection because his progressive outlook, thorough knowledge of the subject, and political and personal good manners had a lot to do with the successful revision of the by this time restrictive McMahon Act.

The government monopoly of atomic energy made sense in 1946. By 1953, it was clear to many that it was time for a change. The monopoly provisions of the McMahon Act were described as creating "an island of socialism" in the sea of free enterprise. Industrialists wanted to operate on their own account, and there was general agreement that greater impetus could be brought to bear on the development of nuclear power if the capabilities of private industry were mobilized in the traditional pattern of American business. The rosy picture painted by some industry spokesmen was a long time coming to full color, but the AEC Commissioners and staff agreed the time had come to open up a bit and try to put some incentive into the industrial participation program that the Commission had inaugurated in 1948.

There was an oft-expressed fear, however, that to open the Act for one kind of revision might invite others, less desirable. The Commission was timid, except for very precise amendments required for operational reasons. It obtained authority in 1953 to enter into unprecedented long-term utility contracts with the electric companies that had committed themselves to build giant new plants to power a new energy-consuming gaseous diffusion plant near Portsmouth, Ohio. A year later, when this authority was transferred to the 1954 Act, it almost derailed the atomic energy legislative train. The obstruction on the track was a contract made by AEC with still another group of utilities to replace power pledged by the TVA for a third gaseous diffusion plant near Paducah, Kentucky. Known as the Dixon-Yates contract (for heads of the private power companies involved), it aroused strenuous opposition among public power advocates and supporters of the TVA. It appeared to them as a secretively developed arrangement to choke off the growth of the TVA as a power supplier. President Eisenhower eventually canceled the Dixon-Yates contract, after $3 million had been spent by the private utilities on a plant to supply the city of Memphis (undertaken for the purpose of releasing the TVA power committed to the city of Memphis). The President's declared reason was an apparent conflict of interest position of an officer of one of the financial backers of the scheme, who was serving as a part-time consultant to the Bureau of the Budget, advising on the funding of the TVA power needs. The abortive deal cost the power companies more than $3 million, for which they sued the government—and lost. More serious damage was done to the career of Adolph Wenzel of First Boston Corporation, widely recognized as the nation's top expert on electric utility financing, who was helplessly entangled in the web wound around him after he had agreed to help the Bureau of the Budget find a way to finance the TVA steam-generating plants, unrelated to the AEC power demands. In a book written after he had left the AEC, Commissioner Eugene M. Zuckert, who had opposed the contract at the time it was before the Commission, said of the proposition:

> Quite aside from whether the Dixon-Yates deal was a good one (history shows that it was not, and, indeed, it may have been the result of something less than exactly open, arm's-length dealing between the government and the private utility combine), to involve the Atomic Energy Commission in what was essentially a fight between private utilities and their most hated (because it was the most successful) public power agency—the TVA—was to deflower the AEC in a political sense.

Much stronger things were said about it during what was called "extended debate" by opponents and a filibuster by defenders (a pertinent filibuster,* according to one observer), when the Atomic Energy Act of 1954 was before the Senate. So threatening was the opposition at one point that Chairman Sterling Cole of the Joint Committee sought to have the Commission withdraw from the Dixon-Yates contract lest it cause the bill to be defeated in the

---

* The eighteen-day debate was the longest filibuster on record up to that time. It was called "germane," and "pertinent" because there was no idle filling of time with Bible reading, etc. The discussion strayed from time to time but stayed on the subject. It was also called a "gentlemen's" filibuster because senators were able to go home at night in accordance with agreements to carry on without altering the parliamentary situation.

Senate. AEC Chairman Strauss said he was willing to take the risk. Ironically, the issue was settled by including in the Act the preference clause favoring publicly owned distribution systems in the sale of any power generated by federally sponsored nuclear plants, a victory the public power advocates could never have gained on their own. The "preference clause" gives first call on hydro power generated at federal dams to publicly owned systems such as rural cooperatives and municipal utilities.

THE COLE-HICKENLOOPER BILL

The names of the two principal authors—they weren't just the sponsors, they were active in the drafting—of the Atomic Energy Act of 1954 didn't stick to the bill, perhaps because the Democrats returned to control of the Congress after the 1954 elections. But while the Republicans were still in control, Chairman Cole and Vice-Chairman Hickenlooper sat for many hours, including some late night sessions, with key members of the staff in writing a wholly new organic atomic energy law. There was a sound reason for this unusual rejection of legislation submitted by the executive branch and substitution of a complete new bill, even though the congressional majority and the executive were of the same party. The Commission, then under the chairmanship of Lewis L. Strauss, who had been called back to duty the year before by President Eisenhower, after three years away from AEC, sent up two bills, each aimed at correcting specific restrictive provisions of the McMahon Act. One was to loosen the restraints against international cooperation, the other to loosen the shackles of government monopoly. Mr. Zuckert gave credit to the staff* of the Joint Committee for the "political sagacity of seeing that, separated, the two parts would have a hard time passing either house of Congress; together they couldn't miss." The committee then decided to recast the legislation.

* When the AEC Commissioners and key staff members were to be advised of the views as to the advantages of combining the two legislative objectives in one act, Chairman Cole had his own staff director, Corbin Allardice, present the case in a closed session, partly because it would make it easier for Cole's close friend, Strauss, to respond to what appeared to be a staff recommendation, thus avoiding a direct Committee-Commission confrontation, and partly because Allardice was the most articulate advocate of the position.

There was really no reason for executive timidity. International cooperation was widely acclaimed national and Republican (or, at least Administration) policy by virtue of President Eisenhower's dramatic presentation of an atom-sharing world to the United Nations on December 8, 1953. Few more stirring speeches have been made in the diplomatic arena than Eisenhower's Atoms-for-Peace proposal before the U.N. General Assembly. In his state-of-the-union message in January, 1954, the President promised legislation to encourage international cooperation and the actual sharing of nuclear materials as well as information. Except for the distribution of isotopes abroad, the U.S. could have no part in international atomic progress until the statutory isolationism was done away with.

Besides the changes in thinking brought about by President Eisenhower's international thrust, another event that contributed to the readiness of the Administration and the Congress to change the Atomic Energy Act of 1946, was the launching on January 21, 1954, at the Groton, Connecticut, yard of the Electric Boat Company, of the first nuclear powered submarine, *Nautilus*. Christened by Mrs. Eisenhower, the *Nautilus* was the forerunner of the nuclear Navy. It was the culmination of years of work, overcoming both bureaucratic problems of traditionalism in the Navy and the technical problems of building a safe and dependable nuclear power system for a war vessel. The credit must go to a fragile-looking, determined, steel-willed, and often controversial officer, Admiral Hyman G. Rickover—father of the nuclear Navy.

On August 30, 1954, fifteen years to the month after Einstein signed his letter to President Roosevelt, President Eisenhower signed the Atomic Energy Act of 1954. That fall, Chairman of the Joint Committee Sterling Cole wrote in the nuclear trade journal *Nucleonics* that President Eisenhower, with that penstroke, had freed the atom

. . . from the confining strictures of total government monopoly and set [it] along the path to commercial development. Perhaps no single law will affect so deeply our way of life—and that of all mankind—as will the new Atomic Energy Act. Domestically, it provides the means of returning this vast new field, so full of import for us all, to the normal channels of industry (excepting, of course, those aspects of the field that are still of high security significance).

Mr. Cole added that, internationally, the new legislation "opens the way for cooperation with friendly nations on the peacetime uses of atomic energy, and provides a channel of information on weapons effects and like matters to our NATO allies and to similar regional defense organizations to which we are a party." In signing the Act, President Eisenhower had stressed the importance of proceeding with the plan for the establishment of an international atomic energy agency. Chapter IX tells the story of that agency and Mr. Cole's subsequent role in the international atomic drama.

Unique Legislation

Effective federal control of atomic energy activities is provided in the organic atomic energy law by vesting the government with power (1) to restrict the possession, use, or transfer of those materials vitally important to or involved in the field either by reason of national security or public health and safety; (2) to control the building, possession, use, and transfer of facilities for production or utilization of atomic energy or particularly sensitive materials that, in the law, are designated special nuclear materials; and (3) to determine what knowledge must be kept secret and under what circumstances that knowledge can be disseminated or used.

There are secondary control points. The law authorizes the Commission to establish health and safety regulations, to enter into agreements with the states for the enforcement and implementation of these regulations, and to use itself or compel the licensing of patents obtained by others in the field of atomic energy. Mr. Cole bitterly opposed the compulsory licensing provision, but it was carried over from the old law. The patent provisions will continue to be an area of argument, but so far, the Commission has administered the patent provisions in a manner that has served the government's needs without serious or, at least, significant dilution of the incentives for industry.

The Atomic Energy Act of 1954, as amended, is still a unique piece of legislation. The only basic change since it was passed has been a provision to permit the private ownership of nuclear fuel materials. Its philosophy remains unchanged. Few pieces of legislation incorporate declarations of their own philosophy and purpose. Chapter I, Section 1 of the Act, opens with the following "Declaration":

> Atomic energy is capable of application for peaceful as well as military purposes. It is therefore declared to be the policy of the United States that—
> a. the development, use, and control of atomic energy shall be directed so as to make the maximum contribution to the general welfare, subject at all times to the paramount objective of making the maximum contribution to the common defense and security; and
> b. the development, use, and control of atomic energy shall be directed so as to promote world peace, improve the general welfare, increase the standard of living, and strengthen free competition in private enterprise.

A remark made at the time—that the Cole-Hickenlooper Act was assured of passage because it carried its own sales pitch—was not far off the mark. The authors of the original Atomic Energy Act in 1946 had said "never before in the peacetime history of the United States has Congress established an administrative agency vested with such sweeping authority and entrusted with such portentous responsibilities." That was democracy's initial response to the atom's challenge, and as much can be said of the atomic energy law as it stands today.

III

The Bureaucratic Atom

There have always been and always will be two Atomic Energy Commissions, one the government agency functioning in the multibureaucracy of the government of the United States, the other the incredible collection of men, machines, and materials carrying out the bureaucratically spawned orders from Washington. All the bureaucracy, of course, is not in Washington—or in the federal establishment. The great universities and the big-name industries that do a lot of AEC work have great bureaucracies, too, and the fact that this complex of politicians and professors, bureaucrats and businessmen, craftsmen and kibitzers, gets so much done is a tribute as much to their good humor as to their high motivation and devotion to duty. AEC works because it has to work and because there are enough people in it who know that it has to. Then, naturally, there's that most elemental of all bureaucratic forces—self-preservation.

Congress didn't invest AEC with such far-reaching powers without reason. The reasons were carefully defined, perhaps as part of a sales pitch for strict Constitutionalists, in Section 2 of the Atomic Energy Act of 1954 under the heading of "Findings." Congress found that:

> The development, utilization, and control of atomic energy for military and all other purposes are vital to the common defense and security.
> The processing and utilization of source, by-product, and special

48

nuclear material affect interstate and foreign commerce and must be regulated in the national interest.

The processing and utilization of source, by-product, and special nuclear materials must be regulated in the national interest and in order to provide for the common defense and security and to protect the health and safety of the public.

The Findings also state that any of the facilities used for atomic energy must be regulated and that the necessity for protection against possible transboundary damage places all of these activities in interstate commerce. Congress "found" in addition that the funds of the United States could be properly expended for all of these purposes under conditions that would "provide for the common defense and security and promote the general welfare." To encourage the development of an atomic energy industry, the Findings further state that U.S. funds may be made available to help relieve sufferers from nuclear "incidents" (read accidents), and that the U.S. may limit the liability of those persons liable for such losses.

Section 3 of the 1954 Act establishes programs to be administered by AEC for purposes of:

—conducting, assisting, and fostering research and development in order to encourage maximum scientific and industrial progress;
—dissemination of scientific and technical information and for control of "Restricted Data" [which means presumed technological secrets];
—controlling possession, use and production of atomic energy and materials and to assure the government's continued ability to enter into and enforce agreements with other nations on controls;
—encouraging industrial participation in atomic energy;
—extending international cooperation in atomic energy;
—keeping the Congress informed in all of these areas.

The actual statutory statement of this mandate is even broader; it clearly sets AEC apart from most government agencies. There is an external restraining influence on AEC, also different from the restraints on other agencies, in the Joint Committee on Atomic Energy, which again is different from other committees of Congress. With the 1954 changes in the basic law, the AEC Commissioners were invested with unprecedented responsibilities in the exercise of judgment in respect to licensing power.

But at the same time, this loosening of the governmental

monopoly over atomic energy was compensated by increases in the authority of the Joint Committee. For example, international agreements for cooperation must be submitted to the Joint Committee for thirty days while Congress is in session before they become effective. Furthermore, all appropriations for AEC activities must be under authorizations that necessarily start with the Joint Committee. Incidentally, many in the Washington atomic energy community—meaning lawyers practicing in the field, contractors' representatives, "atom watchers" and camp followers, consultants and staff members on the Hill and at AEC—just assume that one member of the Commission is selected for purposes of communication with the Joint Committee. Commissioner James T. Ramey, who was appointed to the Commission in 1962, was for seven years executive director of the Joint Committee, having succeeded Corbin Allardice in that position. Before Ramey, John S. Graham was the Commissioner who carried the colors as well as the confidence of the Joint Committee.

Unquestionably, AEC's mission gives it a special status in Washington, a fact that has always been reflected in the quality of the people the agency has been able to recruit. The press guardians of the public weal, however, are sometimes suspicious of the ease with which AEC recruits qualified personnel. Almost any industrial organization or academic institution that has men sought after by AEC considers its interests served by having a friend in the organization. If the employing organization feels the candidate is good, it is often willing to give him up for fear a less good man (possibly from a competitor) might otherwise get the job. The flow has been both ways. Good men from AEC get offers in industry, too, and the real leaders of the nuclear industry are graduates of the government programs. Organizations that may look to AEC for contracts, licenses, or technical data naturally seek the exchange. The situation can hardly be expected to change, if indeed it should, for the cumbersome machinery AEC has set up for selecting sources for services or supplies, not to mention its licensing procedure with its many safeguards, makes it difficult for any participant in the action to exercise influence not subject to scrutiny, either public or congressional.

Although some old hands (like the authors) feel that the gerontological processes affect the Atomic Energy Commission markedly and unavoidably, the agency has maintained a high standard of performance well into its majority. After twenty-five years, AEC still challenges the young. It still presses the frontiers of science. It has developed the skills of bureaucratic self-defense, however, and is therefore subject to the law propounded by ex-Commissioner Eugene Zuckert that a smooth-running period can be a very dangerous time in the life of a government agency. AEC is being carried along on the momentum of success, but it will take more than that to survive unchanged in this era of environmental improvement and participatory democracy.

THE ORGANIZATION

Five full-time members make up the Atomic Energy Commission, which is the name of both the governing body and the agency (see the accompanying chart). The Commissioners are appointed by the President, subject to confirmation by the Senate, for five-year terms, staggered so that there is a new appointment each year. One of the five is designated by the President as Chairman. The Chairman reports directly to the chief executive.

The Commissioners appointed in 1946 (for terms of varying length) established a pattern of avoiding specialization among themselves. David Lilienthal and Sumner Pike, as experienced and expert a pair of public administrators as ever served the government, argued that to make individual members responsible for specific functional areas would dilute the Commission system, which depended on the combined judgment of five competent men, each from a different background and each with his own concept of the public interest. Individual Commissioners would become experts in certain fields, and others would inevitably defer to the specialists. This was what Lilienthal, as chairman of the board of the Tennessee Valley Authority, and Pike, as a member of the Securities and Exchange Commission, had learned to avoid. Pike, a man of rare wisdom and selfless perspective, had not only business experience but a reputation as a voracious reader of history, economics, politics, geology, and the biological sciences.

Despite good intentions and continuous striving for a five-way balance of judgment, a strong chairman will always exercise dis-

Organization Chart of the Atomic Energy Commission

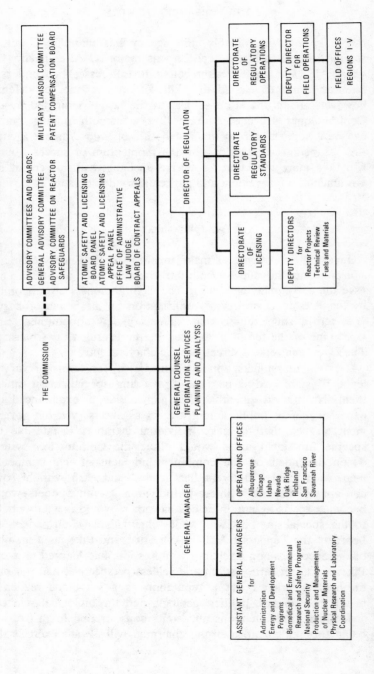

proportionate influence. He may also serve as a kind of bureaucratic lightning rod drawing to the agency as well as to himself the critical charges that gather in the Washington atmosphere as surely as static electricity builds up in the earth's atmosphere. The two Chairmen who served most consistently as lightning rods and exercised the greatest domination over the Commission (until possibly James Schlesinger) were Lilienthal and Lewis Strauss. The two were alike in many ways. Although they approached many issues from one or the other end of the political or ideological spectrum, they always drew fire from the other end. Gordon Dean, Chairman from 1949 to mid-1953, could communicate with both ends of the political spectrum (with Senators Paul Douglas and Joseph McCarthy in a single afternoon) and probably ran the smoothest operation of any Chairman—measured by accomplishment, staff response, relations with Congress, and support by the academic and industrial community. Dean had the help of the unflappable Marion Boyer, who stood behind as well as over his staff during his tenure as General Manager. Boyer once coldly reprimanded a Commissioner, who apologized on the spot, for criticizing a staff member making a presentation at Boyer's side.

Operational Functions

In the beginning, the General Manager was appointed by the President, but the law was changed, partly on the basis of the recommendation of the first General Manager, Carroll Wilson. Wilson had started his professional career as a special assistant to Karl Compton, president of the Massachusetts Institute of Technology, then joined Vannevar Bush and remained at his side throughout the war. He knew the atomic energy business from the inside out. He was not an experienced manager of big enterprises, but he knew how to get the best out of his people. To some old government heads, he wasn't tough enough and would rather preside and persuade than give orders. On the other hand, he could be doctrinaire in his response to the Washington environment. When in 1950, Gordon Dean, ex-law partner of the chairman of the Joint Committee on Atomic Energy, was appointed Chairman of the Commission, Wilson flipped his theretofore very stable lid and resigned in protest over the appointment. He later wholeheartedly apologized to Dean. The latter was incapable of malice or of holding a grudge, and, before Dean's tragic death in an airplane crash on Martha's Vineyard in 1958, their warm and constructive friendship had been restored. Wilson had a lot to do with establishing the tone and quality that the AEC staff has exhibited over the years.

The General Manager of the Atomic Energy Commission now has an organizationally equal partner, the Director of Regulation, who runs his own show and reports directly to the Commission.

The General Manager is in charge of all the operating functions —production, research and development, information, and supporting administrative activities. The job has its difficulties, not the least of which is deciding each day which matters he submits to the Commission and which he will handle himself and inform the Commissioners of later. He naturally deals primarily with the Chairman. The decision-making problem seems to be under control. General Manager Robert E. Hollingsworth, having grown up professionally in AEC, worked closely with Chairman Glenn T. Seaborg for seven years (Seaborg was chairman for ten) and appears to have a good working relationship with Chairman James R. Schlesinger, economist and government-trained administrator, who took over in mid-1971.

Regulatory Functions

Equal in organizational stature with the General Manager, but commanding nothing like the resources, the Director of Regulation heads the nonoperating side of AEC. The regulatory function, growing apace with public interest in the environment, is under fire from a small but vocal and effective number of critics of radiation safety policies and may soon be split off as a separate agency. Harold Price, who had joined AEC at Oak Ridge in 1947 and been brought to Washington by Joseph Volpe, spent seven years as Deputy General Counsel for Civilian Applications designing and building the licensing and regulatory machinery for the peaceful atom. Price headed the licensing organization from the time its functions were separated from the operating side in 1961 until his resignation in 1971. Few men in federal service have ever had such an opportunity to shape the development of a vitally important new function of government and direct it for so long as Price. He was succeeded by L. Manning Muntzing, who brought pertinent state utility regulatory experience to the job but who shouldered a burden beyond anything he could have imagined outside of government.

Both sides of the AEC, operational and regulatory, have big Washington staffs but work through field offices. On the regulatory side, the field offices are concerned entirely with compliance. On the operational side, they are across-the-board administrative offices. While the authority of the field operations managers is far greater than in normal government practice, that authority began to be trimmed back by the Commission following the "incredible mismanagement" investigation in 1949. The freedom of action of the field managers has also varied with General Managers, but generally the growth of the Washington headquarters staff has reflected reduction in the authority and managerial independence of the field offices.

THE BUREAUCRATIC ENVIRONMENT

General Manager Carroll Wilson set up the field office system (see the accompanying map). He expanded on the Manhattan Engineer District pattern, which had been administered chiefly from Oak Ridge but with a number of specialized satellite offices. Wilson established operations offices at New York, Chicago, Richland (Washington), Los Alamos, and Oak Ridge, which he called "geo-functional" offices. Behind his big, horned-rimmed glasses, he merely blinked at the chiding he took for locating direction of the Colorado Plateau uranium exploration program in New York City. The New York office of the Manhattan Engineer District had been the uranium procurement center for uranium from all parts of the world. While the pattern has been changed somewhat, the field offices still have general geographic areas of responsibility as well as assigned operational functions for which they are responsible regardless of location.

At the end of 1971, there were four field offices in addition to the original five: Savannah River, Idaho Falls (for the National Reactor Testing Station), Nevada (at Las Vegas for the weapons testing ground), and San Francisco. The New York office was later closed. The Albuquerque operations office, which replaced Los Alamos, has eight area offices under it. In 1971, the field

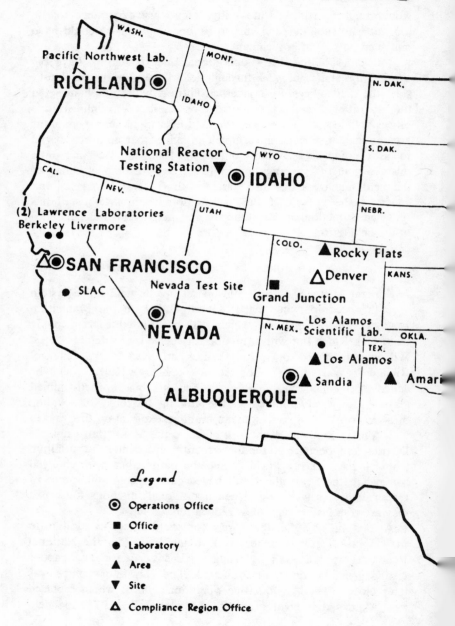

AEC

Pacific Northwest Lab.
RICHLAND ◉

National Reactor
Testing Station ▼
◉ **IDAHO**

(2) Lawrence Laboratories
Berkeley Livermore

△◉ **SAN FRANCISCO**

• SLAC

Nevada Test Site

▲ Rocky Flats

△ Denver

■
Grand Junction

◉
NEVADA

Los Alamos
Scientific Lab.
•
▲ Los Alamos

◉ ▲ Sandia

▲ Amari

ALBUQUERQUE

𝓛𝑒𝑔𝑒𝑛𝑑

◉ Operations Office

■ Office

● Laboratory

▲ Area

▼ Site

△ Compliance Region Office

OFFICES

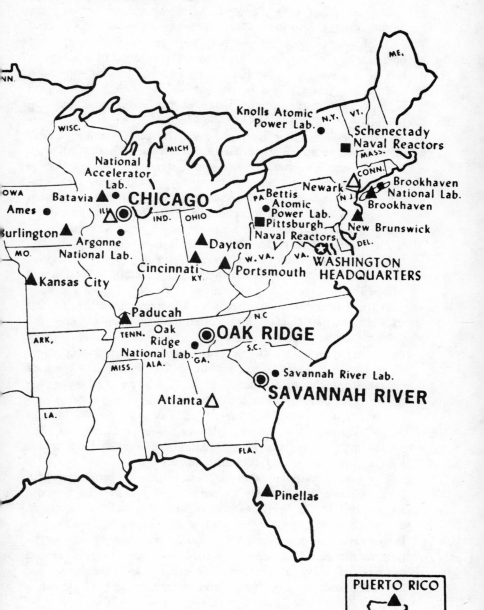

offices had about 4,000 people—and the Washington office some 2,000—on the operational side. The regulatory side had about 550, of which about 20 per cent were in the field compliance offices. The staff of almost 3,000 in the Washington headquarters is a far cry from the 250 that Wilson had for the first two and a half years. He once said he wanted to keep AEC's Washington headquarters in the limited space of the government building originally built for the U.S. Public Health Service at 1901 Constitution Avenue (used during the war by the Combined Chiefs of Staff and most recently home of the Bureau of Indian Affairs). Wilson's reasoning was that if there weren't enough space in Washington, he could put more operating authority in the operations offices and keep the headquarters staff down. He gave up in 1949, when AEC began to expand, first into "tempo's" (temporary buildings) nearby, then into a new building on H Street near the White House. The H Street building is now the "Washington" office of the Commissioners and a few key staff people (the legislation passed in 1954 specified that AEC maintain a Washington office for the convenience of Congress).

When Lewis Strauss came in as Chairman in 1953, he felt strongly that AEC should take the lead in demonstrating the principle of dispersion as a means of reducing the vulnerability of the nation's capital to atomic bombing. He received encouragement from the White House but no backup in terms of pressure on other agencies to do the same. AEC finally settled on a then remote site near the little community of Germantown in Montgomery County, Maryland, about halfway between Washington and a farm owned by General Manager Kenneth D. Nichols. The agency built itself a sprawling, functional but unhandsome office building, which was very soon inadequate.

From the standpoint of the increasing flow of people from all over the country who have to come to Washington on business relating to AEC's licensing and regulatory functions—a traffic almost nonexistent in the agency's first decade—the 35-mile trip to the Germantown location (AEC runs an hourly bus) was downright inefficient. Since separation from the operating side seemed desirable anyway, the Director of Licensing and Regulation and his staff moved in 1966 to a building in Bethesda, Maryland, a

Washington suburb that has changed from a bedroom community to an important commercial satellite of the nation's capital.

The convenience of the Bethesda location was appealing, and AEC during the 1960's continued to acquire space there. Many nonregulatory functions squeezed out of the Germantown building moved into the Bethesda quarters. Whether to consolidate the headquarters operations or to sharpen the separation of regulatory and operational functions, Chairman James Schlesinger, when he took over in the fall of 1971, ordered everybody except the license and regulatory people back to Germantown. He rented additional space near the sprawling Germantown edifice to house the overflow until an addition could be built to the original building. The growth of the regulatory activities probably assures full occupancy of the Bethesda buildings.

The Atomic Energy Commission has continued the Manhattan Project policy of operating through contractors. AEC maintains only one real operating function using government employees. This is the assay and materials control laboratory at New Brunswick, New Jersey. In principle, AEC serves in a goal-setting and policy guidance role, with project definition and auditing responsibility for work done by some two hundred contractors, whose employees number more than 100,000. Some of the research laboratory workers have complained in recent years that this principle has been violated by the degree to which AEC headquarters staffers have gotten into actual research management.

In Washington, the general manager has a deputy and six assistants (reduced from eight in a recent reorganization), each responsible for a number of functional divisions and offices. Despite his immediate prior association with the Federal Office of Management and Budget, the Chairman, James Schlesinger, called in an outside management consultant firm to reorganize the Washington headquarters. The scope and complexity of the managerial job is indicated by the chart on page 52.

There is a dual competence requirement, managerial and technical, in most of the headquarters jobs. The Commission started with a remarkably competent staff and has tried to maintain that level. Recruitment became more difficult with increased competition for technical manpower. Some of the glamor of those heady early days has gone. A big bureaucracy is not as much fun as that tight little group at the beginning. The challenge and demand for innovation are often obscured by the routine and the demand for managerial efficiency. The Washington ambient pressure for bureaucratic equanimity, as contrasted with administrative excellence, means a more peaceful but less progressive bureaucracy. In a mature organization the opportunities for advancement don't seem as bright, but many of the key jobs are now filled by men who grew up in the organization. The driving force of their work compulsions can't be as great as it once was. The outflow of good AEC people to industry has served the national interest but hasn't made the AEC's administrative job any easier. The agency's pattern of growth led to an inevitable peaking of retirement losses in the early 1970's. These forces are at work all the time, but in the late 1950's and early 1960's AEC experienced a jolt to its bureaucratic ego when the glamorous young National Aeronautics and Space Administration suddenly came of age and began to compete with AEC for public attention and money. But it is hard to hold the federal spotlight in the absence of a payoff comparable to nuclear power. In spite of geronto-bureaucratic problems, the AEC still has good morale, a definite momentum toward goals of national importance, a technically fascinating field of work, a challenge for political scientists and administrators, and a real opportunity for rewarding and worthwhile public service.

There has long been discussion of separating the regulatory functions of the AEC from the operational functions. That may occur sooner than later. The possibility was first mentioned during the drafting of the 1954 Act, but the idea was discarded because of the need for technical support for the regulatory function. It was simply a case of not knowing enough about the business. A related question considered from time to time is that of changing from the commission form of organization to that of a single administrator. This may be indicated for the operational side but not the regulatory side, unless swelling public and political concern with the environment should result in the takeover of radiation safety functions by other regulatory authorities.

The Director of Regulation issues permits or licenses for all atomic energy activities that involve the use of radioactive materials and for the construction and operation of reactors and other facilities. His office formulates regulations and inspects licensed installations. Before a license is issued, a determination must be made as to the applicant's capability and financial responsibility. The Compliance staff, which is part of the Office of the Director of Regulation, has to follow up to see that the provisions of the license and of the regulations are adhered to. There are five regional Compliance offices—New York, Chicago, Atlanta, Denver, and Berkeley. The Washington office has, in addition to its compliance function, responsibility for the licensing of reactors and nuclear materials, for establishing standards for reactor operation and safety, for radiological and environmental protection, and for safeguards against unlawful diversion of fissionable materials.

THE KIBITZERS

Since its beginnings under the National Defense Research Committee and the Office of Scientific Research and Development, the national atomic energy program has had a profusion of external, or nonoperational, advisers. General Groves used many scientific consultants effectively and sometimes ruthlessly. The Commission expanded the practice and the Congress added to it, so that AEC now has a large collection of statutory kibitzers who have to be heard.

The first, of course, is the Joint Committee on Atomic Energy itself. Its activities, as much a part of the atomic scene as the Commission itself, are covered in Chapter VII.

Of critical sensitivity in the early years, because it represented a mild compromise with military control, was the *Military Liaison Committee*. Its chairman is appointed by the President, and it has two members from each service, appointed by their secretaries, and a staff of its own, which up until the 1960's worked very closely with the Division of Military Applications staff in Washington and with the weapons laboratories and test groups. The committee was also concerned with international activities, nuclear materials, security, and especially, naval reactor development. The close working relationships with AEC have relaxed in recent years. The Military Liaison Committee and staff spend most of their time in the Pentagon, keeping up with things atomic mostly through documentation—paper shuffling—of one kind or another. The committee's primary function seems to be to keep the Secretary of Defense "fully and currently informed" and to keep AEC informed of Department of Defense views.

The top scientific advisers to the Commission are the nine members of the *General Advisory Committee,* appointed by the President to advise the Commission on scientific and technical matters relating to materials, production, and research and development. This committee meets as a general rule about every three months. While it usually considers an agenda of items submitted by the Commission, it also may probe on its own and has all the authority of a scientific grand jury to look into any part of the scientific and technical activities of the AEC.

Next oldest of the statutory committees is the *Patent Compensation Board,* which, as its name implies, is concerned with the compensation or awards and the determination of reasonable royalty fees for inventors. The need for such a board stems in part from the secrecy requirement.

The *Advisory Committee on Reactor Safeguards* was established as a statutory body in 1957 to review the safety studies and facilitate license applications referred to it by the regulatory office. Its reports on hazards and on the adequacy of measures taken to avoid them become part of the public record on each license application case. The committee has fifteen members representing all of the scientific disciplines involved in reactor operation.

While not a kibitzer in terms of its relationship to the AEC, one of the significant groups helping the Commission from outside the bureaucracy is the *Atomic Safety and Licensing Board Panel,* consisting of more than fifty qualified members from which boards of three are called on to conduct public hearings on matters related to license applications. Two members of each designated board must be technically qualified and the third experienced in the conduct of administrative proceedings. There is an Atomic Safety and Licensing Appeals Board separate from the panel.

This is only the beginning. In addition to the advisory groups provided by law, the Commission, according to its annual report for 1971, uses more than a dozen other boards and panels of advisers from outside its own organization. This may be cumbersome, but the system seems to be workable and useful. Service on these groups is a matter of status, both for the individuals who serve and for the government agency that signs them up. People from the academic world, from industry, from the professions, from other agencies of government, and from labor unions bring in new ideas and suggest new approaches to problems and different, if not always nonbureaucratic, solutions to bureaucratic problems. AEC people enjoy and profit professionally from contacts with the people who serve as advisers on almost everything AEC does. The system helps overcome the ill effects of secrecy-isolation and makes for safer if not speedier administration.

The subject areas in which AEC has external advisory groups are:

Contract Appeals	Nuclear Materials Safeguards
Labor-Management	Reactor Physics
Biology and Medicine	Declassification
Historical	High-Energy Physics
Isotopes and Radiation	Controlled Thermonuclear
Development	Research
Medical Uses of Isotopes	Personal Security Review

Plowshare (peaceful uses of nuclear explosives)

How the System Works

Extensive use of advisers—and AEC recognizes that it will get good advisers only if they are really used—slows down decision-making processes in many cases, adds to paperwork, and is subject to the criticism that it provides alibis for timid bureaucrats. So it might, but AEC is probably not as guilty of shifting responsibility, or diffusing it, as are the military departments in their use of "think tank" contractors. Paperwork is a serious burden. Recordkeeping is the unwelcome essence of government because of the historic, and surely not diminishing, requirement that responsible executives must be prepared to defend and explain before a hostile investigating committee, in detail, giving names, dates, and places two or three years hence, even some of the relatively minor decisions made almost daily.

AEC started with its own special paperwork burden. The initial staff was compact, but history was being made. David

Lilienthal, the first Chairman, was an avid diarykeeper at home and a careful recordkeeper at the office. Well he might be, toughened as he was by the battles in defense of TVA and unquestionably scarred by the tortuous hearings attending his confirmation as Chairman. Since they were pioneering, and since all of the Commissioners took seriously the concept that they were guardians of the public interest without real public scrutiny, there was a tendency to record analyses of issues and problems in great detail, to explain selections and to justify decisions.

One reason the system worked—and it still does— was that so many of the key people involved were themselves skilled language carpenters and demanded clarity and precision in documentation. This doesn't mean that the files of the AEC do not contain painful evidence of the failure of schools to teach English composition to scientists and engineers. The files abound in examples of the difficulty many technically trained people have in presenting ideas briefly and simply on paper. It does mean that—largely because of the schoolteacherish insistence of Roy Snapp, secretary to the Commission in those early years, on good organization and clarity in the staff papers that his office processed for the Commission for formal action—the AEC papermill has been more effective as a management tool than similar type mills in many other bureaucracies, public or private. This standard has been maintained by Snapp's successors, W. B. McCool (1955–72) and Paul C. Bender. The latter can tell quickly, from the files of clearly written papers, just what the Commission has done through all its history.

Internal communication and coordination inevitably present problems in a new organization, particularly one suffering from a secrecy requirement, with functions involving many disciplines and where the ramifications of a decision may extend in so many directions. The secrecy problem seemed serious in the early days. (It was not so serious that, among the suggestions made to General Manager Wilson, was one that he open a bar in the AEC building each day an hour before quitting time to enable staff members to get on paper the initials of colleagues they couldn't get to during regular working hours. Another suggestion—aimed at relief from the time-and-energy-draining, pre-jet-era travel around the operations circuit of New York, Chicago, Hanford,

Berkeley, Los Alamos, and Oak Ridge—that Wilson lease private railway cars and keep two of them circulating weekly in each direction around the country. He appeared to give the idea some thought until somebody asked if the cars would be equipped with secretaries.)

Some of the AEC long-timers, especially those at and near the top of the heap, who have to read so much of the paper generated below, say the paperwork problem worsened with successive General Managers up to Hollingsworth. Despite or because of his having grown up professionally in the organization, Hollingsworth decided to do something about the problem. Shortly after becoming General Manager, he was reported to have reduced the paper inflow to his office by 90 per cent from the peak it had reached under his predecessor, ex-Air Force Major General Alvin Luedecke, who served from 1958 to 1964. Even a cut of 10 per cent would have been a notable achievement.

The basic procedure remains the same. The five-man Commission makes a decision on the basis of a staff paper submitted by the General Manager, containing a statement of the problem, a discussion of possible solutions, and the recommended action. The Commision generally buys the staff recommendation.

Even though the formal procedures continue, significant changes have taken place since Glenn Seaborg took over in 1961. There is much more direct and informal exchange between the Commissioners and members of the General Manager's staff. Hollingsworth has encouraged it. Strauss, who was Chairman from 1953 until 1958, and John McCone, who served from 1958 to 1961, were both strong executives. They didn't encourage the other Commissioners to indulge special interests through direct contact with the staff on their own initiative. Another change from the Lilienthal-Dean days is the practice of each Commissioner concentrating on one field of activity. Lilienthal had believed that such practice undermined the Commission form of organization and tended toward one-man decisions, since the other Commissioners would depend on the judgment of the specialist. Sometimes the effect is not highly noticeable, other times it is. Commissioner Gerald F. Tape, a high-energy physicist, got AEC launched on the huge accelerator project at Weston, Illinois, before he left in 1969. Commissioner Wilfred E. Johnson specialized in raw materials and production of nuclear materials. Commissioner Clarence E. Larson watched over weapons work. Commissioner William O. Doub, the newest member, concentrates on regulatory activities, having been chairman of the Maryland Public Utilities Commission before coming to AEC. Commissioner Ramey has taken a leading role in the field of reactor development. His interest and competence in the field is, in a way, another evidence of the pervading influence of Walter Zinn, with whom Ramey worked closely when he was AEC counsel at the Chicago Operations Office (where he had been assigned by Volpe), and on whom Ramey leaned heavily for technical advice during his seven years as executive director of the Joint Committee. In his several roles and especially in his eleven years on the Commission, Ramey has probably made more nontechnical contributions to the progress of the nuclear power industry than anybody else in government or industry.

The General Manager of the AEC is in a position akin to that of president of a corporation, except that his board of directors (the Commission) is in session full-time. If the Commission is like a board of directors, then the congressional Joint Committee on Atomic Energy is the incarnation of a continuing watchdog committee of stockholders. Few corporate executives would enjoy having a watchdog committee with a staff of investigative-minded trained observers looking into everything they do every day. In the case of the AEC, these observers specialize in various fields of AEC operations and usually know as much about what is going on in the field as anybody in the Washington headquarters. There have been instances when they knew more, and it pays the General Manager to maintain good communications with the Joint Committee. (See Chapter VII for more on the Joint Committee.)

Hollingsworth makes it a policy to attend all of the Joint Committee hearings, and to stay in communication with both the senators and representatives and the staff. He encourages members of his own staff to maintain communications with the committee staff. He may have learned a lesson from observation, if not experience. During the period when the calm and informal but propriety-conscious Representative Sterling Cole was chairman of the Joint Committee on Atomic Energy and Cole's close and greatly admired friend Lewis Strauss—a stickler for manners—

was Chairman of AEC, General Manager K. D. Nichols, who had been General Groves's backup and shadow czar in the Manhattan Project, sometimes seemed out of step, due to his apparent difficulty in concealing his distaste for his obligation to respond to inquiries of the Joint Committee staff members. Nichols had resigned from the Army to take the AEC General Manager's job but remained in the post only eighteen months. He was followed by a fellow West Pointer, Brigadier General Kenneth E. Fields, who also resigned from the Army to take the AEC post. Fields, former all-American halfback and academic star at the U.S. Military Academy, kept the AEC staff functioning smoothly and maintained good relations with the committee staff (and members) for two and a half years, while his Chairman, Strauss, was having increasing difficulty with the Democratic leadership of the Joint Committee.

Not surprisingly, relationships with Congress, its committees, and their staffs are an important factor in the General Manager's daily duties. This function was handled in the AEC General Counsel's office until mid-1952, when Edward Trapnell was assigned as special assistant to the General Manager for the purpose, remaining until after the 1954 Act was passed. The job has always been administratively a part of the General Manager's office. The incumbent under Hollingsworth, Robert D. O'Neill, in his daily activities as director of the Office of Congressional Relations, has continuing access to both the General Manager and the Chairman, whom he must keep advised of goings-on on the Hill. The degree of cooperation between the General Manager and the staff of the Joint Committee varies with the personalities involved. Marion Boyer, for example, was so softly and smoothly evasive with the committee staff that he was good-humoredly derided as the General Manager who never made a decision. Decisions were either not important enough, said a committee staffer, to come to the General Manager, or they were too important, and had therefore to go to the Commission. Even these observers, looking back, eventually agreed that Boyer had done a phenomenal job in the three years during which AEC undertook and carried well along to completion the tremendous facilities expansion program of the early 1950's. Boyer, who came to AEC as an oil company technical operations man and went on to become executive vice-president of the Standard Oil Company of New Jersey, was able to adapt his industrial experience to the Washington environment. He came quickly to understand the exigencies of congressional operations and the particular requirements of legislators (politicians). Hollingsworth learned the same lesson in eighteen years of government service before he became General Manager in 1964.

WORKING WITH CONTRACTORS

General Manager Hollingsworth has followed the management practice of the first two General Managers of using and backing up the field managers in dealing with contractors. Strangely enough, the General Managers trained in the military were less strict on keeping contractor contacts in channels than the civilian-trained academician Wilson, the industrialist Boyer, and public administrator Hollingsworth. Hollingsworth seldom sees the contractors himself. There have been periods, however, when there was almost a steady stream of contractors' representatives seeking relief through the General Manager's office from some restriction imposed by a field manager, or appealing rulings of field managers on costs disallowed.

Hollingsworth is probably the first General Manager who daily works only an hour longer than the regular schedule and who seldom comes in on Saturday. Traditionally, the job has been closer to a sixty- than a forty-hour week, except under the austere Admiral Paul Foster, who served for five or six months between the tenures of Fields and Luedecke. AEC'ers who have been with the agency from the beginning still talk about the constructively rigid staff practice and the smoothness of the operation under Foster. Making the contractors deal with the field managers instead of with Washington is one of the practices that enables Hollingsworth to work only forty-five hours a week. AEC has more than fifty contractors with total annual costs of more than $1 million each and half a dozen or so contractors whose costs run into the hundreds of millions. Contractors operate plants and laboratories, supply ores and special steels, instrument weapon tests, and maintain computers. Their list includes chemical companies, an airline (Pan-Am has done housekeeping for nuclear rocket test work), electrical equipment manufacturers, oil companies, mining companies, special nuclear companies, electronic, metallurgical, and rubber companies, and universities. There are seventy-five contractors engaged in research and development, each doing more than $250,000 worth of work a year, mostly in their own facilities. At any one time, AEC will have around two dozen architect-engineer-construction management firms working on new and expansion facilities or modifying some obsolete plant for a new function.

There is a school of thought, not shared by the authors, which opposes the contract-operation system. The system appears to be economically and politically sound for the management and conduct of those functions that do not have to be performed by a government agency. The record shows AEC has done a creditable and effective job using the contract pattern. There are hazards, of course, to the system, such as the competitive advantages gained by some contractors by virtue of AEC work, and the possible inability of the government agency to stimulate progress and maintain quality at the same time it is trying to police the operation. But some of these hazards exist in government-operated plants too. In some cases, as the military holds in the development field, for example, a mixture may be called for. The government, in these cases, does well to take the smaller portion of the mix. The competition, however, serves to keep both private and public groups on their toes.

Contractor organizations can suffer from bureaucratic arthritis too, and the suggestion has been made that AEC should devise and employ some shakeup techniques to get the most out of its contractors. Harold Orlans of the Brookings Institution in Washington did an exhaustive study of the AEC-contractor setup a few years ago and came to the conclusion that AEC should conduct a continuous evaluation of contractor performance in a manner that would permit orderly change if the performance is below a defined and agreed-upon standard. The standard would apply to research laboratories as well as to production plants. After extended exposure to AEC people, Orlans said that contract operation is all right as a policy but should not be accepted as dogma.

The contract system has sometimes been challenged on the grounds that General Electric (GE) and Westinghouse, the big two of the electric power field since Edison's time and now the biggest two of the nuclear power equipment industry, both have government-financed laboratories, which are almost integrated parts of their own organizations. The Knolls Atomic Power Laboratory at Schenectady, New York, home base of GE, was reputedly designated for the company as part of the postwar arrangement under which GE took over operation of the Hanford Plutonium Works. The Hanford plant had been designed, built, and operated by Du Pont under a contract that provided for Du Pont's release within a year after the cessation of hostilities. The Bettis Atomic Power Laboratory near Pittsburgh, Westinghouse's home territory, was designated for management by the company strictly to further the nuclear propulsion program for the Navy. There was adequate precedent, since General Electric, the principal competitor, already had a commitment for a government-financed laboratory. These two laboratories have not played as visibly a productive role in the twenty years of post-World War II nuclear research and development as have the so-called national laboratories, Argonne, Brookhaven, and Oak Ridge, and the Los Alamos Scientific Laboratory. The justification for Knolls and Bettis is their contribution to defense, since both support naval reactors work. Babcock and Wilcox, venerable boilermakers for generations and now a major supplier of nuclear steam generating systems for the nuclear power business, has provided its own laboratories. So did Combustion Engineering, and Gulf, the latter having taken over the General Atomics Division of General Dynamics, which spent more than $100 million of its own to break into the nuclear power business. These companies have sufficient resources of their own to compete with Westinghouse and General Electric. All of these companies are staffed with talent nurtured in the government program. Combustion Engineering acquired Walter Zinn, and General Atomics was actually started by Frederic de Hoffman, a product of early Los Alamos.

The AEC job might have been done better, if contractors had been prodded more, and changed more often, and if perhaps more of them had been used, but there is no reason to believe the job could have been done any better, or even as well, had the government tried to do everything "in-house." The nation hasn't found a better method than the employment of qualified academic, commercial, and industrial organizations for work that continues to challenge both government and industry. The dissemination of government-trained talent throughout industry constitutes an efficient and constructive subsidization of American business.

According to the 1971 annual report of the Atomic Energy Commission, the agency had total operating expenses of about $2.5 billion. The figure has been nearly the same for a decade. More than 55 per cent of this, or $1.4 billion, went for production operations of the AEC, of which $935 million was for the development and fabrication of weapons. Since most of the nuclear materials produced ($500 million worth) and the raw materials were for weapons purposes, the AEC is still more than half military in over-all operation. The agency has been on a pretty even expenditure rate for a dozen years. Nuclear materials and production costs during the period have gone down, but weapons costs are up. Research and development costs for reactors and for biology and medicine have gradually increased, while physical research expenditures have nearly doubled.

Before World War II, the National Defense Research Council spent $500,000 checking out the fission idea. The Office of Scientific Research and Development spent a little more than $14.5 million, and the War Department (including the Manhattan Project) spent $2.2 billion. The Atomic Energy Commission in its first quarter-century spent $48,957,000,000. Altogether, since Einstein wrote his letter to President Franklin Roosevelt on August 9, 1939, the American people have invested more than $52 billion in atomic energy.

IV

Men, Machines, and Materials

Much of the world has been in an energy revolution during most of the twentieth century. It is revolution in two directions. We have learned to use energy in bigger and bigger and smaller and smaller packages. At the same time that we have been putting energy to work in ever greater quantities to multiply our muscle power, we have been refining our control of energy in a way that permits us to use microsensitive amounts.

Chairman Glenn Seaborg, about two AEC reorganizations back, cited an example of the spread of agency activities over the wide range of energy levels involved in the work of two AEC management divisions:

At one end of the scale is the Division of Peaceful Nuclear Explosives and at the other is the Division of Isotopes Development. I place them at the opposite ends of this arbitrary energy scale because while the nuclear explosives group deals mostly in energies measured in kilotons and megatons—equivalents of thousands and millions of tons of TNT—the isotope group is more apt to be using such power terms as watts and microwatts, or such terms as curies or millicuries, and at times even microcuries and picocuries. The Division of Peaceful Nuclear Explosives administers the AEC's "Plowshare" program—derived from the biblical expression concerning the beating of swords into plowshares. This program involves the development of nuclear explosives, and related technologies, for large-scale excavation such as the digging of canals, mountain passes, harbors and underground storage areas. To give you some idea of the energy involved in such work, or more accurately, the work done with such energy, I might point out that in an early Plowshare cratering experiment—1962—a single 100 kiloton thermonuclear device was able to lift 6.6 million cubic yards or 8.4 million tons of earth in a matter of seconds. Contrast this with the energy of the radioisotopes, perhaps the ten to fifty microcuries of iodine-131 in a glass of water, which a person might drink in the course of a routine diagnostic scan of his thyroid gland. Such an isotope, finding its way to the thyroid, would be emitting a constant signal which only a highly sensitive electronic scanner could detect. And of course even this represents an energy level far greater than many used in other nuclear work.

One of the facets of the energy revolution is the need for precision measurement. Here again is an example of the nature of the work done in the atomic energy field. The ancients sought for centuries a way to change the base metals into gold. Their alchemy failed. It can be done today, but it isn't worth the trouble. On the other hand, it is worth it in a very limited way to change gold into mercury. The reason is that a particular isotope of mercury that can be produced by changing the atomic structure of gold has a light wavelength so sharp that it provides the most precise standard of measurement ever attained. The point is that in the atomic age a good standard of measurement is worth more than gold.

Uranium, the base metal of atomic energy, was little more than a scientific curiosity for the first forty years after its discovery by a German chemist, Martin Klaproth, in 1789, although it did find some use as a source of lovely yellow shades in ceramics. In the 1930's, scientists began to explore the uranium atomic structure by bombarding it with neutrons. The first stage of man's interest in this heavy metal ended with the first successful chain reaction in 1942. During the war, uranium came from the Belgian Congo, a little from Canada and a little from the western U.S. The only reason we thought there wasn't much uranium in North America was that we hadn't looked for it. One of the first things the young AEC did in its early days was launch a massive exploration program. Within a few years, we found so much uranium we had to put purchases on a schedule, modified from time to time, but primarily designed to keep a reasonably healthy mining industry going with government purchases until such time as the development of economic nuclear power would provide a normal market.

In 1950 when AEC first started limiting its uranium purchases, it was expected that the market would develop sometime in the 1970's. It developed earlier. By 1968, it was clear that the mining industry would have to start gearing up for the full-grown demand of the very early 1970's. AEC still buys from South Africa (uranium concentrates separated from gold mine tailings) and from Canada, but most uranium used in the U.S. comes from our own West. Many of the ore deposits are so low in uranium content they would not have been considered workable up until World War II, but improvements in mining methods and in ore processing makes it possible now to mine ores containing just a few hundreds of a per cent of uranium. Milling, essentially a leaching-precipitation process, produces an ore concentrate containing more than 50 per cent uranium, often up to 75 per cent. It is this concentrate that AEC buys, mostly through its Grand Junction, Colorado, field office.

From this point on, AEC operations spread in every direction, some back into the uranium mines where miners are exposed to ionizing radiation. There is serious criticism of the degree of regulatory protection given these miners, whose complaints may someday bloom like the black lung affair in West Virginia. Others, as the Chairman has reminded us, lead into vast earth-moving jobs and down people's throats to their thyroids. A rundown of the headings of AEC's activities in a recent annual report of the Commission gives a slight indication of the range of the agency's operations:

Source and Special Nuclear Materials
The Nuclear Defense Effort
Naval Propulsion Reactors
Reactor Development and Technology
Licensing and Regulating the Atom
Operational Safety
Central Station Nuclear Power Plants
Nuclear Rocket Propulsion
Specialized Nuclear Power Units
Isotopic Radiation Applications
The Plowshare Program
International Cooperation Activities
Informational and Related Activities
Nuclear Education and Training
Biomedical and Physical Research

Industrial Participation
Administrative and Management Matters

It is clear that there is something for everybody in atomic energy.

PRODUCTION OPERATIONS

The uranium concentrates purchased by AEC are shipped to an AEC "feed materials" plant operated under contract by National Lead Company at Fernald, Ohio, near Cincinnati. This plant refines the concentrates into high-purity uranium trioxide. In the normal production chain, this trioxide then takes one of two paths on its way to utilization as fuel to generate energy.

One path is toward the plutonium production reactors, for which purpose the trioxide is processed at the Fernald plant to very pure metal and formed into fuel elements to fit the plutonium production reactors. On some of these, the Fernald plant uses the nearby plant of the Bridgeport Brass Company at Ashtabula, Ohio, for special extrusions, then brings the metal back for final fabrication. For many years, AEC had a second feed materials plant at Weldon Springs, Missouri, operated by Mallinckrodt Chemical Works, but this plant was closed in 1966.

The other path is toward enrichment in the fissionable isotope U-235. The trioxide is shipped to a "hex" plant, where it is converted into gaseous uranium hexafluoride for passage through the filter cascades at Paducah, Kentucky, Portsmouth, Ohio, and Oak Ridge, Tennessee. AEC operates the three plants in very close coordination, usually with Paducah feeding Oak Ridge and Oak Ridge feeding Portsmouth in the case of the very highest assay material. Tailings from both Portsmouth, which is operated by Goodyear Atomic Corporation, a subsidiary of the rubber company, and from Oak Ridge may be sent back to Paducah to start the trip again. Oak Ridge and Paducah gaseous diffusion plants are operated by Union Carbide Corporation.

The product from the gaseous diffusion plants goes into reactor fuel and, in the highest enrichment, into weapons. The plants are probably the largest industrial installations in the world. When in full operation, they used about 4 per cent of all the electric power generated in the United States.

The government requirement for weapons-grade U-235 is predictable and level, and, while it is perhaps a third of the total output of the plants as of 1969, it would be but a pittance of the total requirement for nuclear power reactors by the 1980's. AEC says it can figure out how the gaseous diffusion plants can meet the demand until about 1980. After that, there will have to be new capacity. Already, industrial interest is being exhibited. AEC has been declassifying data about the plants, telling more and more about how they are operated and maintained, and how much they cost to operate. Part of this is related to the "toll enrichment" program, under which AEC will enrich privately owned uranium for a fee. In 1954, the functions and responsibilities of the AEC were expanded to provide for the promotion and development of the peaceful uses of atomic energy in the private sector. In 1964, the law was changed to permit private ownership of special nuclear materials, and authorized AEC to offer a service of enriching privately owned uranium under long-term contracts. The service was started January 1, 1969. This is probably just a step toward privately owned enrichment plants. The Atomic Industrial Forum, the trade association of the atom, issued a report in 1968 urging AEC to transfer its enrichment plants to the private sector.

Although ultimate transfer of ownership of uranium enrichment facilities to private industry had long been discussed, the proposal did not take definite form until late 1969, when it appeared that its supporters included not only the influential Atomic Industrial Forum with its many powerful members but the AEC and the Nixon Administration as well. It developed, however, that there remained in Congress a considerable feeling to the contrary, as became apparent in mid-1970, when a move to bring private ownership nearer to actuality abruptly collapsed.

In September, 1969, the AEC, apparently under some persuasion, recommended to the President that it should be the government's objective ultimately to establish private ownership and operation for the uranium enrichment step of the fuel cycle for civilian nuclear power plants as a part of the private sector. Receptive to this recommendation, the White House announced its conclusion that the uranium enrichment facilities should be transferred to the private sector, by sale, at such times as various national interests would best be served. AEC promptly announced that, in contemplation of ultimate transfer to the private sector, a "new entity," an AEC directorate, was being set up to conduct enrichment activities in a manner closely approaching the way they would be conducted in a commercial enterprise.

These recommendations and proposed organizational steps did not receive the same reception in Congress—and perhaps elsewhere—as in the White House. Indeed, the Joint Committee on Atomic Energy, under the leadership of Representative Chet Holifield of California, refused to authorize any of the requested funds for the directorate, and the House Appropriations Committee, led by Representative Joe Evins of Tennessee, refused to appropriate a single dollar for the intended purpose. Faced with so strong a build-up of opposition, the AEC in July, 1970, announced "in response to inquiries" that the plan to set up a separate uranium enrichment directorate had been dropped, and that there were no actual plans for sale of the facilities. There was no explanation in the AEC release for abandonment of the directorate idea other than that, with the plants operating at a relatively small fraction of capacity, it was doubtful whether industry would view a take-over as an economically attractive venture.

During the period when it seemed that the ill-fated directorate would shortly come into being, AEC quietly brought in John J. Flaherty from the presidency of Atomics International at Canoga Park, California, to head up the proposed entity. A few days before it made it known that the directorate was being dropped, AEC announced "a series of organizational changes" under which John Flaherty would assume the new position of Assistant General Manager for Plans. Thus ended the first attempt to give definite form and shape to the proposed substitution of private for public ownership of the huge, vital uranium enrichment facilities—despite the presence of Flaherty, one of the ablest managers AEC had before he left the Chicago Operations office to manage the power reactor development business of what is now North American Rockwell.

Events in the closing years of the 1960's offer an example of the complexity of AEC's operational responsibilities. The power demands of the gaseous diffusion plants were actually reduced from their normal of 2,700 megawatts for the three plants to around 2,000 during 1969. But AEC predicted a power demand of 4,400 megawatts in these same plants for 1973. Tremendous size and tremendous power demands are characteristic of the gaseous diffusion process. And while AEC was declassifying information with a view to possible industrial participation in the business, another way of enriching uranium in very small units and with comparatively little power was gaining so much ground that the Commission felt compelled to classify it. This was the gas centrifuge process of separating the U-235 atoms from the U-238 atoms. With AEC help, the one company in the United States making progress in this field, Electro-Nucleonics, Inc., of Fairfield, New Jersey, switched its talents and energies in centrifugation to the business of manufacturing and employing (in a laboratory set up at Bethesda, Maryland) the zonal ultra-centrifuge for biological separations on a rental basis. The machine and the techniques had been developed at the Oak Ridge National Laboratory. The production capability of the zonal ultra-centrifuge made possible the rapid production of Hong Kong flu vaccine in the fall of 1968. Possible progress in the use of gas centrifuges for isotope separation in other countries, however, worries the U.S. and its allies because the technology is known, and U-235 can be separated without constructing massive plants.

The metal slugs from the Fernald feed material plant go to the Hanford plant near Richland, Washington, and to the Savannah River plant near Aiken, South Carolina. Principal production contractor at Hanford is (after General Electric had moved out by the end of the 1960's) Douglas United Nuclear, Inc., sharing operations at the site with Computer Sciences Corporation for technical facilities, with Atlantic Richfield Corporation for separations work (removing the plutonium from irradiated fuel elements) and International Telephone and Telegraph's Federal Support Services, Inc., for general facilities housekeeping. At the Savannah River plant, E. I. Du Pont de Nemours and Company does everything, which both AEC and the company like. There are those in AEC who hold that Du Pont is the toughest (in negotiations) and best contractor AEC has used. The relationship is constructively formal. Afterhours, an AEC'er once said to a Du Pont friend, "The trouble with the goddamn Du Pont people is they think they can do any job we have better than anybody else in the country." The quiet response was, "We can prove it!" Having departed Hanford in 1946 under contract terms insisted upon by the company that it be relieved within one year after the cessation of hostilities (rather than the treaty end of the war), Du Pont came back in response to a request signed by President Truman, stating that the company's return was essential to the national defense.

Plutonium-239 is a man-made fissionable material produced in nuclear reactors through a three-step process starting with the capture of a neutron by uranium-238, the nonfissionable isotope of that metal. Plutonium is used primarily—almost entirely as matters stand now—for weapons, but someday it will be an important fuel. Several experimental reactors have been run on plutonium as the nuclear fuel. All uranium-fed reactors produce plutonium, and the power plant operators will either have to sell it back to AEC or use it in their own reactors. The Hanford production reactors were cubical stacks of graphite with horizontal tubes loaded with uranium slugs clad in aluminum. The Savannah River reactors are large stainless steel vessels filled with heavy water. The fuel is loaded in vertical tubes. Savannah River has five reactors, two of which have been shut down, and Hanford has nine, seven of which have been shut down. One of the reactors operating at Hanford is a "dual purpose" reactor, producing weapons-grade plutonium and steam. The steam is fed to an electric generating plant built next door, owned by the Washington Public Power Supply System.

But no atomic energy operation is as simple as it sounds. After the immediately useful products are removed from the irradiated fuel elements in a plutonium-producing reactor, there is a terribly annoying radioactive residue, which has to be treated in various ways to reduce its volume and then stored in underground storage tanks. Cesium-137 and strontium-90 are among the useful radioactive isotopes taken out of the Hanford wastes. One of the things being produced in the Savannah River reactors is californium-252, an unusual radioisotope that lends itself to all kinds of detection and analysis techniques because it is an intense neutron emitter. The neutrons will activate, or make radioactive, atoms like gold, so that even a most miniscule amount of gold in an ore sample can be quickly detected. A piece of californium-252 somewhat smaller than the dot of this "i" can be very useful, so the AEC-quoted "price" of $450 billion a pound still doesn't price it out of the market. It is currently available at $100 for one-tenth of a microgram—one ten-millionth of a gram.

WEAPONS

Under the Atomic Energy Act, development and production of the most important weapon available to the U.S. military was put entirely under the direction and control of a civilian agency that was not even under the supervision of the Department of Defense. Some men in uniform thought this wasn't quite right. It is not just hearsay that an incoming Secretary of Defense, when shown the organization chart of the Pentagon family, asked, "Where is the AEC?" There is no longer any worry among military men as to the quantity, quality, and on-time delivery of atomic weapons from the civilian agency. Here is one of the ironies of the military-vs.-civilian control of the atom. It would be hard to find anybody who would say the military could have done a better job for itself in providing nuclear weapons. As an independent agency, the AEC reports through its Chairman directly to the President of the United States. As a munition-supply element of the military establishment, it would have been headed by a general officer, trained for a variety of duties other than industrial management, reporting through superiors concerned with a lot of other problems. Fortunately, and by wise design, a lot of young officers are continually being qualified in military nucleonics, so there is no real problem when the military services define their "requirements" for nuclear weapons. They know what AEC can do and what makes sense from the military standpoint. With the Military Liaison Committee looking over the Commission's shoulder, and with the Defense Atomic Support Agency fully involved in the testing programs of AEC, there is very little lost motion in the system.

Design and development of weapons are conducted at three installations—Los Alamos Scientific Laboratory in New Mexico and Lawrence Radiation Laboratory at Livermore, California, both operated by the University of California, and Sandia Laboratory at Albuquerque, New Mexico, operated by the Sandia Corporation. Sandia Corporation is a subsidiary of the Western Electric

In the presence of seven U.S. senators, President Harry S. Truman signs the Act that brought the Atomic Energy Commission into being on August 1, 1946. *(All photos from the U.S. Atomic Energy Commission unless otherwise noted.)*

General Leslie R. Groves, left, and David E. Lilienthal, first Chairman of the Atomic Energy Commission, on the occasion of the transfer of the U.S. atomic energy project from military to civilian control.

Henry DeWolf Smyth, whose famous "Smyth Report" first revealed to public scrutiny details of the wartime work of the Manhattan Project.

Above: Admiral Hyman Rickover, in dark trenchcoat, center, with members of the congressional Joint Committee on Atomic Energy and the skipper of the *Nautilus,* the world's first nuclear-powered submarine. *Below:* Members of the Joint Committee wave from the fin of the *Nautilus* prior to a meeting on the submerged submarine.

Oak Ridge National Laboratory at Oak Ridge, Tennessee, one of the AEC's largest research and development installations.

Interior of an AEC contractor-operated gaseous diffusion plant. This series of cylindrical converters for enriching uranium comprises a gaseous diffusion cascade.

STG 2

STG 1

erial view of the $834 llion gaseous diffusion nt at Oak Ridge, oper- d for the AEC by the ion Carbide Corpora- n.

The Atomic Energy Commission sponsors research in many fields. *Above:* Effects of radiation on plant materials are studied in the Brookhaven National Laboratory's Plant Radiobiology Laboratory.

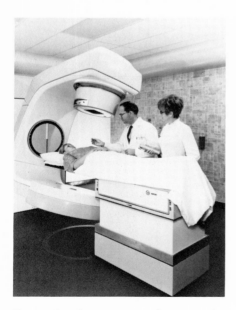

Preparation for treatment of a tumor in a device using a section of an accelerating structure invented for use in an AEC accelerator.

A worker at the AEC Lawrence Berkeley Laboratory conducts research on the cancer-producing properties of hydrocarbons found in cigarette smoke and auto exhausts.

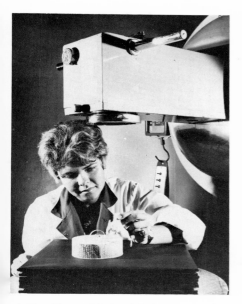

A Brookhaven National Laboratory technician places a mouse in a radiation chamber to study the effects of X-irradiation on aging.

Electron microscope research by scientists at the Lawrence Berkeley Laboratory may eventually make life structures visible at the molecular level.

Heat dissipation patterns in the Great Lakes are studied in research sponsored by the Argonne National Laboratory near Chicago. Water temperature measurements taken close to a coal-burning power plant will be used in determining the effects, if any, attributable to nuclear power plants sited along the lake shore.

The main accelerator ring at the AEC National Accelerator Laboratory in Batavia, Illinois, four miles in circumference. The central laboratory, with its circular cooling pond, is in the foreground.

Aerial view of the Stanford University Linear Accelerator Center, used in AEC research. The accelerator is two miles long.

The Los Alamos Meson Physics Facility, which produces meson beams 1,000 to 10,000 times more intense than any previously obtainable.

The feasibility of controlled fusion for generating electricity is studied at the AEC Los Alamos Scientific Laboratory. The arc segment above, part of a 49½-foot doughnut-shaped device, is capable of producing ion temperatures close to 10 million degrees centigrade for ten-millionths of a second at a time.

This nuclear generating station at Fort Saint Vrain, Colorado, is the world's first commercial high-temperature, gas-cooled power reactor. *(Gulf General Atomic photo)*

One of the four planned North Anna Power Station units under construction at Mineral, Virginia. The four units, expected to be operational in the 1970's, will deliver between 3 million and 4 million kilowatts of power for distribution by the Virginia Electric Power Company. *(Virginia Electric Power Company photo)*

The General Advisory Committee meets with members of the Atomic Energy Commission at the AEC's Germantown, Maryland, headquarters. Atomic Energy Commission Chairman Dixy Lee Ray is second from the left.

Company, set up at the request of AEC to combine the production talents of Western Electric and the developmental talents of its corporate brother, the Bell Telephone Laboratories. A number of industrial contractors play important roles in the weapons production complex, managed and directed from the Albuquerque Operations Office and the Oak Ridge Operations Office. AEC weapons-manufacturing activities are directly responsive to military requirements approved by the President, who specifically orders the level of activity. One of the continuing activities is the retirement of obsolescent weapons. Weapons development and fabrication has been costing in the range of three-quarters of a billion dollars annually since 1968, having crept up from a half-billion in the previous five years.

The research and development phase of the weapons program provides for the specific development requirements of the Department of Defense, for the basic research needed for continuing advance in weapons technology, and for a wide range of other activities that are necessary to maintain the vigor and momentum of the laboratories. These "other activities" add up to one of the basic safeguards under the test ban treaty. Underground nuclear weapons testing is conducted at the Nevada test site on a former Air Force bombing range in southern Nevada. Supplemental sites are maintained in central Nevada and on Amchitka Island off the coast of Alaska. Testing in the atmosphere, in space, or under water is banned under the treaty signed August 5, 1963, by the United States, the United Kingdom, and the Soviet Union, and subsequently by other nations. Atmospheric testing in the U.S. had been stopped the year before. The AEC maintains today, however, a capability for any kind of testing on short notice. One of the critically important weapons-related programs of the AEC is the Vela project, supervised by the Advanced Research Projects Agency of the Department of Defense to provide the means and capability for the detection, location, and identification of a nuclear detonation anywhere in the world.

PLOWSHARE

The Plowshare program was established to develop peaceful uses of nuclear explosives. Many such uses have been proposed, ranging from canal construction and the excavation of harbors to the recovery of minerals and the production of new elements. One of the first payoffs may come from the artificial stimulation of gas wells. Further off is the possible use of nuclear explosives to create deep aquifers for storage and transfer of water. Of all the potential applications, the one most likely to have early economic value is earth moving. The technology for excavation is being refined through AEC-sponsored field work and laboratory studies. A nuclear explosion deep underground also provides a unique opportunity for basic research through the generation of electromagnetic radiation with more heat and pressure than are available from any other source. Applications to mining are being explored, as are industrial-scale chemical reactions not attainable any other way.

One of the objectives of the Plowshare program has been to determine whether nuclear explosives can be used to dig a new sea-level canal across the American isthmus to replace the Panama Canal, but the Canal Study Commission recommended against it. The big problem in surface excavation, of course, is to reduce the amount of radioactivity released to the atmosphere. The Soviets claimed more than a decade ago that they had moved mountains and changed rivers with nuclear explosives, but the rest of the world has not seen the work. The first U.S. explosion in the Plowshare series, Project Gnome, was set off underground near Carlsbad, New Mexico, in 1961. The second, 1962's Project Sedan at the Nevada test site, had the explosive equivalent of 100,000 tons of TNT. It dug a crater more than 1,200 feet across and 300 feet deep, displacing 10 million tons of earth in a few seconds.

RESEARCH

The charm of AEC, a scientist once observed, is its research policy. Chairman David Lilienthal and all of the members of the first Commission named by President Truman emphasized that they knew that one of the primary requirements of the job was to restore a constructive environment for research for American scientists, who were sick of war and its misuse of their talents. Sumner Pike understood the importance of research to the people in it; Bill Waymack understood the importance of research in terms of its social impact and contribution to the life of the nation; Bob Bacher, a researcher at heart, understood its significance from every standpoint, and Lewis Strauss understood the technique as well as the value of research. No succession of commissioners has changed the initial staff concept of research. No bureaucracy consciously or willingly gives up a good thing. This is why AEC has been a continuously successful government research administrator.

Admittedly, the bureaucracy has had help. Harry Smyth, who followed Bacher as the scientific member of the Commission, did more than help maintain the traditional standard of professional integrity of science; he upgraded it. In terms of mental brilliance, the line of scientific members of the Commission probably peaked with John von Neumann, one of the mathematical geniuses of all time. Willard F. Libby was the first Nobel Prize–winner to serve on the Commission. He was succeeded by John H. Williams, who was one of the great teachers of science but who served less than a year. Leland J. Haworth came to the Commission for a few months from a post he had held with distinction—director of Brookhaven National Laboratory—and moved on to the directorship of the National Science Foundation. He was succeeded at Brookhaven and on the Commission by Gerald F. Tape, who was the model of the new scientist—a combination of manager of programs and master of his field.

The longest-serving member of the Commission, the longest-serving scientist, and the longest-serving chairman, was Glenn T. Seaborg, discoverer of plutonium, Nobel Prize–winner, and successful administrator—somewhat to the surprise of those who helped him along in the early stages of his career as a chemist. He was appointed Chairman by President Kennedy in 1961 and reappointed by Presidents Johnson and Nixon. The progress and accomplishments of the Commission since his first appointment were sufficient tribute to his tenure, which ended in 1971.

Research is an essential part of any technical effort or undertaking, whether it be steelmaking, space exploration, or the manufacture of modern munitions. Atomic energy research cuts across the entire spectrum of scientific subject matter. Nuclear technology is a means as well as an end. Atomic energy research has always followed three distinct, constantly mixing, but still identifiable lines—to learn more about nuclear structure and behavior; to exploit nuclear technology and all its appurtenances in an effort to learn more about everything else; and to determine the response of everything else to the nuclear radiation environment. On this knowledge base, the practical applications of atomic energy are built: weapons, submarine propulsion, space propulsion and auxiliary power, thyroid treatment, plant mutations, activation analysis, electric power plants, and age-detection techniques. There is clearly no limit to AEC's search for new knowledge, as long as it bears some relationship to atomic energy. In 1967, Congress extended the AEC realm in order to permit the great talent of the national laboratories to be applied to current social problems that might respond to technical attack. One of the things that came out of the Argonne Laboratory was a computerized braille tape for the blind. Even the National Science Foundation, bastion of unfettered search for knowledge, has financed environmental studies at the AEC National Laboratories.

AEC's research is carried on in two different ways, in its own laboratories and through hundreds of research contracts under which individual scientists and organizations pursue specific projects of interest to the Commission. The principal AEC in-house research facilities include Ames Laboratory at Ames, Iowa, operated by Iowa State University and rooted in the metallurgical work of Dr. Frank Spedding; Argonne National Laboratory, Illinois, successor to the wartime Met-Lab, now operated by the University of Chicago with heavy kibitzing by an association of some thirty universities; Brookhaven National Laboratory on Long Island, operated by Associated Universities, Inc., which has a tradition of no classified—no secret—work and was once considered as a possible gift to the U.N. to help launch President Eisenhower's Atoms for Peace program; Lawrence Radiation Laboratories at Berkeley and Livermore, California (named for E. O. Lawrence, developer of the cyclotron and proponent of electromagnetic isotope separation); the Los Alamos Scientific Laboratory at Los Alamos, New Mexico (the last three are operated by the University of California); and the Oak Ridge National Laboratory at Oak Ridge, Tennessee, operated by Union Carbide Corporation.

These are all multidiscipline laboratories. Some of them have a higher proportion than others of AEC-assigned work, or programmatic research. The difference can be understood if one takes programmatic research to mean research aimed at solving specific problems encountered in the AEC program. Pure research is the search for knowledge without a necessarily understood utilization, much less a profitable or practical application. A lot of people in the AEC have spent a lot of time thinking up ways to convince members of congressional Appropriations Committees that pure or basic research has to be done, whether or not the Commission knows what will be done with the knowledge produced. They haven't done too badly, since the AEC physical research budget climbed from a little over $100 million in fiscal 1959 to more than $300 million in fiscal 1968. It has, of course, suffered with all federally sponsored research in the budget squeeze at the beginning of the 1970's.

The directors of the national laboratories have always been among the most effective performers before committees of Congress in support of AEC requests for research funds. Walter Zinn of Argonne carried the brunt for years, and Norman Hilberry, who succeeded him, was almost as effective. In recent years, Dr. Alvin Weinberg, director since 1955 of Oak Ridge National Laboratory, has been a champion of broadening the research programs of the national laboratories to deal with national needs outside of the atomic energy field. He has been an inspiration to many young researchers who believe their talents should be applied to problems of the whole society.

Physics is the basic science of atomic energy, even though it takes the chemists to put it to work, and AEC conducts many kinds of studies in nuclear, atomic, and classical physics. Much of the work requires specialized—and usually very expensive—equipment, including reactors and accelerators. In addition to basic studies on the structure of the nucleus and the properties of matter, AEC physicists also work on improvements in isotope separation methods. High-energy physics is concerned with the elementary particles of matter, their interactions, and their place in the basic structure of matter. High-energy work gets more than a third of the physical research budget. To further extend the frontiers of work in this field, AEC has built at Weston, Illinois, not far from Argonne, a new National Accelerator Laboratory, which will have a 200-BEV (billion electron volts) particle accelerator with a magnet ring a mile and a quarter in diameter. Under certain conditions it can be punched up to 500 BEV, the scientists hope. Its initial price tag was $250 million, also subject to being punched up.

In addition, AEC does a lot of medium- and low-energy physical research. Most of the work in the medium range from 50 MEV (million electron volts) to 1 BEV is aimed at a better understanding of the nucleus itself. Low-energy physics, below 50 MEV, provides more immediately useful knowledge for use in the reactor and weapons programs and also produces interesting new evidence as to the formation of heavy elements in the interiors of stars, formed very slowly in some cases and relatively quickly in certain types of stellar explosions. All three levels make use of accelerators, which are machines to accelerate charged nuclear particles up to very high speeds, or energies, and to aim them at target nuclei. AEC is supporting research at seven accelerators of various sizes at Brookhaven, Lawrence, and Argonne National Laboratories, at the California Institute of Technology, and at Harvard, Princeton, and Stanford universities.

Research in chemistry as it serves atomic energy emphasizes the properties and reactions of radioactive materials, the chemical effects of radiation, the behavior of materials under both thermal and radiation stress, and chemical theory. There are two objectives: applying atomic energy to chemical problems and applying chemistry to atomic energy problems. A great deal of chemical engineering work goes into the study of fuel processing of irradiated fuel elements. The work labeled as chemical in atomic energy laboratories has necessarily had to bridge the gaps between chemistry and physics, between chemistry and metallurgy, and between chemistry and biology.

One of the major problems of the atomic energy business since its beginning has been the separation of the disciplines of science. There is probably no way to avoid this specialization, which means some have to be trained as biologists, some as chemists, some as physicists, and some as specialists within each general field. Yet, to achieve progress, all have to work together because nature doesn't recognize disciplines. In the field of the biological effects of radiation, for example, one of the areas of greatest concern in applying nuclear technology beneficially to man's problems, biologists need the help of both physicists and chemists. That's why we have such specialized areas of study now as biophysics, biochemistry, physical chemistry, and nuclear this and nuclear that. All are involved in studies of the biological effects of radiation. All are involved in the application of nuclear science and its techniques to the study of basic life processes, and all are involved in environmental interactions. Science educators today recognize the problem, but bureaucratic jealousies in universities make for slow change.

The AEC's biological, medical, and environmental research is concerned with radiation as a research tool, with understanding the interaction of radiation and biological systems, and with providing guidance for control of radiation exposure. Scientists use radiation to solve practical problems in medicine, biology, agriculture, and food processing. There is no field of knowledge of nature, no discipline concerned with the structure of matter or the processes of life in any form that is not subject to probing with the tools of atomic energy. Of course, one cannot escape the fact that atomic energy itself creates some of the problems that have to be studied. Research in health and safety, including radiation measurement, radiation protection, and investigation of the chemical toxicity of nonradioactive materials involved in atomic energy processes, are programmatic requirements.

Don't be surprised that AEC supports research in history—geological history, that is. It is important to the studies of the behavior of uranium and thorium. And studies of the natural occurrence of radioactive and stable isotopes are important to our knowledge of all the materials of the earth and the planets and the stars. Research in metallurgy is closely related to geological studies. Our ability to make constructive use of the energies of nuclear reactions depends upon our knowledge of the physical behavior of materials. Corrosion and the stability of alloys are of critical importance. It is not just the new problems that arose with atomic energy applications that have given us trouble in, for example, the power field. We've known about rust for a long time. We haven't known about fission for very long. Yet, in the design and operation of nuclear power plants, corrosion has given us a lot more trouble than neutrons. The metallurgical research in the AEC program is aimed at learning more about the structure of metals and their properties and responses under the stress of heat and radiation.

Nearly 10 per cent of the AEC research budget goes into thermonuclear research—not a very good term to describe the field. Controlled fusion is much better. The fusion (or joining) of the nuclei of atoms of the lighter elements liberates many times more energy than the fissioning (or separation) of the nuclei of the heavy elements. Like nuclear fission, fusion can be employed in weapons to create an explosion. In these systems—A-bombs and H-bombs, respectively—the reaction of fission in the former and fusion in the latter is allowed to proceed in accord with the laws of nature, without interference by man (although he provoked it), or, in other words, the process, once begun, is uncontrolled. We have learned how to control the fission reaction. As a matter of fact, we learned how to let it proceed under control— as in the first pile at Chicago—before we learned how to sustain an unrestrained reaction, as in the first weapon test at Alamogordo.

Researchers hope to learn how to control the fusion reaction. If they succeed, man's energy-need problems will all be solved, practically forever. One material that shows promise as a fuel for fusion reactions is deuterium, a heavy form of hydrogen, occurring as one heavy hydrogen atom out of every 6,000 hydrogen atoms in water. That doesn't sound like very much, but, considering the amount of water in the earth's biosphere, there is enough of this valuable raw material to meet man's energy requirements for millions of years. The fusion process has the advantage of not producing the residue of radioactive debris that we get from the fission process.

The U.S. effort to achieve controlled fusion for the production of electric power is known as Project Sherwood. The principal work is going on at the Oak Ridge National Laboratory, the Plasma Physics Laboratory at Princeton University, the Los Alamos Scientific Laboratory, and the Lawrence Radiation Laboratory. Supporting work is done at the National Bureau of Standards, New York University, a number of other universities, and in industrial laboratories. The "line" being followed by researchers in this field is the creation of a small "sun," in terms of the attainment of temperatures of hundreds of millions of degrees. It is generally agreed that we simply have to learn more about the laws of physics in order to be able to contain a plasma of such thermal intensity. Significant progress has been made in the first decade of this effort, but it is truly a long-range project.

REACTOR DEVELOPMENT

The program and progress in the development of nuclear reactors for the production of power, the main objective of the reactor development program, are covered in Chapter V, but the AEC effort in this field is concerned with basic research as well as with the applications of the technology to the generation of power. The big power plants described in seven-digit "name-plate-ratings" are the glamorous and visible demonstrations of the peacetime applications of atomic energy. There are necessarily many brilliant behind-the-scenes researchers in AEC laboratories who must provide the answers the power plant designers will need for the next generation of power plants.

The backstage work in the field of reactor development falls into six main categories. Probably the most important is reactor safety. Every component of the reactor system is under study all the time. Evaluations are constantly being made on properties of materials, fracture characteristics, irradiation effects, leakproofing of every kind, and techniques for testing such things as 12-inch-thick sections of exotic steels that might be used in future pressure vessels for water reactors. The safety people try to find something wrong with what everybody else does. Their job is to find a way for something to go wrong, then help find the way to prevent it. One of their special assignments is to devise techniques to find out whether something is going wrong before it does, or before damage shows up. For example, they have developed a way of using supersonic echoes—acoustic emission techniques—for the detection and location of incipient failures in the walls of piping and reactor vessels. It is still a laboratory technique, but it looks very promising.

Closely related to the safety work, and pushing it for first place in reactor technology programs, is the business of figuring out what to do with radioactive wastes. In typical bureaucratic style, it is called the management of radioactive wastes, although it is a technical, as well as a management, challenge. There are two main purposes to the research and development and operating effects. One is to prevent, or at least control by holding to minimal levels, radioactive emissions of any kind into the environment—into the air or into water resources. The second is to find ways to hold in absolutely inviolable, nonsoluble, immobile solid form the wastes that are the unavoidable product of fission. Atomic fuels have their ashes just as coal does, but they can't be used for ballast or cinderblock or paving materials. AEC has found a way of converting liquid radioactive waste into glaze-surfaced solids, but there are those who say we can never be absolutely sure of protective measures against the hazards of radioactive wastes. The safest storage for long-life radioactive wastes is believed to be in deep salt mines. An attempt to establish such a facility as a demonstration project in a deep salt formation in Kansas was blocked by local environmental protectionists. AEC is now seeking a site elsewhere.

The third and fourth areas of reactor development technology are fuels and materials. They are closely related. The stability under irradiation of the fuel element itself is a critical factor in reactor operation, but then so are the stability and integrity of all the materials surrounding it. The work involves a search for new alloys and for new ways of combining, coating, sandwiching, and compressing materials, including the development of a new class of materials called cermets, or semimetals with the strength of metals and the heat resistance of ceramics. These materials have been developed further and applied in the space program.

Fifth is the area of fluid dynamics and heat transfer. This work sometimes gets pretty basic. When the boiling water reactor concept was first being investigated, a theorist was explaining to a group of listeners one day how the system could be expected to behave under certain conditions. A skeptic interrupted with, "How can you say that? We don't even know how water boils." The result, believe it or not, was that, in the middle of the twentieth century, an AEC laboratory had to do special research to find out how water boils. But this is typical of the nuclear power business. One of the problems of liquid metal coolants, which is being worked on as the most promising way of removing the heat from very small spaces in a breeder reactor, is the uniformity of heat distribution in the materials. A balanced and predictable transfer of heat per unit of surface exposure between coolant and fuel element is essential. New things are also being learned about the heat pickup capabilities of gas, which has many advantages (and disadvantages) as a coolant for very high temperature systems.

The sixth area of reactor technology development is control and instrumentation. It has been learned that there is a fixed and definable relationship between the sound velocity and temperature in materials. This makes possible new temperature-measuring techniques and the use of instruments that employ ultrasonic waves. In liquid-cooled reactors, boiling of the coolant is very objectionable. A "hearing aid" has been developed that enables the reactor operator to hear bubbles collapse. Such an acoustical detector warns the operator of boiling and permits reduction of power or shutdown to halt undesirable boiling of the coolant. And for the inspection of materials, X-ray techniques and principles have been carried to a new level of effectiveness through neutron radiography, a technique in which neutron bombardment permits very precise plotting of the response of the material being inspected. Any variation in the section, even the tiniest vestige of a crack, is detectable.

In addition to the six principal categories of reactor technology development, there is a seventh that outshines all the others, and that is reactor physics, the essence of the business. This, practitioners insist, is the purely nuclear end of the business, the rest is hardware and plumbing. But all of the hardware and plumbing affects reactor physics. The problem is to determine exactly how the reactor will behave and how well it will operate when all of the materials have been put together—the coolant, the fuel element, and the structural materials that hold the fuel in place. The reactor physicists have to figure out how the thing will work, for example, after various amounts of fission debris have accumulated in the fuel elements. It is not a simple business.

SPECIALIZED NUCLEAR POWER

The most significant, perhaps the truly distinctive, characteristic of nuclear fuels compared with all other energy sources is that of energy concentration. The energy packed into a pound of ordinary fissionable material such as U-235 or plutonium is just about two million times the amount of energy in a pound of high-grade coal. In other terms, a pound of uranium has the energy content of six thousand barrels of oil. A nuclear power plant may get a year's supply of fuel in one charge.

One other characteristic of uranium as a fuel makes it an ideal energy source for one important military application—the fact that it "burns," or fissions, in the absence of oxygen and without emission of any product into the atmosphere. For submarines, this is ideal. Despite these obvious advantages, the road to acceptance by the Navy of nuclear power for the propulsion of undersea vessels was not always a smooth one. It was laid out by a determined and often ruthless nuclear surveyor. The wiry, tough, and technically brilliant Admiral Hyman Rickover, who could be both cantankerous and ingratiating at the same time, had a way of irritating Navy brass. Had it not been for people in AEC and, especially, on Capitol Hill, who had faith in him and his ideas, his naval career might very well have ended in 1953, when he was about to be passed over for promotion to admiral.

Congressional supporters of nuclear propulsion helped propel the career of the restless Rickover. Right after World War II, he went to Oak Ridge to study reactor technology. He formed an unshakable conviction as to the potentials of nuclear propulsion and became its almost fanatical advocate in a Navy that sometimes found it hard to respond with alacrity to the proddings of this excited Jules Verne in a blue uniform. What might have been a normal Navy development effort was aborted by Rickover's administrative deftness in drawing upon his credit with the Joint Committee on Atomic Energy (which at all times has been an aggressive proponent of applications of nuclear science) and upon AEC's eagerness to fulfill its defense obligations by setting up an AEC-funded submarine development program under a dual AEC-Navy policy guidance structure. Admiral Rickover wore two hats and, by playing the two agencies with both skill and daring, he got what he wanted—a nuclear navy.

The first nuclear submarine power plant was a land-based prototype, erected in a big tank filled with seawater in the middle of an Idaho desert on the AEC's National Reactor Testing Station. The tank contained the center section of the submarine, with the nuclear engine and essential parts of the propulsion and control machinery, which AEC built and turned over to the Navy. Through this strange and circuitous route, the Navy came by its extraordinary capability in the application of specialized nuclear power. Even into the early 1960's, the Navy had hard-boiled reasons for going slow on development of power plants for surface vessels. In its January, 1969, report to Congress, however, AEC was able to describe the naval propulsion reactors program as a "joint effort of the AEC and the Department of the Navy which has as its objective the design and development of improved nuclear propulsion plants and reactor cores for installation in Navy ships ranging in size from small submarines to large combatant surface ships."

The report went on to say that Congress had authorized 108 nuclear-powered submarines, including forty-one of the Polaris missile-launching type and one deep-submergence research vehicle, in addition to seven nuclear-powered surface ships. By the end of 1972, 104 subs were in actual operation with nuclear power systems, as were four surface ships—the aircraft carrier *Enterprise,* the guided-missile cruiser *Long Beach,* and the guided-missile frigates *Bainbridge* and *Truxton;* two nuclear frigates and one aircraft carrier (the *Nimitz,* with twice as much power as the *Enterprise*) were in the water, being outfitted; and two more carriers and three frigates were under construction.

The next most significant specialized application of nuclear power, at least in terms of the investment, is the nuclear rocket propulsion program for space flight. It is a joint AEC-NASA effort aimed at providing a substantial increase in propulsion capability for future space missions. The program has finally settled down to the NERVA (Nuclear Engine for Rocket Vehicle Application) project to develop a 75,000-pound-thrust engine, which could perform most of the advanced missions seriously considered by NASA. It works by heating hydrogen to more than

4,000°F and exhausting it to produce thrust. An extensive development effort in support of the NERVA project is under way, involving the reactors to be used to heat the hydrogen and the specialized fuel elements able to withstand the thermal stresses encountered. Full-scale testing of a ground-based engine was successfully completed in 1969.

In reporting on the rocket propulsion program, AEC in 1969 pointed out a lesson that had been learned at great cost in dollars and time: "Programs which provide basic technology usually have general goals or objectives; the development of systems for space flight missions requires a clear statement of requirements. Therefore, the first step in NERVA development has been to determine engine requirements from a detailed definition of likely missions and to document all studies and decisions that pertain to the process of determining requirements." An aircraft nuclear propulsion program stumbled along for some fifteen years at a cost of hundreds of millions, but little came of it that the Air Force could use, largely because the military planners and fliers could never agree on the mission requirements. The AEC-NASA effort in space has suffered from similar administrative wheel-spinning.

The Los Alamos Scientific Laboratory has had the lead among AEC laboratories—although all have contributed—in the NERVA project, with industrial backup of major and substantive participation by Aerojet-General Corporation, Westinghouse, and Rocketdyne Division of North American Rockwell.

Propulsion is only half the story in the development of nuclear systems for space. Space vehicles, manned and unmanned, need power on board. The energy concentration of nuclear fuels has long since paid off for this purpose. One SNAP (System for Nuclear Auxiliary Power) generator, albeit a small one delivering less than 5 watts of power, has been operating in a navigation satellite since June, 1961. Another, delivering 25 watts, has been in orbit since 1963. Both had been designed and built for five years of operation in space by the Martin Company Nuclear Division (since taken over by a new company called Isotopes, Inc.). The same people had another SNAP generator ready in 1970 for a weather satellite. Its use was delayed because the launch was aborted due to malfunction in the guidance system. The plutonium fuel elements were ejected and recovered from the

Pacific Ocean undamaged. One Apollo lunar landing crew left on the surface of the moon an Apollo Lunar Surface Experiments Package (ALSEP), which included a plutonium-fueled SNAP generator with a design life of one year, delivering a steady 50 watts of power for experimental equipment placed on the moon. It had been built by General Electric and tested for up to 25,000 hours of dependable operation.

One secret of the dependability of these systems is that they have no moving parts. Electricity is generated by thermocouples, loops of dissimilar metals, joined to a heat source. Electricity will flow in the loop circuit when the two junctions are at different temperatures. The radioactive plutonium-238, with a half-life of eighty-seven years, supplies the heat. These thermoelectric systems have the advantage of very long life and dependability, but the disadvantages of low power output and weight. For higher power needs, AEC is working on thermionic systems, in which a selected metallic or semimetallic cathode material is subjected to very high temperatures in a reactor, "boiling off" electrons that can be gathered on a collector plate in a flow of electricity. The thermionic systems can generate more power per unit of weight than the thermoelectric type. They are being worked on by Gulf General Atomic, General Electric, Thermo Electron Corporation of Waltham, Massachusetts, and the Los Alamos Scientific Laboratory. For still higher power requirements of long-period manned flights or orbiting vehicles, AEC and its contractors are working on compact, self-contained power plants that are virtual miniatures of big plants in that a coolant takes heat out of the reactor and transfers it to a turbine-driving gas, as in a Rankine heat cycle. In other types, the gas goes direct from reactor to turbine, without going through the evaporation-recondensation cycle, in a direct pass known as the Brayton cycle.

In another of those semantic ironies of the atomic energy program, the biggest demand for what AEC calls its Terrestrial Isotopic Power units comes from underwater users. In the spring of 1968, the second report of the Congress on Marine Resources and Engineering Development said the most critical unmet need of underwater technology was for power sources with longer endurance, since underwater missions, except by military nuclear submarines, were limited by the capacities of batteries.

The unique characteristics of radioisotope devices, the same in principle as the space units, makes these systems highly useful for activities involving underwater surveillance, for weather buoys, for navigational aids, seismic stations, undersea platforms, and commercial exploitation of marine resources. An extensive development program for power sources to meet these needs is under way, with Oak Ridge National Laboratory taking the lead in technology development and Minnesota Mining and Manufacturing Company and Westinghouse providing industrial backup.

Somewhat farther down the spectrum of power applications projected by former Chairman Seaborg as part of his scholarly promotional efforts is the nuclear-powered cardiac pacemaker— the little stimulator that can be implanted in the chest to help maintain a steady heartbeat rate. Present batteries for these little instruments, representing an incredible advance in electrical accumulation and storage in the past two decades, have a useful lifetime of from 1.5 to 2 years. AEC is working on a plutonium unit that will last 10 years. Somewhat behind the pacemaker in state of development is the nuclear power system for an artificial heart. Nuclear Materials and Equipment Corporation is working on the pacemaker. Parallel design studies on the artificial heart engine are being carried out by Aerojet-General, Donald W. Douglas Laboratories at Richland, Washington, Thermo Electron Corporation, and Westinghouse.

V

Energy

The wartime success of the United States in developing methods of releasing the tremendous energy locked in the nucleus of the atom brought more than the reward of military victory. It brought exciting promise of the release and application of this energy for civilian needs. It was precisely for this reason that civilian control of the atomic energy program was finally established. The probable civilian requirement for nuclear power, more felt than foreseen at the time of the debate on atomic legislation, was a more persuasive argument than the dangers of continuing military control.

In addition to the importance they attached to the unique applications of nuclear techniques and products in scientific research, medicine, agriculture, and industrial operations, it was believed by many, but not all, of the experts in the field that nuclear fuels would be of very great economic significance in widespread utilization for the generation of electric power. It was also recognized, but not emphasized, that the availability of nuclear fuels as an energy source might someday be critically important to the conservation of our finite supply of irreplenishable fossil fuels. The ultimate energy content of the nuclear fuels, if they could be fully exploited, would be sufficient not just to supplement the energy available from coal, oil, and gas but actually to release these fossil fuels for the uses that they are uniquely able to fill.

97

THE FUEL ENERGY GAP

Next to land, water, and air, which are essential to existence, energy is the most important terrestrial resource. An industrial society depends upon it. In common with the other three, it has no substitute. Today's society depends almost entirely upon energy originating in the sun. The vast bulk of this has been stored during hundreds of millions of years in the form of fossil hydrocarbons such as coal and oil. But these materials are increasingly important for more than just their energy content. Nature's accumulation process proceeds so slowly that, in terms of foreseeable human history, replenishment is out of the question. Although the supply is vast, we are consuming these materials at such a rapidly increasing rate that, if not supplemented, they will approach exhaustion within the span of a few generations.

The total energy contained in our recoverable fossil fuels of all grades is variously estimated to be between 30 Q and 130 Q.* The reason for such a spread apparently lies in differences in estimates as to the quantity of "marginal resources" (such as coal in thin veins or at great depths, or both) and differences in assessments of the feasibility and cost of recovering such marginal resources and in assumptions as to the fraction actually recovered in a given operation. There is little disagreement as to the amount of readily recoverable reserves. The Department of the Interior claims that about 6 Q can be mined at present cost levels with known technology, and something like an additional 25 Q could be recovered at 10–15 per cent higher cost, provided the technology of mining exploration and extraction is improved by further development. Decreasing accessibility would make the remainder increasingly expensive, to a degree depending upon the effectiveness of new technology.

Although our current consumption is small compared to the above figures, "the rate is increasing so rapidly as soon to be far

---

* In order to avoid unwieldy numbers, planners use a very large unit, the Q (for quintillion Btu, equal to a billion billion British thermal units). This is equivalent to the energy available in about 40 billion tons of average high-grade coal. The United States currently uses about one-twentieth of a Q per year.

from negligible," to quote from the AEC report to the President on civilian nuclear power, issued back in 1962. Estimates of future consumption are based on experience in population growth and per capita use of energy. So far in this century, fossil fuel use has doubled every thirty years. This rate may be too conservative for the rest of the century, since past increases would have been much greater had it not been for improved efficiency of use. The upward slope of the efficiency curve cannot continue for both practical and theoretical reasons.

Authoritative estimates of fossil fuel reserves, of population growth, and of future per capita energy use differ widely but generally indicate that, without the use of some supplementary source of energy, our low-cost supplies of readily available fossil fuels will be exhausted in from seventy-five to one hundred years, and the "guestimated" total supplies will be exhausted in about double that time. Even if ultimate exhaustion of these materials were made tenable by the introduction of acceptable substitutes for every purpose, the transition would not be made suddenly. At some time, long before the point of exhaustion of the fossil fuels, we would be obliged to begin to taper off their use, perhaps within the life-span of persons now living.

The fossil fuel resources of the world at large may be relatively more limited than those of the U.S. An energy study by the Committee on Natural Resources of the National Academy of Sciences has estimated that, with only 6 per cent of the world's population, the United States has approximately 30 per cent of the world's reserves of fossil fuels. The remainder of the world is consuming its reserves at approximately the same fractional rate as the U.S. but is increasing its consumption, with the exception of petroleum, at a much faster rate. The rapid growth of technology in the less advanced areas will tend to accelerate this relative increase. Hence, unless new fuel sources are found, the non-U.S. supply will probably be exhausted before our own. In any case, it seems certain that dependence upon foreign sources cannot assist materially the long-range conservation of our domestic resources of fossil fuels. This may not apply across the board, as for example, with petroleum, which accounts for only a small fraction of the world's total resources.

In qualitative terms, this coming fuel energy "gap" was sensed by the framers of the McMahon Act. Subsequent quantitative data, summarized above, has confirmed their "gut feeling." Continuing examination of the long-term prospects makes development of the nonfossil fuels imperative and, now that we have adequate data as to their availability, not only attractive but downright exciting.

In many important applications, the fossil hydrocarbons have special advantages that are not matched by their foreseeable large-scale substitutes such as fission, fusion, or solar energy sources. Such substitutes are not directly applicable, for example, to small mobile power units for automobiles and aircraft, although in time effective energy schemes may be developed to make them indirectly so. For example, battery technology may be so improved as to permit their use in private passenger cars subject to recharge from utility distribution systems drawing power from nuclear electric generating plants. But, as we have emphasized, the fossil hydrocarbons are important for more than just their energy content. They are essential in the iron and steel industry and in other metallurgical applications. They are the key raw material for plastics and synthetic fibers and represent a priceless heritage of complex molecular substances, the possible uses of which are only beginning to be recognized. For all of these reasons, we should supplement the use of fossil fuels and replace them as energy sources as soon as possible in those applications for which technically satisfactory and reasonable economic substitutes can be utilized on a significant scale.

AEC has recently been very concerned about conservation of these premium fuels. This has not always been so. Sometime about 1948, the Commission approved the conversion of the wartime Oak Ridge power plant from coal to natural gas despite protestations by some of the staff that the use of natural gas under boilers to generate electricity was "economically immoral."

THE NAME OF THE GAME

From the day of the announcement of the first use of atomic energy as a weapon, it was clear to many—and to some from the first confirmation of fission in 1939—that the energy of the atom's nucleus could be harnessed to do man's work. Every attempt to look into the future, then and now, reveals a growing need for new energy sources. But the ability of any potential nuclear or other source to supplement appreciably our total energy supply necessarily rests upon positive answers to two questions: (1) Can technically feasible and economically reasonable ways be found to utilize the new source? (2) Are the potential demands for energy and the available supply of nuclear fuels of sufficient size to be quantitatively significant?

In the early days, quantitative answers, that is, actual demonstrations justifying investment, were hard to come by. After the veil of military secrecy was lifted, everybody started to work with a firm conviction that the answer to both questions would be definitely affirmative. The public's confidence rested in large part upon the declarations of the Acheson-Lilienthal Report. Surely a way could be found to use efficiently the immense amounts of heat produced in a nuclear reactor. But at what price? From the beginning, there was confidence in the technical feasibility of utilizing the heat from the nuclear chain reaction. The economic feasibility, however, was highly speculative. The speculative element was laboriously reduced in the first decade and a half of the AEC program.

Similarly, the answer to the demand half of the second question (Are the potential demands significant?) was clear from the beginning: There would be an ever growing requirement for the heat produced in reactors. The two biggest markets are electric power generation and process heat. The power market, at least, continues to grow.

The supply half of the second question (Is the supply of sufficient size?) relates to the amount of source material available at acceptable cost. The answer seems now to be clearly affirmative. When AEC started working on this part of the answer, there were only a few known deposits of high-grade uranium ore in the world. But the geologists knew there was lots of uranium in the then less-than-economically-workable deposits, and the metallurgical chemists knew they could find ways to extract the uranium. They even found economically acceptable ways of taking uranium from gold mine tailings.

But even so, all this uranium would not be enough if we were limited to the amount of energy we can get from the fissionable isotope U-235, which, as we have seen, constitutes only seven-tenths of one per cent of the uranium found in the earth. AEC, in its 1962 report on civilian nuclear power, stated that

> . . . the fission energy derivable from this isotope in the known and estimated reserves of uranium that could be mined at costs not much in excess of those of the high grade ores being mined today is estimated to be less than 1 Q. Thus, if this were our only source, the contribution to our total energy reserves would scarcely be worth the developmental cost.

Fortunately, this is only part of the story. The real promise for the future is in the technique of "breeding" nuclear fuel. U-238, the common or garden variety of uranium, and thorium, which is even more plentiful in the earth's crust, can both be converted into fissionable material. Plutonium can be made from U-238, and U-233, also fissionable, can be made from thorium. In a breeder reactor, more fuel (fissionable material) is made than is burned, so the surplus can be reclaimed to serve as fuel for other reactors. The breeding business multiplies the energy potential of a given amount of uranium by at least 100, so the supply picture is radically changed. Very marginal ores become economic assets.

The energy potential of the nuclear fuel reserves dwarfs that of the fossil fuel reserves. Nuclear power development and exploitation thus are matters of increasing and long-lasting national importance. Nuclear fuels will account for a larger and larger share of our total energy consumption and ultimately will predominate. They can meet our needs for the indefinite future. It is evident now, even to the last die-hard militarists (whose nuclear material demands are finite and are effectively satisfied) that what the original band of supporters of civilian control could only feel in 1946 is now abundantly clear and true—that the name of the game is energy. Putting the civilian purposes and the military requirements under the civilian management, with industrial objectives but responsive to military needs, had been the principle of the McMahon Act. It was clarified and confirmed in the Cole-Hickenlooper Act of 1954, which effectively opened two doors for U.S. atomic developers, commercial opportunities at home and commercial opportunities abroad.

The Industrial and International Atom

The Atomic Energy Commission had seven good years, from 1947 to 1954. It restored to the atomic energy program the morale and much of the momentum that the program had demonstrated in developing the bomb. In 1947, the Commission had launched a long-range research and development program for peacetime uses, with electric power as one of its major facets. It had greatly expanded fissionable materials production in response to military demand but obviously without impairing its ability to meet civilian or industrial needs. The first nuclear-powered submarine had been launched, and the first fusion-type weapon device had been detonated.

But to many who had responsibility as well as cognizance in the atomic energy field, the good years would be followed by lean, unless the importance of industrial capability and motivation were brought to bear on the power development effort, and unless the industrial sector could receive training and specialized experience in nuclear ways. The government monopoly had to be relaxed, and some incentive for private investment, first of brains then of dollars, had to be devised within the framework of government responsibility for public safety, military needs, and security.

President Eisenhower took up another idea that had many supporters in the atomic energy community and throughout the public-interest citizenry. He decided it was time for another try at some kind of international control. In lieu of the internationalization of all facilities, services, and materials, proposed in 1946–47 by Bernard Baruch, President Truman's representative to the United Nations Commission on Atomic Energy, President Eisenhower, in his historic appearance before the U.N. General Assembly on December 8, 1953, made a counterproposal. In his "Atoms for Peace" speech, he proposed a pooling of nuclear materials by the "have" nations, then almost exclusively the U.S. and the U.S.S.R., and a sharing of technology with the so-called underdeveloped nations, for whom low-cost atomic power seemed to promise a panacea for many of their troubles.

The results of President Eisenhower's advocacy of international participation are reported elsewhere in this book (see Chapter

IX), but his proposal had a significance of its own in connection with the domestic power program. It happened that many of the supporters of the industrialization of the atom were lukewarm about the idea of internationalization, while many who favored extensive international cooperation expressed fear for the public interest and the consumer if the admittedly socialistic aspects of the McMahon Act gave way to private enterprise.

In one of those intriguing demonstrations of the pragmatic flexibility of our politico-economic system, the Joint Committee on Atomic Energy stepped in to solve the problem by the straightforward approach of combining the provisions for international cooperation and industrial participation in a single law. The AEC had proposed revision of the McMahon Act in two steps. The solution was advanced by Executive Director Corbin Allardice* of the staff of the Committee, with the backing both of Republicans, who then controlled the Congress, and of Democrats. The bill was almost lost, despite approval in all quarters, due to the injection of the extraneous Dixon-Yates issue (see Chapter II), but finally passed on the basis of a midnight compromise proposed by the then minority leader of the Senate, Lyndon Johnson, and the minority whip, Hubert Humphrey, and worked out by Allardice with Humphrey's staff.

The complete rewrite of the nation's organic atomic energy law paved the way for an epochal atomic power development program, whose progress by the late 1960's had exceeded the predictions of all the promoters except the 1948 predictions of the sober-sided General Advisory Committee. Many AEC watchers thought it pessimistic of the committee, of which J. Robert Oppenheimer was then chairman, to say it would be twenty years before any significant amount of electric power would be generated from nuclear sources. Oppenheimer interpreted "significant" to mean 3 per cent or more. (The amount generated from nuclear fuels in 1968 was less than 2 per cent of the total.)

Because he was one of the world's outstanding electric utility operators, AEC used Philip Sporn as an adviser on nuclear power

* Allardice and Edward Trapnell (the authors of this volume) who had worked together in both the Manhattan Project and the Atomic Energy Commission, were chided about a possible conflict of interest because, at the time of the drafting of the new legislation, Trapnell was legislative liaison representative of AEC. They claimed a commingling of interests.

from the very beginning. Sporn, for many years head of American Electric Power, had a hard time convincing the young nuclear power enthusiasts that all other generating technology was not going to stand still while they developed nuclear fuels. At first, some of them thought he was just "anti-nuclear." When their difficulties became clearer, he encouraged and urged them on, citing the inherent advantages of nuclear fuel and the even then foreseeable national need for a new fuel energy source.

The point is that during the mid-1950's, the predictions were quite optimistic. In the early 1960's, they were pessimistic. The year the nuclear power business actually "took off" was probably 1967. That was the first year in which more than half of the new plant commitment, in terms of generating capacity, was nuclear-fueled.

Despite the ups and downs, as measured in the speeches and publicity of the promoters, the accomplishments of the AEC and its industrial partners over the decade and a half since the change in the law are a tribute to the managerial and technological strength of the nation. They are also a tribute to the sagacity of the political managers in the Congress.

In carrying out the responsibilities assigned to it by the legislation, the Atomic Energy Commission has conducted a vigorous research and development program in its own facilities, has stimulated work in industrial facilities under contract, and has helped to build and maintain an environment in which industry could do its own work in its own facilities.

The 1962 special report of the AEC to President Kennedy stated:

> The Commission has conducted and encouraged a national program, aimed, first, at obtaining the basic scientific and engineering data needed for proof of technical feasibility and safety of the more promising approaches to nuclear power generation and, second, at demonstrating the actual or potential economic feasibility of such approaches. This program has been strongly backed in both the executive and the legislative branches of government.

The vast Sunday supplement dreams in the early months of the atomic age—such as running the then new *Queen Mary* across the ocean on the energy contained in a glass of water—soon gave way to the nitty-gritty of inventive progress. It is significant that the first major reactor project thought up by the new civilian Atomic Energy Commissioners was a materials testing reactor. They were forced to this decision by the barriers to nuclear progress erected in every other direction they wanted to go. The proponents of nuclear power simply didn't know enough. One of the important things they didn't know well enough was the behavior of materials under neutron bombardment. The materials testing reactor was referred to by Carroll Wilson as a reactor development reactor.

THE TECHNOLOGICAL STAIRWAY

The nuclear power program started with what had been learned through the wartime effort. But that was a single-purposed effort with a short-run goal. The Du Pont engineers, who had had to take the minimal Met-Lab data and—at the same time that they were gaining experience on the Oak Ridge pile—blow it up to provide engineering specifications for the huge production reactors at Hanford, were chided at the end of the war for "over-designing." The chiding was short-lived. Over-design was a good thing. A few years later, the Hanford production reactors had to be practically rebuilt, because final engineering had been done on the original reactors before anyone understood the graphite problem, and graphite blocks actually grew as they accumulated energy under irradiation. "Over-design" provided a margin of a couple of years of production.

Each time the planners of the atomic power era began a new line of development, they found they had to start with some fundamental materials testing. They didn't know enough about how steels and other materials would behave under intense neutron bombardment. High-grade boiler plate, for example, proved dimensionally unstable in the reactor environment.

Strangely enough, the nuclear problems encountered in the development of nuclear power have been much more readily susceptible to planned solution than the conventional problems of rust and leaks. For a variety of reasons, all very straightforward, it was decided at the earliest stages of the submarine propulsion program to use pressurized water as a coolant. But the problem of rustproofing and leakproofing against very hot water under very high pressure made even the traditional high standards and rigid specifications of the Navy seem something less than adequate.

For example, about halfway through the building of the pioneer nuclear submarine the *Nautilus,* Admiral Rickover, who managed the naval reactors program with the rigid discipline of a very tight ship, ordered all of the piping that had been installed before a certain date ripped out. Two types of piping, welded and seamless, had become mixed in the yard, and no one was sure which type had been installed. The admiral took no chances, even though the unsatisfactory pipe was better than any that had ever been available before.

Believe it or not, we've had a lot easier time with the new problems of neutron behavior than with old problems of rust and leaks. One never speaks of rust in nuclear circles; it's corrosion. Rickover was taking no chances on submarines. Fantastic detection techniques have been developed, and total X-ray examination of a reactor vessel is commonplace. During the planning stage of the experimental boiling water reactor (EBWR), craftsmen at Argonne said they could build a system so tight that the total leakage would never be more than three drops a minute. Thinking of the possibility of having to operate the reactor with heavy water as a moderator, the lab director said, "Hell, I'm talking about three drops a year." In designing the fuel elements for that reactor, Argonne had to conduct experiments to find out how water boils.

The first civilian nuclear power plant to go on the line of a utility and stay on the line as a dependable commercial supplier was the Shippingport, Pennsylvania, plant of the Duquesne Light Company. It is a pressurized water–type plant, taken directly from the design of the early submarine reactors. The Navy adopted the pressurized water system, which Rickover had learned about at the Oak Ridge school. Walter Zinn, the protégé and successor to Fermi—and director of the Argonne National Laboratory—agreed with Rickover that such a system could be brought to a state of practical application and naval standards of dependability quicker than any other. Admiral Rickover, again with Zinn's blessing, chose Westinghouse as prime contractor to design, develop, test, and manufacture the first submarine nuclear propulsion system. That is why today Westinghouse is the leading proponent and producer of nuclear power plants using water under pressure as the coolant to remove the heat from the region of the fission process. Nearly eightly nuclear power plants with pressurized water reactors have been built or are under construction—or committed—by Westinghouse, Babcock and Wilcox, and Combustion Engineering. The latter firm acquired Zinn as a vice-president in charge of research and development when it bought up General Nuclear Engineering, a company that Zinn founded when he left Argonne.

Zinn's name should probably be mentioned next after Fermi's in any list of contributors to the development of nuclear power. He sat up all night in the Hotel Washington in Washington, D.C., one night in the winter of early 1947 and wrote a paper that became, with little substantive change, the first reactor development program of the AEC. His paper was prepared as a recommendation to the General Advisory Committee. It proposed that AEC build the materials testing reactor first, then proceed with intensive developmental programs on pressurized water systems, heavy water moderated reactors, homogeneous systems, and fast breeders.

The program adopted by AEC in those early days was simply a matter of doing first things first—not necessarily the easiest things first but the things that AEC seemed most able to do in the light of available knowledge and that seemed to provide the soundest platform for subsequent developments. The U.S. nuclear power developmental program grew over the years in a quite orderly program of the AEC. His paper was prepared as a recommendationsciously shaped—by the people like Walter Zinn, his deputy Norman Hilberry (later Zinn's successor as director of the Argonne Laboratory), and Lawrence R. Hafstad, the Commission's director of reactor development in Washington and later engineering vice-president of General Motors. The four steps were described in the electric companies' national Public Information Program (PIP) *Nuclear Fact Book* as:

1. The development of basic nuclear technology and materials by the Federal Government and various research and development groups supported by the electric utility industry.
2. Testing of nuclear concepts through construction and operation by AEC of experimental plants.
3. A power reactor demonstration program, in which both government and private industry participate in the construction and operation of prototype nuclear power projects.
4. The building of nuclear power plants through private financing alone.

Every new reactor concept will go through something like these four steps. First to start the process was the breeder system, which the Commission actually authorized in 1947. The first model, EBR-I, became operational in 1951 and demonstrated the feasibility of breeding in 1952. A second, completely contained model, EBR-II, has been operated almost faultlessly since 1964. This technology is now being applied to full-scale commercial operating requirements in the breeder to be built by TVA and a consortium of power companies, led by Commonwealth Edison of Chicago, to feed the TVA network. Thus, the liquid-metal cooled breeder will have taken three decades to go through the first three steps.

During the early 1950's, while work in the first two steps was under way on breeders at Argonne and on homogeneous reactors and organic moderators at Oak Ridge National Laboratory, the water cooled systems took on another life. The pressurized system had been pushed at the beginning because water was the most convenient, most available, most familiar coolant. The system had to be pressurized to increase the heat-carrying capability, because the scientists thought that water could not be allowed to boil in a reactor vessel. The physicists reasoned with great confidence that the bubble voids would make the reaction unstable. They reasoned with confidence, that is, until a Friday evening in 1953 when Zinn, himself a proponent of the pressurized concept and unquestioning defender with all his peers of the can't-allow-boiling theory, suddenly questioned it. A staff member's casual dismissal of an idea in conflict with the no-boiling principle was met with Walter Zinn's shattering, "How do we know?"

On Monday morning, physicist Sam Untermeyer came into the laboratory director's office after a no-sleep weekend with sheets of detailed calculations and said, "Wally, my figures indicate we've been wrong. A boiling system should be inherently safe and stable." Subsequent field tests at the Idaho facility and increasingly sophisticated experiments proved the point.* In 1955–56, Argonne built the EBWR (Experimental Boiling Water Reactor) to demonstrate the principle. It worked like a jeweled watch.

---

* A series of experiments called BORAX I, BORAX II, etc. (for Boiling Reactor Experiment) was carried on under Zinn's direction at the Idaho Testing Station, including one experiment carried to destruction. Sometime later, reports from Europe indicated that Russian scientists had tried to figure out how and why the U.S. was using borax in a nuclear reaction.

The next step in the boiling system progression was a full-scale, privately financed, utility-oriented nuclear power plant on the system of Commonwealth Edison, serving Chicago, designed and built by General Electric, which took up the boiling concept—and Untermeyer with it—in wholehearted fashion. Some forty-five plants of all sizes have since been built or committed, most using General Electric designs. The boiling system enabled GE to overcome the lead that the Navy experience had given Westinghouse in building pressurized-water power plants. With continuing improvements, the two systems continue in competition. Which system a utility selects is usually based on some other consideration than cost.

Other systems have not fared so well. The only full-scale power reactor using sodium as a coolant, the Hallam, Nebraska, plant of Consumers Public Power District, was shut down in 1964 because of major technical difficulties and has since been dismantled. One organic-moderated reactor, built by Atomics International Division of North American Rockwell, delivered some 12,000 kilowatts to the municipally owned system of the city of Piqua, Ohio, in 1964, until it was closed down for a combination of economic and technical reasons. No other organic-moderated system has been put into service, although work continues on the development of organic moderators because of their desirable quality of low neutron absorption. Work has continued at Oak Ridge on molten salt systems, which have the advantage of very high heat transfer capability, and prospects seem to be brightening.

The first full-scale breeder system, designed and built by Power Reactor Development Company, a combination of electric utilities, engineering groups, and hardware suppliers, was named for the pioneer of reactor technology, Enrico Fermi. The power was to be purchased by the Detroit Edison Company, but the plant never reached its design capacity of 150,000 kilowatts. Most of the trouble has been in the complex heat removal system. Again, this is a case, consistent wth experience, in which problems of nuclear physics were easier to solve than problems of leakproofing and mechanical dependability. Some of these problems doubtless stemmed from the fact that the Fermi project may have been launched prematurely, at least in the light of the long-range nature of the program imposed in the mid-1950's by the early selection of the fast-breeder system. The sponsors hardly expected to begin construction work so soon, but then they hadn't counted on being coaxed or pressured into making the project a demonstration of industry good faith, a kind of antidote to threatened federal investment in nuclear generating plants. Then the sponsors had to fight a costly legal battle against opponents who claimed the safety of the system had not been established in accordance with the requirements of the Atomic Energy Act. More than $125 million has been spent on the project, all but a small part from private sources.

Nevertheless, the Enrico Fermi plant, at the west end of Lake Erie near Monroe, Michigan, was a significant project in terms of its technical contribution. It represented an imaginative and courageous approach to the breeding problem, and its sponsors demonstrated a staying power becoming to their vision. As a matter of fact, AEC has committed its commercial fast-breeder development effort substantially to the liquid-metal coolant system, so much so that some say the Commission has put far too many eggs in one basket. Utility engineers are far from unanimous that this type of breeder has the long-term promise that justifies such a concentration on a single system.

One other system should receive special mention because of its technical importance and the unwavering support provided by a single non-AEC advocate. This is the gas cooled system promoted exclusively in the U.S. by Gulf General Atomic, formerly the General Atomic Division of General Dynamics. Its higher efficiency pays off in lower thermal pollution as well as lower costs. The British have built many successful nuclear power plants using gas as primary coolant. Gulf General Atomic, under contract to a group of some fifty utilities headed by Philadelphia Electric (High Temperature Reactor Development Associates) designed and built America's first gas (helium) cooled plant. This is Peach Bottom Unit No. 1, on the Susquehanna River, which feeds 40,000 kilowatts to the Philadelphia electric system. A larger gas cooled plant of 333,000-kilowatt design capacity is due to go into service in 1973 on the lines of the Public Service Company of Colorado. Both are actually Step 3 projects—demonstration plants with costs shared by government and industry. These plants may be significant for more than technical reasons. The gas cooled system—so steadily advocated by Frederic de Hoffman (now with the Salk Foundation), who worked with Edward Teller as a graduate student at Los Alamos during the war and who launched General Atomic (as a division of General Dynamics) under Gordon Dean's tutelage after both had left AEC—subsequently became the basis for Gulf Oil Company's entry into the nuclear power plant business. Here came a third giant to compete with GE and Westinghouse, putting its blue chips on gas as a primary coolant, hoping eventually to be able to pass the coolant straight into a gas turbine. That may take a long time to accomplish, but after all, says Gulf, we're in the energy business, and the utilities should welcome more competition among their suppliers. Despite expressions of concern about the oil companies threatening to dominate the energy field, it was one of the policy objectives of the Atomic Energy Act of 1954 to "strengthen free competition in private enterprise." The tens of millions invested, first by General Dynamics and then by Gulf, surely modify the meaning of "free" as used legislatively.

THE ECONOMIC STAIRWAY

The technological progress on the nuclear front has been accompanied by (or, it might be more appropriate to say, has been measured by) a surge of progress on the economic front. The pace was not exactly predictable, but the actual advance was in response to a planned series of projects. First came the experimental program, then the demonstration projects. The latter included projects under which AEC built and owned reactors that supplied steam to utility systems, projects under which utilities were given AEC research and development assistance for privately owned reactors, and others under which AEC leased nuclear fuel at no cost.

Midway through the demonstration program, the Joint Committee on Atomic Energy recommended, on the basis of studies by its staff members, the expansion and extension of the nuclear power development effort. In 1958 and 1959, AEC conducted detailed analyses and evaluations of all reactor concepts that seemed to hold promise of economic nuclear power. The national laboratories as well as the nuclear industry took part. It was the first major revision of Carroll Wilson's four-reactor program of 1948, based on Zinn's winter-weekend paper of the year before. On the basis of these studies, the Commission published a series of reports that set forth what came to be known as the Ten-Year Program, establishing short-range as well as long-range economic goals. Two summary reports issued since then, the 1962 report on civilian nuclear power to President Kennedy and its 1967 supplement, provide a measure of progress. The latter report claimed that "the promise shown for nuclear power in the United States has developed beyond expectations."

The Commission also claimed that the known and estimated domestic resources of uranium were adequate to meet predicted needs of light water reactors for about twenty-five years, pending development of breeders and advanced converters (which do essentially the same thing). When the breeders are commercially available, they will provide a "virtually unlimited source of energy with uranium costs constituting a very small fraction of the energy cost."

The Commission predicted total energy consumption would increase 50 per cent by 1980, over the 1965 figures used in the report, and 150 per cent by the year 2000. The proportion of energy consumed in the form of electricity would increase from about 20 per cent of the total in 1965 to about 30 per cent in 1980 and 50 per cent in 2000. The expectations of such large increases were predicated on the use of electricity as a substitute for many of the present industrial and transportation uses of fuel and on large increases in the per capita consumption for residential and commercial use.

AEC also predicted that from 23 to 30 per cent of electric power generation would be from nuclear fuels by 1980, and 50 per cent by 2000. The rate of increase appeared to depend "largely on the technology and economics of advanced converters and breeder reactors, on developments in mining and transportation of fossil fuel, and on the extent and rate of discovery of low cost uranium resources."

American utilities maintain an unrelenting effort to hold down generating costs and would not hesitate to switch to a lower-cost fuel. Fossil fuel generating costs were steadily coming down until environmental quality factors began to limit usage to low-sulfur coal and oil. Acceptance of nuclear power by the utilities is therefore due mainly to over-all economics, according to the 1967 AEC supplementary report. According to the report, "the [1962] estimated cost of producing electricity in a 500 MWe [megawatts, electrical, or 500,000 kilowatts] base load nuclear plant was 6.2 mills per kilowatt-hour, whereas the current [1967] estimate for large size investor financed base load plants is 3.5 to 4.2 mills per kilowatt hour." The 1967 values for nuclear kilowatts correspond to a range of 17 to 25 cents per million Btu for delivered coal. In a reasonably comparable period of three years, 1962–65, the price of fossil fuels delivered to steam electric plants decreased from an average of 26.4 cents to 25.2.

Costs are no longer on a downward trend. Generation from fossil fuels cannot hold its own cost levels, even if gradual improvement in thermal efficiency continues. Increasing public pressure to reduce air and water pollution (stack emission to air and thermal pollution of streams by discharge of condenser water) is bound to result in an over-all increase in the cost of generating electrical kilowatts. Both capital and operating costs will be higher in a plant that cannot dump waste heat in some nearby flowing body of water. Cooling towers and plant cooling ponds are costly. Back in 1967, AEC hedged a bit by saying nuclear plant pricing might be affected by the backlog of nuclear plant orders, but little was said about the possible increase in power plant costs due to measures to protect the environment. Nuclear plants have an advantage over fossil plants in terms of air pollution but today's water-cooled steam-turbine nuclear plants constitute a significantly greater thermal pollution threat to lakes and rivers than do the most modern fossil-fueled plants. They also carry a tremendous cost burden due to health and safety requirements. From the standpoint of economics and conservation of resources, nuclear power is clearly here to stay, but the problems of public acceptance are not all solved. Meeting the criteria of public acceptance will undoubtedly add to the cost of nuclear power but probably won't change the basic economic relationship to power from other fuels.

For some years after 1957, when electricity from nuclear fuels first began to be fed into the nation's power network, many forecasts, including some by reputable scientists and engineers, continued to be pessimistic, predicting that it would be decades before competition would become effective. By the end of 1962, private industry and the electric utilities working with AEC had gained experience from half a dozen power reactors. But "as reliable as these reactors proved to be," said Chairman Seaborg, speaking at a Financial Forum on Nuclear Energy in October, 1968, "they were not economically competitive with conventional power plants, and therefore utilities were in no hurry to contract for nuclear plants on their own."

A turning point came in 1963, when Jersey Central Power and Light Company decided on the basis of a careful and thorough economic comparison to "go nuclear." It contracted with the General Electric Company for a 515,000-kilowatt boiling water system to be built at Oyster Creek near Toms River, New Jersey, after having weighed the fuel cost with that of a coal-fired station at the same location and another at a mine-mouth location. This was the first case where a utility had selected a nuclear plant on purely economic grounds, without government assistance, in direct competition with a fossil-fueled plant. The Oyster Creek project was plagued with construction problems and GE is reported to have lost heavily on the job, but it will remain a landmark if not a milestone on the road to economic feasibility.

At the Financial Forum on Nuclear Energy in 1968, Chairman Seaborg, after characterizing the growth of the nuclear industry in the previous four years as nothing short of remarkable, claimed that the key to the economic success for nuclear plants was their size. Units ranging from 500,000 kilowatts up to and exceeding 1 million kilowatts could compete with fossil-fueled plants in some areas and would later compete successfully even in areas where these fossil fuels were naturally abundant. The historic example was the decision by TVA in 1966 to build two 1,064 MWe nuclear power units at the Browns Ferry station in Alabama. The bus-bar power cost for these plants was estimated to be 0.46 mills per kilowatt hour less than the competitive coal-fired plant. Seaborg continued:

TVA's decision during 1967 to construct an additional 1,065 MWe* nuclear plant and the choice of a 1,300 MWe coal fired unit, both

* Megawatts-electrical, as distinguished from thermal output.

to be placed in service in 1972, reflected the finding that the relative cost of nuclear and coal-fired units was approximately a standoff at that time on the TVA system. During 1968, TVA evaluated bids for both coal-fired units and nuclear units; the quotations indicated increased costs in both types of plants, and it appeared that coal would be the winner. However, during the process of negotiation it turned out that a nuclear plant was more attractive and TVA ordered two nuclear plants from Westinghouse for operation in 1973 and 1974. The three previous nuclear plants were ordered from General Electric for operation in 1970, 1971, and 1972.

The atom had arrived at economic parity with fossil fuel energy sources at the end of a good twenty years of planning and stimulation by AEC and plenty of hard work in the government laboratories and in the development and production facilities of industry. The capital cost of nuclear plants is high, and the fuel cost low, compared to fossil-fueled plants. The "parity" is attained over about two decades.

Between 130 and 140 nuclear power plants had been sold by mid-1972, by five companies offering nuclear steam supply systems. The plants had a generating capacity of more than 130,000 MWe, or 130 million kilowatts. More than a score with a total capacity of nearly 15 million kilowatts were "on the line." Around 110 with a total capacity of nearly 100 million kilowatts were under construction or committed in one way or another. Estimates of the total capacity of plants expected to be in operation by 1980 vary from 150 to 200 thousand megawatts. (See accompanying map.)

THE STAIRWAYS CONTINUE

AEC Commissioner Wilfred E. Johnson in a speech at Oklahoma City reminded the homefolks of an Oklahoma lawsuit in the early days of flying. The suit sought to prevent the issuance of municipal bonds to build an airport. A local judge dismissed the suit on grounds of his conviction that "aviation is the comin' way of goin'." The U.S. Atomic Energy Commission continues to demonstrate its faith and conviction that nuclear fuels are the comin' way of making electricity.

The business of making power from nuclear fuels reached a major goal in the first twenty years of effort, but it is only an interim goal. The effort would hardly be worthwhile if the goal of economically competitive nuclear power from simple fission reactors were the end of the line. There are still two great goals. The really long-range one of the two is useful electric power from the fusion reactor. That one is sure to be reached, as sure as man's technological progress continues in an environment of sociological progress befitting his destiny. To be sure, if he cannot solve the problem of people living peacefully together in an increasingly crowded and threateningly poorer world, he hardly deserves to find the answer to the problem of constructive uses of fusion energy.

On the other hand, unless man does solve the controlled fusion problem, he may lose his chance to solve the people versus resources problem. Both population control and better use of resources are essential. Cutting losses due to waste is essential. Burning high-grade hydrocarbon-rich fossil fuels under boilers to make electricity is no way to cut waste losses. "Burning" uranium and thorium in breeder reactors is a giant step toward better use of resources. The sequential goals of breeder and fusion systems for generation of electric power are necessarily a part of the foundation of the technological structure within which man must live in the future.

The closer, shorter-range goals—the attainable nuclear goals—are sure to help us attain the people goal. The next and necessary technical goal is the attainment of nuclear fuel breeding.

BREEDERS

Breeder reactors, AEC Commissioner Gerald F. Tape once said to an American Power Conference, represent the ultimate in production of power from the fission process. Their importance is, he said, "their unique capability to create more fissionable material than they consume."

There are two routes to nuclear fuel breeding, one via thorium to uranium-233, the other via uranium to plutonium. In the former, thorium-232, with which the planet earth is plentifully endowed, is changed into thorium-233 through capture or absorption of a neutron in the fission ambience of a reactor. Thorium-233 decays to protoactinium-233, which in turn decays to fissionable

NUCLEAR POWER REACTORS

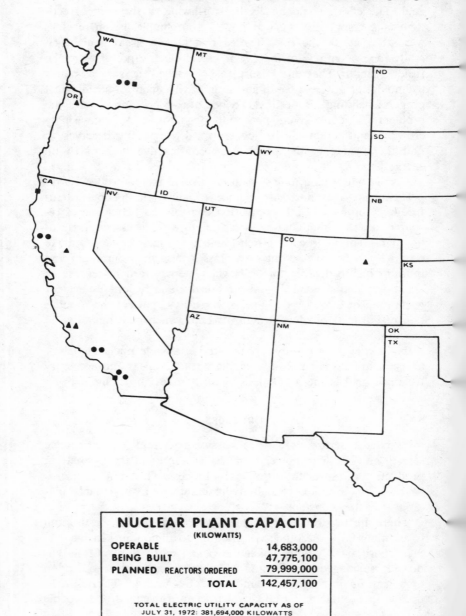

NUCLEAR PLANT CAPACITY
(KILOWATTS)

OPERABLE	14,683,000
BEING BUILT	47,775,100
PLANNED REACTORS ORDERED	79,999,000
TOTAL	142,457,100

TOTAL ELECTRIC UTILITY CAPACITY AS OF
JULY 31, 1972: 381,694,000 KILOWATTS

IN THE UNITED STATES

PUERTO RICO

LEGEND

OPERABLE	■	(29)
BEING BUILT	▲	(55)
PLANNED (Reactors Ordered)	●	(76)

U.S. Atomic Energy Commission
December 31, 1972

uranium-233. This process has the indicated advantage of working with either thermal or fast neutrons.

In the uranium-plutonium breeding cycle, the relatively plentiful uranium-238 is changed by neutron capture in a reactor into uranium-239, which is very shortlived and decays to neptunium-239, thence to fissionable plutonium-239. The process depends upon fast neutrons, giving rise to the term "fast breeder."

Breeder reactors are important for two reasons. First they promise to produce electricity at lower cost than by any other method, either nuclear or nonnuclear, and second they will effectively extend the supply of fuel by a vast increase in the efficiency of utilization of the fissionable or fertile materials. The so-called high-gain breeders should make it possible to use nearly all the uranium and thorium we can find and feed into the nuclear furnace. The reactors that AEC and the power industry learned to build in the initial twenty-year effort can burn at best but a very small percentage of the nuclear fuels put into them. It is possible, with recycling of the fertile materials produced in breeder reactors—fast breeders in combination with thermal "converters" —to use all of these fuels except for that small amount lost in reprocessing and refabricating the fuel elements. Breeder reactors as electricity producers are practically freed from adverse economic effects of fluctuation in the price of ores. The nonbreeding light water reactors by which nuclear power came into its own in the United States are definitely susceptible to the effects of any significant increase in the price of uranium ores.

Breeders offer hope of keeping up with the national increase in the use of electricity, which doubles about every ten years. There is every reason to believe that one type of breeder reactor— the liquid metal-fueled system, which is the expensive centerpiece of the third-decade stage of the AEC reactor development program—should have a doubling time of six to seven years, give or take a year. The doubling time is the time necessary for the reactor to produce a surplus amount of fissile material equal to that required for its initial fuel loading. The rate of breeding of new fuel could very well provide enough fuel to keep pace with the increase in demand for electricity. According to an AEC report issued in December, 1967 ("Forecast of Growth of Nuclear Power"), water reactors developed in the second decade, fueled with uranium and producing plutonium as a by-product, will, in the course of commercial operation through the third decade, provide additional supplies of plutonium for start-up fuel for a reasonable number of economically practical breeders due in the fourth decade.

In the first two decades of the nuclear power development, the federal government, through AEC, spent $2 billion to bring the light water cooled reactors to a state of economic practicability. More will probably be spent on the liquid-metal cooled fast breeder, which will require a correspondingly larger commitment of scientific and engineering manpower. AEC is supporting studies of several concepts that hold varying degrees of promise to meet the next goal of making full use of the available nuclear fuels. This cause is being followed for three reasons. First, the LMFBR (Liquid Metal Fast Breeder Reactor) may encounter technical difficulties. Second, the long-run economics of one of the other systems may turn out to be more attractive, and third, competition is served. Commissioner Wilfred Johnson acknowledged some years ago, however, "that competition based on quality is not very practical in an industry where the quality standards are necessarily imposed by regulatory agencies."

While developmental work has been steadily increasing since Zinn started work on the fast breeder in the late 1940's, intensive work really started in the mid-1960's, when AEC realized that, if the demand for power continues to grow, and if competing technologies don't offer more promising alternatives than were then in sight, then breeders had to be pushed. The decision was made to concentrate on the LMFBR for a variety of declared reasons, but the most obvious is that more was known about the system or, as the Commission said in its January, 1972, annual report, "there is a body of available base technology and organizational and operational experience."

Two programs are under way, one for establishing the technology, another for setting up a 300- to 500-megawatt demonstration plant to be built on the TVA system not far from Oak Ridge, as a joint TVA/Commonwealth Edison of Chicago venture. About fifty other electric utilities are participating in the demonstration. Each will contribute money and engineering brains and experience through an entity called Project Management Corporation. The plant should be in operation by 1980. Construction is due to start in late 1973.

If the schedule holds, it will be some kind of tribute to Chairman James Schlesinger that, within twenty years from the start of the Dixon-Yates attempt to deny TVA its needed power-generating capacity, the AEC joins forces with the New Deal-spawned regional public authority in undertaking the most technically complex nuclear power development project in AEC history.

The technology development program is concentrated in a new Liquid Metal Engineering Center, operated by Atomics International at Santa Susanna, California. It will have an elaborate array of test loops for sodium circulation, pump test beds, steam generators, and facilities for the cleaning, handling, assembling, and inspection of components.

The critical nuclear work for the LMFBR demonstration will be performed at a Fast Flux Test Facility being built on the AEC Hanford reservation. It will be the primary irradiation facility for testing LMFBR fuel specimens and assemblies, as well as providing facilities for testing fuel elements for other types of fast reactors.

Every possible step is being taken by AEC to solve any technical difficulties Commissioner Wilfred Johnson may have had in mind, and they are many, but since he made his statement, the horse that he called "the long-run economics of one of the other systems" has been gaining on the outside. This is the Gas Cooled Fast Breeder (GCFB), which is showing increasing promise from the technical work being done by Gulf General Atomic, backed by a group of some forty power companies. The gas system seems to have more appeal for foreign builders, especially in Germany.

The claims of the backers of the gas system, whether demonstrable or not, are such that AEC would be well advised to hedge its bet on the liquid metal system. The ratio of funds going into development of the liquid metal system as compared to other systems now under study is so disproportionate as to lead to a serious question of AEC's technical judgment. Through 1972, the private investment in the gas system was greater than AEC's. This in itself is significant. Some independent appraisals of the gas system indicate its doubling time and breeding ratio (mass of nuclear fuel produced to that consumed) would be as good as the liquid metal system, its capital costs less, and the coolant medium—helium—much easier to handle safely. Backers of the molten salt system are urging AEC to hedge further by investing in a third breeder coolant, lest fuel elements cannot be built to withstand the high temperatures of the liquid metal and gas cooled reactors.

One of the reactor types that AEC is supporting at the Bettis Atomic Power Laboratory, but with little input up to 1972 from private industry, is the light water breeder concept. Interest in this system stems in part from the possibility that, if the cost of uranium should increase significantly, many light water reactors now installed as first generation commercial power systems might be converted to use thorium and eventually, after several loadings, reach the thorium–uranium-233 breeding cycle. The Shippingport plant might be the demonstration guinea pig.

Another system considered but not supported by industry is the thorium breeding molten salt cooled reactor under development at Oak Ridge National Laboratory. It is a slow breeder in terms of its specific rate of reproduction of new fuel, but, because it has a low fuel inventory that may be recycled rapidly, its doubling time is acceptable. The light water and molten salt breeders lack industrial support mainly because of many unsolved technical problems. In other words, these systems are still in the first step of the developmental process described earlier in the PIP *Fact Book*.

NONTECHNICAL AND NONECONOMIC PROBLEMS

By most standards of government activity, AEC has an impossible job in the energy field. The staying power of the agency in its struggle with the nontechnical and noneconomic aspects of its job is no less remarkable than its efforts to make nuclear power both technically and economically practical.

The Atomic Energy Commission has responsibility, under the organic atomic energy law of the country, for both the development and regulation of nuclear power. AEC is supposed to stimulate the use of atomic energy and at the same time enforce the conditions of use imposed by its own regulations. There is sound basis for the argument that the two roles are incompatible. AEC, which has been blessed from the beginning with a staff of precedent-making quality, shrugs its bureaucratic shoulders and, without admitting the dichotomy, asks, "What are the alternatives?" The disarming but not humorous grin that accompanied the bureaucratic response for ten years, almost becoming its symbol, was that of Harold Price, the first AEC Director of Regulation.

Price was involved on the AEC side in the recasting of the original atomic energy law to relieve the government monopoly and open the field to private enterprise under regulation. From 1954 to 1971, he guided the AEC in establishing a regulatory environment that would permit the private sector, particularly the private electric utility sector, to grow and flourish. There has been almost continuing complaint about the red tape burden of the AEC licensing procedures but little valid criticism of the actual operation. None of the applicants for licenses have been more aware of the hazards of bureaucratic processes than the responsible AEC people, and the rules and regulations have undergone constant revision and improvement. The AEC regulatory process proved workable and successful for the initial period of growth, as indicated by the number of nuclear plants in operation or under construction in the 1967–69 period. But the 1970's have changed things. Recent public concern with the environment presents a challenge of which the AEC licensing and regulatory staff is only too well aware. AEC hopes that the greatly expanded demand for licenses can be met by shortening the issuing process on the basis of the safety experience and record of the plants licensed in the 1960's and early 1970's. But concerned members of the public, some technically qualified spokesmen for environmentalists, and new government groups like the Environmental Protection Agency and the Council on Environmental Quality are not so sure the standards applied to the plants built during the 1960's were what they should be. L. Manning Muntzing has the job of seeing that they are adequate for the 1970's.

In order to minimize the possibilities and implications of a conflict of interest within the AEC growing out of responsibilities having to do with regulation on the one hand and developmental activity and operations on the other, the licensing and regulatory staff is completely separated from the rest of AEC, organizationally and geographically. (It is about twenty miles from Germantown to Bethesda, Maryland.) The quasi-judicial function of licensing and regulating is completely removed from other AEC functions, but the five-man Atomic Energy Commission, sitting *en banc,* is, of course, the ultimate grantor of a license, and only at this final point does the AEC as an operating agency face any possible conflict with the AEC as the licensing agency in its own field of operations. There is irony in the fact that the licensing and regulatory function increasingly has more need for a five-man panel of especially qualified citizens sitting as a court than does the sprawling operations organization conducting the research and development, production, and other functions of AEC. There are those who argue that the operations could be better managed under a single administrator. Eventually this switch will be made, despite the argument that the regulatory staff is helped in staying technically abreast of atomic progress by virtue of its affiliation, if not association, with the other side of the house. The congressional Joint Committee on Atomic Energy favors the argument that the regulatory staff needs the support of the technical operators (see Chapter VII).

The regulators make more extensive use of the technical people in the family of AEC contractors than they do of the members of the AEC staff. Sometime during the late 1950's and early 1960's, the community of technically qualified people outside of the AEC structure grew bigger than the community within it. So, for such purposes as service on Atomic Safety and Licensing Boards, which conduct the public hearings on AEC license applications, the Director of Regulation and his aides do not have to depend upon their AEC colleagues. The people who serve on these boards make the determination for the public record as to the adequacy of the license application as regards safety standards and make sure that all requirements of the licensing procedure have been met.

Looking independently at the safety and technical factors is the Advisory Committee on Reactor Safeguards, made up of the best-qualified men available. Collectively they have competence in all disciplines bearing on the safety of reactors. As the committee's name implies, it is advisory and it performs not only a review function but may also probe into things it thinks need attention, like a grand jury. In the beginning, the committee did the principal reviewing and examination of applications for license, digging into every single one. As the experience and competence of the regulatory staff grew, the number of applications grew too. Today, the real digging job is done by the regulatory staff, while the part-time senior technical citizens on the Advisory Committee on Reactor Safeguards give advice and consent. The real responsibility is necessarily in the regulatory staff while the boards, the advisory committee, and the Atomic Energy Commission itself provide safeguards. The five-man Commission has the legally established responsibility. The performance of the AEC Regulatory Division in the first full-load decade of its activity affords reason for confidence in democracy's continuing response to the challenge of the atom.

ATOMIC POWER AND THE ENVIRONMENT

Ecology, biosphere, biodegradable, dieldrin, toxaphene, heptachlor—words once familiar only to the scientist and the technician—today have achieved common newspaper, if not household vocabulary status. Talk of environmental pollution is heard on every side. Politicians have rushed in to raise the STOP POLLUTION banner, and in a remarkably short time (so short that dedicated environmentalists fear the public outcry may prove to be only a passing fad) protection of the environment—of our air, our water, our open spaces— has become a major goal of our time.

Atomic energy, especially for generating electricity, inevitably is caught up in the great popular uprising against further despoliation of the Good Earth. Ironically, the atomic energy industry, the first in U.S. industrial history to be developed with public safety as the prime consideration from the very start, is now viewed by many as an industry pushing ahead without adequate knowledge of its actual or potential effects on the environment. Insofar as radiation effects are concerned, such a view is little short of maddening to the many research scientists, doctors, and technicians in AEC and among its contractors. Their lifetime work in the biological effects of radiation, complemented by similar research by others in this country and abroad, has developed a body of information about the effects of ionizing radiation on man that far overshadows the information available on the effects of common environmental contaminants due to coal, oil, chemicals, and dirt. The extent of this research effort was indicated in the response of AEC Chairman Seaborg to questions directed to him during a House Appropriations Committee hearing in May, 1969:

> Since its establishment, the Atomic Energy Commission has supported an extensive research program on the biological effects of radiation. For example, the operating budget administered by our Division of Biology and Medicine for FY 1969 alone was about 90 million dollars. In addition, research programs on the biological effects of radiation are supported by HEW and many private organizations in the United States and by many other nations of the world. Our knowledge on this subject is extensively documented in research reports and publications and in scientific publications by such groups as the International Commission on Radiological Protection, the National Council on Radiation Protection and Measurements, the Federal Radiation Council, the National Academy of Sciences, and the United Nations' Scientific Committee on the Effects of Atomic Radiation. In addition, this has been the subject of extensive hearings by the Congressional Joint Committee on Atomic Energy. The publication of the record of the hearings held in 1960 on radiation protection criteria and standards and the hearings held in 1967 on the nature of radioactive fallout and its effect on man are highly informative compilations of information on the biological effects of radiation.

Extensive worldwide research has provided the basis for the radiation standards adopted by the Federal Radiation Council, which AEC requires its licensees to observe. Conservatism has been the rule followed in the development of these standards. AEC claims that levels of the releases of radioactivity permitted in streams are set so low, for example, that a person could drink water from the receiving stream for a lifetime without noticeable effects. With regard to marine life, permitted releases take account of the fact that concentrations of radionuclides in some plants and animals may enter the food chain. The regulations contain tables of radionuclides with corresponding maximum limits on concentrations for each radionuclide and, if needed, reconcentrations. Similarly, permitted discharges to the air are such that only small amounts are added to natural background levels over the lifetimes of persons living near installations such as nuclear power plants.

In recent years, as power utilities plan and build greater numbers of ever larger electric power plants to keep pace with demands for electricity, actual and potential waste heat discharges into lakes and streams and other bodies of water have given rise to considerable public anxiety. Indeed, the growing protest against what has come to be known as "thermal pollution" threatens to bring about a very serious slowdown in the siting and construction of steam electric power plants. The consequent power shortage in the U.S. could be serious.

Warm water discharges are characteristic of all steam electric plants, those that draw their heat from fossil fuels and those that use the heat of atomic fission. Thus far, it is true, first generation nuclear power plants do discharge larger amounts of waste heat to streams than do the most modern fossil fuel plants, but the most efficient nuclear plants soon to come on the line will narrow and perhaps close the gap. AEC emphasizes this point whenever possible, but the public continues to worry more about nuclear plants as dischargers of waste heat for two reasons. They not only discharge more heat per unit of capacity but they are also several times larger than most fossil plants.

AEC is no newcomer to the problems associated with discharges of heat into the aquatic environment. At Richland, Washington—site of AEC's plutonium production reactors, which for years discharged sizable volumes of warm water into the Columbia River—the physical and biological impact on the river water has been studied since 1946 under the direction of the Applied Fisheries Laboratory of the University of Washington. Particular attention has been given to possible effects on salmon, and the studies have shown that the river in the vicinity of the Richland reactors has continued over the years to offer conditions not noticeably harmful to the salmon. The salmon population, in fact, has tended to grow rather than to diminish.

An interesting offshoot of the work at Richland is that a computer program developed for predicting temperatures of Columbia River water has been applied to other rivers providing cooling water for power plants.

AEC also sponsors research at the Chesapeake Bay Institute of Johns Hopkins University in the physical process of movement and dispersion of waste heat in tidal areas such as estuaries, and supports studies at the University of Miami on the effects of heat on the ecology of South Biscayne Bay in Florida.

While a great deal of attention is being given nowadays to technological development that will increase the efficiency of steam power plants and thereby reduce discharges of waste heat, and to alternative methods of disposal such as cooling ponds and towers, which themselves involve other environmental effects and economic penalties, studies are also under way on the possible beneficial uses of the waste heat. In Oregon, the Eugene Water and Electric Board is considering the use of warm water from a power plant to irrigate crop lands. Use of heat from power plant effluent water to increase the oyster harvest through doubling or tripling the spawning period is also under consideration. Whether these and other possible uses will prove beneficial and practical remains to be seen, but in the light of present knowledge, AEC questions the prudence of extensive investment in systems for putting to use the large amounts of heat to be dissipated by steam electric plants. AEC does not believe warm water should be regarded as a pollutant in the same sense as industrial wastes or municipal sewage. It is clear that changes in water temperature affect aquatic life, but it is not yet clear that these effects always must be adverse.

"At AEC," Chairman Howard Pyle of the National Safety Council has said, "safety is a way of life." The Atomic Energy Commission, long conditioned to thinking in terms of avoidance of environmental hazards, has had to adapt its programs and procedures to the National Environmental Policy Act of 1969 and the even more stringent water quality control legislation passed since. The federal court ruled in the landmark Calvert Cliffs case, brought by Chesapeake Bay environmentalists who objected to locating the Baltimore Gas and Electric Company plant at Calvert Cliffs, that AEC had to file environmental impact statements before approving construction of a nuclear plant. AEC requires public issuance of a broad statement of environmental considerations involved in every new steam power plant proposed for licensing and requires that the applicant, as a condition of his license, furnish a certification from the appropriate state or federal agency that all applicable water quality standards will be met. AEC holds public hearings at the construction permit stage and provides another opportunity at the licensing stage for a hearing at the request of any person whose interest may be affected.

AEC keeps reminding the environmentalists that steam-driven turbines, whether the plant is fossil or nuclear fueled, are the most effective machines available and must be relied on to meet constantly increasing electric power needs. But efficient as they are, AEC readily acknowledges, they present environmental problems, and it is evident that something must be done about those problems. A statement on environmental effects of steam electric plants, prepared by AEC in connection with hearings of the Joint Committee on Atomic Energy held in 1969, concludes with these words:

> It is imperative that we examine these environmental matters with some sense of overall perspective. We must start with the basic premise that power plants and associated facilities will be built to meet the energy needs of this country. Accepting this premise, we must then look for ways to minimize any detrimental impact they will have on the environment. The views of all affected parties must be sought and reconciled. Extreme positions on either side cannot be accepted. We all have a stake in protecting and preserving the environment, while at the same time recognizing that advances in technology are necessary for human progress.

Progress seems to be in the making as this volume goes to press. In the confrontation between environmentalists and technologists, recognition seems to be growing that both sides are in the same boat, and the confrontation shows signs of losing some of the rancor associated with unfriendly adversary proceedings. The techno-economic expansionists have finally begun to learn that environmentalists have been justified in questioning the way "overriding energy needs" is defined. It may be a lot cheaper to pay more for the energy if it enables us to preserve the biological support capabilities of estuaries and the water-gathering capabilities of covered slopes with strip-minable coal underneath. "Ecology should be a required course for engineers" is the way one educator put it. If there is improvement in the quality of the dialogue between the environmentalists and the technologists, some of the credit should surely go to the American Nuclear Society and the Atomic Industrial Forum, both of which have carried on steady programs of public education characterized by the assumption of intelligence on the part of the public and restraint on the part of the promoters of the atom.

There remains one area of serious concern among even the most knowledgeable of the environmentalists, such as Carroll Wilson, now professor at the Alfred P. Sloan School of Management at M.I.T. This is the area of very long-term safe waste storage and the safe management—to use the euphemistic terminology of the nuclear community—of the plutonium produced in breeder reactors. Plutonium is a very hazardous material, highly toxic with an extremely long radioactive half-life. It is a bone seeker, that is, it is held very strongly in the body in the bone structure.

TOUGH GOING AHEAD

As AEC began its second quarter-century, the arguments advanced by the earliest proponents of nuclear power development —that the country would need the new source of fuel energy— had come true with a vengeance. The situation that faced the nation in the early 1970's was frequently referred to as an energy crisis. Chairman Schlesinger didn't like to call it a crisis, but he acknowledged its seriousness. It was, he said, in an interview in the *Washington Post* in July, 1972, a combination of continuing increase in energy demand, a "topping out" in domestic oil production, an adverse balance of payments that makes increased imports a questionable solution, limitations on coal use due to environmental objections to expanded strip mining and the burning of high-sulfur coals, timid research and development efforts on the part of utilities, inadequate natural gas supplies, and delays in the licensing and construction of nuclear power plants.

He might have listed also the subsequently imposed AEC restrictions on the temperature permitted in pressurized water reactor fuel elements—in plants already in operation or well along in construction—as a result of questions raised in months-long hearings on emergency core cooling systems for water reactors. The effect is a corresponding reduction in power output for the 18–24 months required for replacement of fuel elements. The problem stems from the possibility that sudden loss of coolant in case of a rupture of the circulatory system might lead to such overheating of the fuel as to melt the structure that holds the fuel in place inside the reactor vessel and permit release of radioactive material.

According to Schlesinger, it takes eight years to bring a nuclear power plant on the line in the U.S. but only something like half that time in some other countries. It is hard to escape the implication that the ponderous licensing procedure and the environmental considerations are largely responsible. On the whole, however, he claims the environmental focus on nuclear power would prove constructive because it brings to light the fact that nuclear systems are environmentally the cleanest. The net effect of all the problems involved in energy generation and distribution is an upward pressure on ultimate costs to the consumer, which may mean 40 per cent higher prices within the next decade. The speed with which nuclear plants can be brought on the line will be an important factor in damping this increase.

To the AEC, all of these factors add up to a challenge that is just as great as that which confronted the spirited gang that took civilian control of the atom in 1947. The Atomic Energy Commission has had competent leadership, perhaps more consistently than any other department or agency in Washington since the end of World War II. But the job is tougher. There is no way to give an organization starting its second quarter-century the same zest and spirit it had in the beginning. The public, to a large extent, has caught up with AEC and authoritative pronouncements are seldom left unchallenged. As the atomic energy business has matured, AEC's public responsibilities have expanded. The early promise of atomic energy has changed into a challenge to deliver. The country needs the power.

Part of the response to the challenge is to extend AEC's horizon so as to cover more than just atomic energy. The agency is quietly but carefully expanding its activities in the total energy field. AEC has gone into research on the electrical side of the picture, an area traditionally left to the equipment manufacturers in the power field. Commissioner William O. Doub has said that the Atomic Energy Commission is increasingly concerned with the energy generation and transmission problems that affect the use of nuclear fuels as energy sources, and the congressional Joint Committee on Atomic Energy has begun in such a way that it should perhaps be renamed the Joint Committee on Energy.

The reason for this is simply recognition of the fact that the earth's resources are finite and the rate of utilization keeps going up. Population and the per capita use of energy increase at faster rates than ever before. Something has to be done, and the people in the Atomic Energy Commission are not given to handwringing. Neither are they panacea seekers. They believe the nation must have a more coherent energy policy and are ready to go along with President Nixon in trying to bring it about, partly through a shuffling of federal agencies to reduce the number—sixty by one count —of federal entities with a role of some kind in the national energy drama. In such a reshuffling, AEC could well find its civilian side split into several parts, each becoming part of a larger family of governmental units bound together by the common interest of meeting the nation's energy needs while preserving natural resources, safeguarding the public health, and trying to maintain economic order.

VI

Public and Secret Information and Security

The Atomic Energy Commission was born amidst a conflict of views that reflected basic differences in attitudes toward democracy. One view has roots in institutions, the other in individuals. The one view holds that strong government must protect people from their own foibles and foolhardiness. The other holds that the only solid foundation for government of a free people is a fully informed people. Democracy's response to the challenge of the release of the energy of the atom's nucleus is a continuous working out in pragmatic fashion of the essential accommodation between the institutionalists and the individualists—those who have confidence in secrecy as the key to national security and those who put confidence in attainment through broad participation in the national effort.

There was no simple resolution of this conflict in the worrisome period of the late 1940's and early 1950's. Secrets were important. Security was the term applied to all the means of preserving the secrets. But public information was important too, partly because the atomic energy field was expanding so fast it was hard to delineate areas requiring security, partly because an ever broadening range of new brainpower was needed—and partly because taxpayer support and public recognition of goals and objectives could be sustained only by an informed public. Ironically, the Smyth Report was at one and the same time the single most important

134

contribution to public understanding of atomic energy and the single most important security safeguard.

A monument in the field of scientific reporting, the Smyth Report provided a secrecy boundary line, the starting point for the AEC technical information program, and the first paving block on the road toward public acceptance of nuclear fuels as an everyday energy source. It picked up at the point at which American physicists decided to go underground in 1939 and brought the public knowledge of nuclear physics up to date—as of the nuclear-imposed end to hostilities of World War II. It established a barrier or baseline behind which the data left unpublished was to remain restricted until specifically released and provided a starting gate for the public information needed for such things as a legislative foundation for peacetime control and management of the atom. Smyth's work has stood the test of time. It has not even drawn complaint from any of the hundreds of scientists (including the expected number of prima donnas) about whom Dr. Smyth wrote one of history's great adventure stories. Two organizations that have been traveling the route he laid out—the American Nuclear Society and the Atomic Industrial Forum—finally in 1972 created jointly the Henry D. Smyth Award, with Dr. Smyth as first recipient in recognition of his great service to the atom.

The possibilities of military use of atomic energy had been recognized from the earliest days after the advancement of the hypothesis of fission and its experimental confirmation in January, 1939. American scientists, however, were, as Dr. Smyth pointed out, so unaccustomed to the idea of using their science for military purposes that they hardly realized what needed to be done. One group had actually turned down an offer of a grant of $1,500 from the Naval Research Laboratory, whose director at the time, Admiral Harold G. Bowen, thought there might be more possibility of using nuclear fuels to propel submarines than there was of making a nuclear weapon or bomb that could be carried in any known or proposed aircraft. It took the foreign scientists, many of whom had fled the terrors of Naziism, to arouse American physicists to the fact that Hitler could and would utilize the fruits of science and to convince them that they had better forgo for a time their cherished right to publish the results of research. Fermi, Szilard, Teller, Wigner, and Victor Weisskopf, all Europeans, buttonholed their New World colleagues at every opportunity and urged a stop to publication. Both British and American scientists agreed, particularly after Niels Bohr took up the cudgels. He, too, was used to free science. It took nearly a year to make the ban fully effective, even though a number of scientists voluntarily withheld reports on their own work. One event that slowed down imposition of the ban was the refusal for a time of Frédéric Joliot-Curie, France's foremost nuclear physicist and husband of Eve Curie, daughter of the discoverer of radium, to go along because of a letter-report submitted to the *Physical Review* and published before all of the Americans had been brought into the agreement.

In the spring of 1940, the National Research Council set up a so-called Reference Committee to pass on all scientific publishing, with a subcommittee on uranium fission, chaired by Dr. Gregory Breit and including Briggs, Pegram, Urey, and Wigner. There has been such a group at work ever since. Today it is an official AEC-appointed committee, and its judgments are just short of having the force and effect of law. It is known as the Committee of Senior Reviewers. As of this writing, it is headed by Dr. Warren Johnson, retired vice-president for Special Scientific Programs at the University of Chicago and onetime chairman of the AEC's General Advisory Committee. The committee studies the major technical activities of the Atomic Energy Commission program and advises the AEC on classification and declassification matters, making recommendations with respect to classification rules and guides for control of scientific and technical information. So, the scientists started the secrecy business and have continued to control its substantive application. The young scientists who at the end of the war were so exercised over Army security and secrecy would have swallowed hard had they known that, when Vannevar Bush proposed Army takeover of the work from his Office of Scientific Research and Development organization, President Roosevelt replied that he had no objection if Bush was satisfied that the Army made adequate provision for secrecy.

SCIENTISTS AND PUBLIC INFORMATION

When the next big effort on the application of nuclear science to a weapon came along, the development of the H-bomb, American scientists recognized the importance of secrecy, but they spoke out clearly against the hazards of concealment. Shortly after President Truman had ordered the go-ahead on the development of fusion weapon systems, Dr. Robert F. Bacher, then head of the Department of Physics at California Institute of Technology but previously the scientific member of the first Commission and one of the architects of the A-bomb at Los Alamos, had this to say on the subject of secrecy:

> It is most important in our democracy that our government be frank and open with the citizens. In a democracy it is only possible to have good government when the citizens are well informed. It is difficult enough for them to become well informed when the information is easily available. When that information is not available, it is impossible. While there may be some cases in which the information which the citizen needs, in order to make an intelligent judgment of national policy, must be kept secret, so that military potential will not be jeopardized, the present use of secrecy far exceeds this minimum limit. These are the methods of an authoritarian government and should be vigorously opposed in our democracy. . . .
>
> The citizen must choose insofar as that is possible. Today, if he tried to come to some conclusion about what should be done to increase the national security, the citizen runs up against a high wall of secrecy. He can, of course, take the easy solution and say that these are questions which should be left to the upper echelons of the military establishment to decide. But these questions are so important today, that to leave them to the military men to decide is for the citizen essentially to abrogate his basic responsibility. If, in time of peace, questions on which the future of our country depends are left to any small group, not representative of the people to decide, we have gone a long way toward authoritarian government.
>
> The United States has grown to be a strong nation under a Constitution which wisely has laid great emphasis upon the importance of free and open discussion. Urged by a large number of people who have fallen for the fallacy that in secrecy there is security, and, I regret, encouraged by many, including eminent scientists, to prophesy doom just around the corner, we are dangerously close to abandoning those principles of free speech and open discussion which have made our country great. The democratic system depends on making intelligent decisions by the electorate. Our democratic heritage can only be carried on if the citizen has the information with which to make an intelligent decision.

Dr. Bacher's words, extracted from a speech made at the Los Angeles Town Hall, were used by William L. Laurence in his book *The Hell Bomb*. Laurence had heard about the H-bomb when he was selected by General Groves to witness and write about the first explosion at Alamogordo. So impressed was he that his account had to be "color-reduced" by George O. Robinson, a former Memphis newsman, who was wartime public information officer at Oak Ridge, in order to get clearance from both the scientific and military heads of the project. Robinson later wrote a book, *The Oak Ridge Story,* dealing with the people side of the atomic bomb story at its largest and most important center.

Another ex-Memphisian who played a key role in keeping the wartime secret was Jack Lockhart, assistant to the deputy director of the U.S. Office of Censorship. Until General Groves got the idea that Lockhart had to be fully informed about the Manhattan Project, the atomic secret was in constant danger from inadvertent news references that might be very useful to knowing "collectors," who combed American publications as carefully as Groves's own intelligence staff combed foreign publications. By the time of the Hiroshima announcement, a number of newsmen and others who had nothing to do with the atomic bomb project had either deduced its existence for themselves or had to be told of it. Lockhart, one of the few newsmen to completely gain Groves's confidence, convinced the general in the spring of 1946 that he should have his own public relations staff, and the general hired the authors of this volume. A competent and congenial military man was in charge of the Manhattan Project public relations office. He was Major Robert J. Coakley, a quite unmilitary-minded officer in the parlance of the day, who shared philosophically and good-naturedly the not inconvenient isolation that the public relations staff suffered as a result of the intrigues of General Groves, first against passage of the McMahon Act and next against the confirmation of David Lilienthal as Chairman of the AEC.

As we look back on that period, the summer and fall of 1946, without benefit of diaries, it seems we spent a good deal of our time on internal "public relations" problems, worrying about the evident disenchantment of so many scientific people, and writing speeches (mostly for use outside the Manhattan Project) in support of President Truman's position on the legislation, with General Groves's clearance but not necessarily with his agreement. We convinced the general that he should not permit contractors' names to be put on the list of government-owned facilities (such

as Monsanto Clinton Laboratories at Oak Ridge and the General
Electric Atomic Power Laboratory at the Knolls outside of Schenectady) and helped Dr. Norris Bradbury get Los Alamos de-
militarized and renamed the Los Alamos Scientific Laboratory.
We helped Zinn and Hilberry get the Metallurgical Laboratory
renamed (and eventually relocated) and opened to the press and
wrote an aborted report of General Groves's stewardship of the
program between war's end and transfer to the AEC of the whole
function. We helped publicize radioisotope distribution from Oak
Ridge and wrote a story on the first controlled nuclear chain reaction for publication as a War Department press release on the
fifth anniversary of the first nuclear chain-reaction, which Groves
said was the "outstanding scientific achievement" of the Manhattan Project.

The two civilians in General Groves's public relations office became the second and third Manhattan Engineer District trans-
ferees to the new civilian Commission in November, 1946. The
first was Miss Virginia Olsen, who was also the first civilian employee of the District and had served throughout the war as secretary, first to Colonel James C. Marshall and then to Colonel Kenneth D. Nichols.

The aborted report on the really very solid planning done under
General Groves's direction between the late summer of 1945 and
the summer of 1946 never got security clearance, nor policy
clearance for that matter, but it served a useful purpose years
later when General Groves wrote his own story *Now It Can Be
Told*. It was useful in other ways because it showed how many
of the "name scientists," some of whose names were familiar to
the public in connection with the legislative battle of civil versus
military control, were still making constructive contributions to the
management and future policy directions of the atomic bomb
project. We watched the battle of the young scientists against that
day's equivalent of the "Establishment" from a position of
heightened interest, if not vantage, and thought then that some of
them were frustrated because politicians didn't behave with the
predictability of protons. The young scientists made their point by
the intensity and integrity of their arguments, and they taught
some of their elders in science that the fraternity could no longer
thrive in quiet cloisters and comfortable removal from the worka-

day world of gritty, grim, and sometimes grueling politics. A no less locked-in member of the Establishment than the Director of the Bureau of the Budget, however, had calmly assayed and stated the change. Harold D. Smith, in testimony on the Hill in another connection, had said, "I believe that science has far more to gain than to lose by being brought into the mainstream of public affairs as a more active force in our governmental system. For research requires the support that only our public resources can provide, and the power of science can be too far-reaching for it to grow in a state of irresponsible detachment."

WHAT MEANS SECURITY?

Proponents of military control of the atom argued in 1946 that security required that the atomic energy program be kept under strict military supervision. Civilian management and control would jeopardize national security. The two terms, "security" and "national security," were cleverly used interchangeably as though they meant the same thing. They do not. One is a means, the other is an end—the objective of the several kinds of security. In lieu of "national security," Congress finally settled on "common defense and security."

Proponents of civilian control argued that the surest path to national security was through achievement, not through safes and locks and electric fences. The scientific progress to be made by dissemination of technical data and the new discoveries sure to come from more people working in more laboratories would make greater contribution to the national security than trying to protect what was already known.

Congress listened to both arguments—and bought neither. It imposed civilian control and security, too. The civilians, of course, then had to demonstrate they could maintain security in the narrow sense as well as pursue it in the larger. In most aspects of security, they would end up being "more royalist than the King."

"Security" is a word like "science." It is both philosophy and motivation to some. It is a system, a technique, a method. It is also a body of knowledge, an expertise, a corporate professionalism. It is both apparatus and accoutrements. It can provide compelling reasons for doing almost anything. And it can be a helluva thing if misused.

As stated in earlier chapters, security occupied a lot of the time and talent of the AEC in its early days. Out of the self-consciousness resulting from being watched by the hawks and doves of the day, AEC evolved on the one hand an effective system to produce and disseminate scientific data and, on the other, an effective system for the protection of physical property and information. We will deal first with the protective aspects of security. In this sense, security has three areas of practice—personnel security, security of classified information, and physical security.

The area of personnel security is the most difficult and complex of the three. Its purpose is to assure the reliability—or integrity in its broadest meaning—of the people who have access to the facilities and information that are considered worth some trouble to protect against sabotage or, in the case of scientific data and other sensitive information, to prevent transmission to hands that would employ it to the disadvantage of the United States. Simply defining such information is the job of the declassification office. Determining whether and to what extent such transmission may have taken place or whether security information has been compromised is one of the critical security problems.

Security measures imposed by the fledgling AEC were not a matter of supercaution or enchantment with the secrets of nuclear weapons. Early in 1946, the Canadian Government revealed to the world the existence of an elaborate spy ring that had operated during the war, and a few weeks later announced that a young British nuclear physicist, Alan Nunn May, employed on secret nuclear work at Montreal, had passed information to Soviet agents. Not until 1949 was it known that a key British scientist serving at Los Alamos during the war, Klaus Fuchs, was an active Soviet agent, and that a master machinist, David Greenglass, was supplying information from the weapons center to a New York-based pair, Julius and Ethel Rosenberg, who went to the electric chair in 1953 for their espionage activities. The degree to which security had been compromised was indicated by the speed and success of the Soviet weapons programs.

Outright disloyalty, of course, is not the only criterion for determining security risk. Any pattern of behavior that might point to emotional instability or vulnerability to backmail, any associations that might expose one knowingly or unknowingly to channels of espionage are relevant to a security investigation based on what the Atomic Energy Act calls "character, associations and loyalty." Ordinarily, the Civil Service Commission now makes these investigations, but the case must be turned over to the FBI if any question of loyalty shows up.

The new employee first encounters the system when he is asked to fill out a personal security questionnaire (or P-S-Q), on which he is supposed to put down everything he knows about himself— where he has lived, gone to school, or been employed during the previous fifteen years. Fingerprints are taken and a photo made. The investigating agency takes these data and usually makes a quick "agency check" to see whether any other government agency has derogatory information of any kind about the applicant. This might take three weeks, if the record is clean, and then AEC can grant an interim clearance if filling the job is urgent. The full background investigation can take two to six months. This report is read and evaluated by a staff of trained AEC security evaluators who, if they find nothing questionable, simply recommend to the General Manager (if in Washington headquarters), or one of the Operations Managers in the field, that clearance be granted. If the security evaluators find derogatory information they are unable to resolve (sometimes things can be cleared up in an interview and a recheck), a recommendation against clearance is made and the applicant is so informed. He is told what the derogatory information is and that he can have a hearing before a personnel security board with the right to confront his accusers and be represented by counsel. The judgment of that board is subject to review by a personnel security review board, whose action is subject to appeal to the Commission itself. Few go so far. One that did, by a strange route, was the case of J. Robert Oppenheimer, the wartime head of Los Alamos. His story is told in Chapter VIII.

The AEC security people have striven honestly and with real understanding of the effects of the security machinery to improve and refine the basic system set up on the recommendation of a panel headed by former Supreme Court Justice Owen J. Roberts in 1948. Justice Roberts was succeeded on the Board by Charles Fahy, a former Solicitor General of the United States, who, in 1949, was succeeded by Ganson Purcell, once Chairman of the Securities and Exchange Commission. Purcell served for eighteen years. He was a guarantor of integrity, justice, and privacy in the AEC system. The operating heads of the system deserve mention, starting with Rear Admiral John E. Gingrich, who was suggested by Commissioner Strauss to get things started. Francis R. Hammack, a career professional security man, was acting director of Security for nearly two years during the difficult 1948–49 period. He was succeeded by Captain (later Admiral) John A. Waters, who served nearly twenty years. Bryan LaPlante also helped make security palatable, at least in Washington. As head of the headquarters security operations, he so smoothed many of security's otherwise raw edges that he was known as the "Maitre D' of 1901" (1901 Constitution Avenue, the original AEC headquarters office building).

The outward aspects of security are the passes and badges, the classification stamps and the safes, the windows barred or taped with conductive detection circuits, and being called back after hours to check the contents of a safe that the guards have found open. Some safes are so sensitive they are tied into an alarm system that can detect the presence of a human body after the safe is locked and checked for the night. One learns to be very careful about document inventories and recorded receipts for transmission, lest, when the time comes to leave the agency, one finds a top-secret document charged to him. The documents control people have been good at preventing such hang-ups. The Washington classified document control center was run with ruthless efficiency for many years by Mrs. Jeanne O'Leary, who had been General Groves's private secretary during the war. Not even super-security-conscious General Groves could complain about the way AEC took care of the documents transferred to it.

Just keeping tabs on the classified material in AEC files is a mountainous job, but the proportion of classified papers circulating today is far less than it was in the early days. The Security Division carries on a continuous and intensive education program. The director of security is responsible for security operations at all AEC facilities and for the security of all materials in transit. All the contractors, of course, have their own, or contract, guard forces, but in this area contractors are not encouraged to demonstrate imagination and innovative management. They stick to the security regulations.

The security education effort operates on the principle of advertising techniques—constant repetition. AEC staff members can't pass a bulletin board, or even walk around the halls of their ungainly building, without being reminded of their obligation to protect classified information. The posters change, but the message doesn't.

NEW PROBLEMS

AEC's security program, like many another such program involving large industrial and research complexes, underwent a reordering of priorities in light of the phenomenon of civil protest frequently characterized by large-scale, disorderly demonstrations and disturbances, campus unrest (sometimes erupting into violence and resulting in takeovers of university buildings), bomb scares, and actual bombings. In these circumstances an increased share of attention has necessarily been given to physical security, that is, the protection of property.

For the Atomic Energy Commission the potential for destruction of lives and property posed by the new accent on violence was pointed up sharply in April, 1970, when dissident students at New York University occupied the university's computer center and threatened to destroy an AEC-owned $34-million computer and other equipment used in AEC-contracted research unless the students' demands were met. Although the threat did not materialize, the two-day occupation, which ended with issuance of a court injunction, did result in damage in the computer area estimated at $50,000. The gravity of the developing situation was further emphasized for AEC when, in August, 1970, a bomb explosion at the University of Wisconsin caused the tragic death of a young researcher engaged in AEC contractual work and resulted in damage to AEC-owned research equipment estimated at more than $1 million. Following the trouble at New York University, AEC security issued basic standards for protection of university-based equipment. Since maintenance of elaborate protective forces and facilities is impractical for most universities, AEC security procedures provide for a series of emergency backup steps designed to enlist an increasing number of personnel and protective resources—local, state, national—depending on the nature and severity of the threat or incident.

Although 1970 ended without further incidents such as those at New York University and the University of Wisconsin, occasional bomb scares at such widely separated places as Las Vegas (Nevada Test Site), New York City (the AEC Operations Office), Princeton (the Forrestal Laboratory), and Washington, D.C. (the building housing AEC's downtown offices and other government offices has had to be vacated a number of times) have served to keep those engaged in physical security activities very much on the alert.

The prominence given to security considerations in the wake of threatened and actual violence has served to put a brake on action proposed from time to time to improve AEC's public image and bring it from "behind a wall of secrecy," as one newsman put it, by making the security operations less pervasive or, at least, less visible. Although half or more of AEC money and effort has for a good many years gone into wholly unclassified activities of high importance designed to promote peaceful uses of atomic energy, security guards and signs admonishing people to be close-mouthed lest classified information be inadvertently released are still much in evidence. Employees of high and low station must wear picture badges constantly while on duty and cannot enter or leave the buildings in which they work without displaying their badges to the guards. Visitors are carefully checked in and identified and pinned with temporary badges. Unless they have a "Q" clearance, they are escorted at all times, even, as *Newsweek* magazine noted in an article on AEC's twenty-fifth anniversary, when they go the bathroom. The impression gained by visitors, it is feared, is one of employees going about shush-shushing each other and carefully excluding the uncleared public from all but the merest fragments of unclassified information.

Such a reputation is sometimes a bit galling to AEC people, proud of the remarkable growth of peaceful uses of atomic energy that they have helped to foster. The world has benefited from the vast body of information developed over the years, including much having to do with radiation effects, made freely available in the open literature. More than galling, this appearance of secretive bureaucracy is becoming a matter of active concern within AEC as protests mount against AEC practices and standards—protests generally based on misunderstandings nurtured by what appears to be the secrecy fetish.

No one contends that criticism directed at the Commission can be quieted by so simple a means as merely pushing security operations out of view. There is, however, support for the argument that it would help to soften the charge of secrecy and at the same time would save a good deal of time, money, and energy invested in some security practices still observed more from tradition—a whole generation of it—than from need. Possible remedial steps of this sort that have received consideration include removal of classified work from the national laboratories and use of an "island" concept at AEC headquarters by concentrating classified information and work in limited areas. These and other steps to add to employee and visitor convenience and to make AEC people more easily reachable by the public have been seriously considered at one time or another. It is a fair guess, however, that further moves in this direction must await a clearing of the air and a relieving of the tensions that characterized the start of the 1970's. Violence of quite another sort, but still explosive in character, may postpone removal of the trappings of secrecy which were fastened on the atom amidst the violence of World War II.

SECURITY AND SECRECY

The story of the attempt to protect the wartime atomic bomb project from penetration by saboteurs and spies, to prevent inadvertent leaks of information by careless employees, and to stop publication of anything that might indicate the direction or involvement of the U.S. in atomic energy pursuits is now more legend than history, simply because it was never pulled together under the Manhattan Project and was not made a defined objective of the AEC's official history. It was a great subject for feature stories in the period immediately after the war because so many people were surprised that such a massive industrial and construction effort could have been carried out in apparent secrecy. But such secrecy was only relative. Bush, Conant, and Groves were urgently aware that the Germans probably had an eighteen-month lead in the drive for an atomic bomb. They knew that the Nazis had tried desperately to increase the output of the world's largest heavy water production plant at Rjukan in Norway when they overran that country in 1940 and had removed all the product on hand. The fear in the U.S. was that the Nazis were collecting heavy water for a reactor to produce plutonium for a bomb.

The Nazi scientists never did build a reactor that worked. The technical intelligence teams Groves sent to Germany as the hostilities ceased in Europe found that the top German scientists totally disbelieved that the Americans, with the help of the British and the great foreign scientists who had come to America on their own, had actually contained and controlled the nuclear chain reaction. One explanation for the German failure was that they had not detected the delayed neutrons produced by fission that made it possible to control the reaction. Zinn and Szilard had detected them in a basement laboratory at New York University. But every piece of intelligence that could be gleaned from Nazi-occupied Europe and every deduction that could be made as to what the Germans were probably doing led the whole atomic bomb community, civilian and military, scientific and industrial, to assume that we were in danger of losing the race for the atomic bomb. Groves's analysts in Washington found something almost every week in the flow of war news and intelligence data that indicated the Germans were working hard and making progress.

A basic principle of security in the Manhattan Project was compartmentalization. Nobody but Bush, Conant, Groves, and a very few of their closest advisers knew everything that was going on. Undoubtedly, there were things, especially in the security and intelligence fields, that not even Bush and Conant knew. The compartmentalization was an essential security measure, but it had its costs. There were times when the patience of men of great brains and goodwill was tested beyond that of Job because overwork was piled on overwork and somebody hadn't got the word. One of the wartime heroic attainments of Arthur Compton (an unsung hero of the wartime effort) was the overcoming of a crisis in the plutonium project that threatened to undermine not just topside confidence in the plutonium route to the bomb but reflected on the very competence of his men. He was able to hurdle the security barriers that blocked an exchange of views and data on how pure the plutonium had to be.

This compartmentalization practice was most resisted at Chicago—and most effectively. The Met-Lab people held a weekly colloquium, where there was an exchange of reports and data of which some of General Groves's security advisers did not approve. One of the things that annoyed some of the Chicago people was that General Groves somehow always knew what was going on. Oppenheimer, on the other hand, despite the colloquia and the spirit of the Chicago scientists, thought there was too much compartmentalization at the Met-Lab. He had responsibility for the fast neutron work dealing with an explosion, as contrasted with the Chicago work dealing with slow neutrons for production of plutonium. As head of weapons development, he decided that all the people involved in fast neutron reactions had to be brought together where they could compare notes and check each other's work. It was partly for this reason that he proposed to Groves a separate weapons laboratory with no internal information barriers. Instinctively security-minded, Groves bought the idea, which had an added appeal because the possibility of a super bomb, utilizing hydrogen, had already gotten over the compartmentalization barriers.

Locating the weapons laboratory at the most inaccessible, yet livable, place any of the scientists or military leaders could think of was both a positive and a preventive security measure. Some of the work required remoteness for safety as well as security reasons. But the location selected (Los Alamos) was still not totally secure. Despite the high fences, the single mountainous access road, the guards, the checking, the surveillance of travelers throughout a wide area, and monitoring of all sorts, one of the key scientists brought from Britain, a topflight physicist who had advised on the gaseous diffusion process as well as on fast neutrons, was revealed nearly five years later as having served as a conduit to the Soviets, who got everything he thought they needed in order to keep abreast of the military applications of atomic energy. This was Dr. Klaus Fuchs, whose scientific associates at Los Alamos estimated, according to William L. Laurence's *Hell Bomb* account, that the information relayed by this brilliant schizoid—by Fuch's own finding—enabled the Soviets to build an A-bomb at least a year earlier than otherwise would have been possible. (Laurence's estimate was from three to ten years.) Groves, before he knew about Fuchs or Allan Nunn May, who was revealed in early 1946 as having fed the Gouzenko spy ring in Canada, had said it would take the Russians from five to ten years to develop their own atomic weapons. May, also a British physicist, had been on the staff of the Montreal Project set up to work on heavy water reactors. The May revelation was a serious setback to British-American cooperation in 1946, and the Fuchs revelation in January, 1950, put an added order of urgency into President Truman's directive to build the H-bomb.

These events all had a bearing on the posture and policy of the new civilian Atomic Energy Commission, which assumed responsibility for security along with everything else on January 1, 1947. The McMahon Act required the Commission to report to Congress each January and July. The first semiannual report, dated January 31, 1947, included the following section on security—but none on public information:

> The Commission has maintained in full force the security measures of the Manhattan District and has under consideration the adequacy of those measures in terms of the requirements of national defense and of the act.
>
> The Commission has met with the Attorney General and with the Federal Bureau of Investigation for the purpose of establishing procedures for the investigation of personnel and of security violations.
>
> The Commission has been able to obtain the services of Mr. Frank J. Wilson, Chief of the Secret Service, until December 31, 1946, as consultant on security policies and problems.
>
> The Commission also has obtained the services of Mr. Thomas O. Jones as special assistant for security to the General Manager. Mr. Jones was formerly an officer assigned to the Manhattan District. He served as security officer at the Los Alamos installation and was designated by General Groves as the security officer at the Bikini tests.

Tom Jones, or Tojo, as he was known to his friends, was a revelation to some of the newcomers who had been through the summer fight on the atomic legislation and had formed some strange ideas about General Groves's security men. At the time, Jones weighed in at about 135 pounds soaking wet, a wiry but not athletic type, who spoke softly with a wry sense of humor topped off by impeccable manners. He didn't care for the security business himself but he helped make it endurable for many others and he served the new Commission and General Manager well in steering them into a shadowy realm where they were quite unsure of themselves. He retired from AEC in 1970 after spending something more than a decade in the international operations field—and in the process becoming an authority on Gilbert and Sullivan, with a wide repertoire of roles.

In its July report of 1947, the Commission reported to the Congress that it had actually strengthened some of the Manhattan Project security measures, not just continued them "in full force." AEC had also started a reinvestigation of all the people who had been "cleared" for secret data in the Manhattan District organization, since the law required that all employees who might have access to Restricted Data as defined in the Atomic Energy Act had to be investigated by the Federal Bureau of Investigation. The Commission also said it was instituting new document-accounting procedures and had established a new inspection system for all aspects of security.

The July, 1947, report also reflected the Commission's awareness that the information program had to be positive as well as protective. The section on Control and Dissemination of Information quoted the relevant provisions of the McMahon Act, stating:

> The maintenance and improvement of the United States position in the field of atomic energy requires a careful balancing of control and dissemination of information. In our desire to prevent unauthorized transmission of scientific information of military importance, we must not go to the extreme of permanently locking up all our information. We must inspire talented men to enter the new field and we must give them the information they need in order to proceed. To overconfine today's knowledge is to stifle the development which would provide security tomorrow.

The report added that the "Commission has reaffirmed the declassification policy established by the Manhattan Engineer District."

INFORMATION SERVICES

For the first half of the AEC's first year, Chairman Lilienthal vainly sought a "big name" to head the Commission's very important and, many felt, very vulnerable Division of Public and

Technical Information Services. With the guidance of the realistic William W. Waymack, who had come to the Commission as one of the nation's most respected journalists, the Commissioners established the criteria for the job. It would require: a skilled craftsman in government information work, who had the proper concept of the responsibilities and obligations of the job; a man who by performance and service had earned the confidence of the Washington press corps; and, finally, a man who was known on Capitol Hill as a professional in the field and not a grinder of axes for any official or policy. One man, long known to Waymack, fitted the bill. He was Morse Salisbury, whom Lilienthal finally recommended to the Commission. Salisbury at the time was with the Committee for Economic Development. His federal credentials originated in the Hoover Administration and included service as Director of Information for the U.S. Department of Agriculture and for the United Nations Relief and Rehabilitation Administration. Trapnell had worked with him in both agencies.

In its third (January, 1948) report, the Commission was able to tell of the support provided by its technical information program for its own research and training activities and those of contract industrial facilities throughout the country:

The Commission established late in 1947 a unified Public and Technical Information Service to insure, in accordance with the Atomic Energy Act, adequate control and dissemination of the information that is the lifeblood of scientific and engineering progress—and of public understanding of that progress and its implications. The Public and Technical Information Service combines five independent functions relating to the control and dissemination of information:

1. Preparation, reproduction, and controlled distribution within the project of classified reports to personnel requiring such information.
2. Declassification through analysis by qualified scientific reviewers of material which then becomes available for public use.
3. Editing, preparation, and reproduction of technical information materials, including indices, abstracts, project reports, and declassified papers.
4. Security guidance service—aid to publishers, editors, reporters, broadcasters, leaders of citizen groups, or others issuing material relating to atomic energy—in order to prevent compromise of restricted data; and assistance to contractors of the Commission and other agencies of government to safeguard restricted data.

5. Public information service—assisting representatives of the press, radio, picture services, citizen and trade organizations, and educational agencies in obtaining a full range of declassified and unclassified data currently available from the national atomic energy program.

The assistance given wasn't always to protect restricted data. Fred Blumenthal, a "leg man" for columnist Drew Pearson, came into the office one day about the fall of 1948 to say that his boss had a story to the effect that the private utilities had obtained a conspiratorial grip on atomic power and were holding back its use to prevent expansion of the public power program and to protect themselves against the economic consequences of power that, as Lewis Strauss said, regrettably, many years later in a quite different context, "would be too cheap to meter." It was a juicy tip, said the leg man, but the story didn't make sense. After a bit of a lesson on the fundamentals of nuclear power and a description of some of the technical problems confronting the people in the power development effort then just beginning, Blumenthal asked if the AEC staffer would have lunch with his boss the next day and tell him the same thing. The lunch was held and Drew Pearson was thereafter one of the regular "checkers" with the AEC information office.

At about the same time, the educational director of the boilermakers union, a key craft group in power plant construction, came in to talk about the low morale of some union members who feared their jobs would disappear with the advent of this new, cheap, simple, practically free fuel. That was the period when the Sunday supplement feature writers were talking about sending the *Queen Mary* across the ocean on the energy contained in a glass of water. The AEC information people spent a good deal of time with the representative of the boilermakers union, who in turn spent about three weeks reading and studying a comprehensive selection of books on the subject, as well as some recently declassified AEC technical reports. One day he brought back an armload of textbooks he had borrowed and made a remark that was prophetic of some of the problems encountered in the next decade of nuclear power development: "Atomic energy isn't going to do away with the boilermakers," he said, "but it sure is going to call for a lot better boilermakers than we've ever had before." The prophet was Charles F. McGowan, later head of the Office of Saline Water of the Department of Interior.

After about two years, Salisbury recommended the separation of the declassification function from the Information Service, because the specialized nature of the declassification work didn't gain anything, management-wise, from the affiliation and he felt there was a possibility of conflict of interest if the declassification function was under the same directorship as the issuing of information. The declassification work load had begun to build up. The first year, the 120 scientists and engineers serving as reviewers recommended declassification and general release of more than 1,000 out of 1,200 documents submitted, after changes and deletions. The business has grown steadily ever since. It doubled almost yearly for those first few years, finally growing to 25,000–30,000 documents a year, with an accumulated total nearing 700,000.

DECLASSIFICATION

The declassification function is a continuing one, despite the declarations of whole areas of work as unclassified. In 1948, AEC began to practice "classification" in order to try to keep the flow of materials through the declassification machinery within bounds. There will always be three categories of information; that which is unclassified from the start; that which is declassifiable through official review; and that which is clearly classified and retained as Restricted Data under the Atomic Energy Act.

There is a very specific AEC declassification guide. It is used by the reviewers who are full-time scientists and engineers in AEC facilities, although, in some cases, they work outside; each is selected for competence and stature in the designated fields of interest. A paper is usually read by two reviewers. If they disagree, or if the author appeals, then the paper is sent to at least three of the members of the Committee of Senior Reviewers. Their word is final.

The declassification guide is under constant review. In the early days, considerable difficulty was encountered in the military area, but the problem was solved by the adoption of a joint classification on certain data that were of military importance but could not be defined as Restricted Data under the Act. It was a thorny problem for a time, involving long (and deeply) held prerogatives on the military side and zealous adherence to the letter of the law on the AEC side. The security people, not just the declassification people, had strong views on both sides. When the impasse reached the General Manager's office, Carroll Wilson told them to sit down and define the problem areas clearly. A joint classification guide for the military applications of atomic energy was worked out under the guidance of Harold Fidler, first chief of the Declassification Office, a Corps of Engineers ex-officer with a Ph.D. in soil mechanics, whose patience and wisdom were important factors in the establishment of confidence in the civilian Commission's ability to protect atomic secrets. There has been no real problem since. Fidler is now associate director of the Lawrence Radiation Laboratory at Berkeley, having left the Declassification Office late in 1949 for a post in the AEC's San Francisco Operations Office. He had worked with the Berkeley group during World War II and eventually moved into the Laboratory. The second head of declassification was Dr. James G. Beckerly, who left AEC for private industry in 1954, and later spent two years with the International Atomic Energy Agency. Charles D. Luke filled the spot for about a year and was succeeded by Charles Marshall, who had started out as Fidler's deputy. A chemist by training, he once taught chemistry, then served in the Army, and came into AEC from a spot as research chemist for United Fruit. His deputy is Murray Nash, who has been with AEC since the Manhattan Engineer District days. Marshall heads a staff of thirty-one technical and clerical people who keep the machinery working to grind out papers that have been found, often after extensive editorial negotiation and manipulation, to be clear of atomic secrets as they are defined at any given time.

Except for the technology of power reactors, which was classified throughout the early years of AEC, the definitions of areas of data to be held back are now pretty much as they were when AEC first defined them in 1948. The general areas were: information on the production of fissionable materials, specifically all quantitative and qualitative output data; information on nuclear weapons, their components and testing; technical data relating to military application; and certain information relating to operations and facilities of the AEC program. The last has to do with information useful for sabotage purposes or having to do with strategic vulnerability of the United States.

Because information was needed for civil defense purposes, one of the big problem areas was the effects of atomic weapons. The first series of tests conducted by the AEC in the spring of 1948 at Eniwetok produced explosions more than double the power of any of the detonations up to that time—Alamogordo, Hiroshima, Nagasaki, Bikini—and clearly pointed the way to higher yields. Information as to the destructive effects of the more powerful weapons had to be made available to the public. On the recommendation of the public information people a Weapon Effects Classification Board was set up, under the chairmanship of Norris Bradbury, the director at Los Alamos, including the key people on both sides of the problem, military and civilian. The Board recommended the publication of a handbook or guide, to be prepared under the direction of the Los Alamos Scientific Laboratory. Ralph Carlisle Smith, chief of documentation at Los Alamos, came up with the idea that solved the problem of getting out data on more powerful weapons without revealing the actual power. He suggested using a "nominal burst" (the explosive equivalent of 20,000 tons of TNT, close to the known power of the Japanese bombs) then extrapolating to any number of times that yield with data consistent with the test results already obtained and still to come. He also served as the secretary of the board of editors that finally pulled the difficult volume together. Due more to his efforts than those of any other, AEC finally produced in 1950 the first edition of *The Effects of Atomic Weapons*. It was a difficult job, and as in the case of so many publication problems of those days, literally scores of people were directly involved. The volume was edited—and practically rewritten to overcome the usual effects of committee composition—by Samuel Glasstone, but the acknowledgments listed nearly a hundred contributors, reviewers, and technical advisers, as well as five authors.

One of the organizations that had come to AEC for help and guidance in those early days was the American Textbook Publishers' Institute, which sought an authoritative source book on atomic energy for use by textbook authors and editors. There was simply no place to go for basic reference data. Alberto Thompson, the brilliant first Director of Technical Information for AEC, turned to his friend "Sammy" Glasstone—this was before the Weapons Effects book—a professor of physical chemistry at one point but by then a professional textbook writer in related fields. With representatives of the Textbook Publishers' Institute they worked out a plan for a book which Dr. Glasstone wrote from scratch in little more than a year. AEC's input was a consultant's fee to the author, provision of basic documents for reference, and declassification. This source book on atomic energy, a significant and important volume, was published in 1950 by D. Van Nostrand Company. It has been revised and updated and remains a monument in its field.

Technical Information

The AEC technical information program ranks with the big publishing enterprises of the country, with more than 120 million pages a year. Its publishing activities include a $42-a-year periodical called *Nuclear Science Abstracts, NSA* for short, available from the Superintendent of Documents. It annually abstracts and indexes more than 50,000 items of the world's nuclear literature. Not surprisingly, items from other countries, less than 2 per cent in the first year, were nearly 55 per cent of the total in 1969.

The program also includes four series, published irregularly— as they become available or a need is defined—books, monographs, symposia, and critical reviews. AEC sponsors from one to a half-dozen books a year, about half of which are commercially published and distributed, the others being reproduced in government facilities or under contract and distributed through the National Technical Information Service of the U.S. Department of Commerce, Springfield, Virginia. The Service was set up and brought to full effectiveness under the direction of Bernard Fry, who had succeeded the late Alberto Thompson as Director of Technical Information for AEC. Fry is now head of library sciences at the University of Indiana and is one of the nation's experts on automated information storage and retrieval systems.

In addition to book-length works, AEC sponsors monographs each year on a wide range of subject matter, usually with a cooperating professional society, as, for example, the 1968 monograph *Fabrication of Thorium Fuel Elements,* produced with the cooperation of the American Society for Metals and published by the American Nuclear Society. AEC itself publishes the proceedings of a continuing series of symposia on various subjects.

Since 1962, more than 6 million copies of an AEC series of some sixty booklets, "Understanding the Atom," have been distributed. There is one of these useful little books on every phase of the atomic energy program. The series is in heavy demand in secondary schools throughout the world and has been translated into many foreign languages and transcribed into braille for the blind. Well illustrated and simply written, usually by professional writers, each booklet is reviewed for technical accuracy. Full sets are available to schools and libraries, and single copies of titles in the series are available from AEC, P.O. Box 62, Oak Ridge, Tennessee, 37830. The oldest booklet of them all is a dressed-up version of the December 2, 1946, War Department press release, now titled *The First Reactor,* with added chapters by Fermi and his wife Laura.

Between $6 million and $7 million is spent by AEC each year in providing materials to schools. One program, "This Atomic World," operated by Oak Ridge Associated Universities, runs a score of exhibit trucks, each with a lecturer-driver, that visit from 3,500 to 4,000 schools a year and reach 3.5 million students. Universities are cooperating sponsors in most states, and two have reported benefits in terms of increased admissions. In the state of New York the cooperator is the Empire State Atomic Development Associates, a utility group, which keeps two units in service to schools throughout the state.

The volume of scientific and technical materials being produced is now so great that twenty-seven specialized AEC data centers have been set up around the country. They serve as data banks, reference centers, and even provide consulting service in their fields of specialization. All are in AEC facilities, except the Oceanographic Data Center in the Naval Oceanographic Office in Washington and the Liquid Metals Information Center at the Atomics International Division of North American Rockwell, Canoga Park, California.

The organizer and manager of the AEC technical information operation for its first five years was the late Alberto Thompson, who left the agency to set up the science information service for the National Science Foundation. He had vision far beyond the norm for either academic or governmental bureaucracy and the patience and skill to build lastingly toward the goals he could envision (all the while educating his less imaginative colleagues, including the authors of this volume).

PUBLIC INFORMATION

One of Lilienthal's greatest contributions to the national atomic energy program was his insistence upon a public information program of substance. He believed that the only safe and dependable guidance for a free people is their own informed judgment, and he made a personal effort to establish a true basis for public policy guidance in the atomic energy program. He gave government public information people a new sense of duty and destiny when he wrote in 1949 (in *This I Do Believe*) such things as:

> If the American people are not acutely aware of the vital importance of this technical development to them, to their children, to their security, there is a real hazard that neither our great scientific talents, nor engineering nor administrative skills nor huge sums of appropriated funds can maintain the kind of indisputable and unquestioned atom lead in the world we need.

> We are a people with faith in each other, and when we lose that faith we are weak, however heavily armed. We are a people with a faith in reason, and the unending pursuit of new knowledge; and when we lose that faith, we are insecure, though we be so heavily armed.

> I look forward to atomic development not simply as a search for new energy, but more significantly as a beginning of a period of human history in which this faith in knowledge can vitalize man's whole life.

> There is not a single one of us who is a mere spectator, who can turn a knob and tune himself out, or leave if he is bored, or horrified, or is more interested in his private affairs. We are all participants in that future chain of events that these epochal discoveries have set off. There are no supermen to solve these problems for us.

> For the citizens of the world's leading democracy to be in the dark as to the nature of the fundamental structure and forces of the atom—and of the great good as well as evil this knowledge can

bring—would be for them to live in a world in which they are, in elementary knowledge, quite blind and unseeing.

These things and many more like them were originally said in speeches—and in earnest. Lilienthal was a believer because he knew that only a public informed by such reporters as Alfred Friendly of the *Washington Post,* Carl Levin of the *Herald Tribune,* and Thomas L. Stokes of Scripps-Howard could have bolstered the senators and congressmen who saw him through the attack by Senator Kenneth D. McKellar in the confirmation hearings and the charges of Senator Bourke B. Hickenlooper in the "incredible mismanagement" hearings. Lilienthal's faults were never entirely obscured by his declarations, but he established one policy that government information men always strive for but seldom attain—an open press policy that means what it says.

The Joint Committee on Atomic Energy also played an important role in building public understanding. Its publications have always been an important source of information, and its hearings, thanks to the chairmen it has had, have been designed to provide useful public information. Senator Clinton P. Anderson of New Mexico, when serving as chairman in 1955, named a publisher, Robert McKinney of Santa Fe, as head of a panel to survey the entire field of atomic energy. Each year the Joint Committee holds hearings (under provisions of the Atomic Energy Act of 1954) just to get a perspective on the state of the program.

The public information activities of the Joint Committee and of the AEC were effectively if informally coordinated during the time Gordon Dean was Chairman of AEC. Dean considered the external communications of AEC very important, having the same appreciation of public information obligations—and opportunities —as did Lilienthal. Dean saw those external communications in three areas: first, the government, including the Congress and the rest of the executive branch; second, the press—print and electronic—including general and technical periodicals; and third, what might be termed the agency's constituency in industry, education, and the scientific community. Dean had excellent relationships on Capitol Hill, he gave Morse Salisbury unstinting support in the public information field, and he appointed a special assistant, Oliver Townsend, to handle communications in the third area. Townsend had a master's degree in public administration and had acquired public communication experience under Shelby Thompson, chief of public information. Thompson, an ex-AP reporter and photo editor who had worked with Salisbury before either came to AEC, had standards of public information and reportorial decorum that sometimes rubbed even workaday newsmen the wrong way, but there was never a more competent or zealous guardian of the public interest. His pupil did well. Townsend left AEC in mid-1953 to help set up and manage, for several years, the Atomic Industrial Forum. He later helped organize and became first chairman of the New York State Atomic and Space Development Authority. He died of cancer in the fall of 1969, just as the Authority's ambitious program was gaining momentum.

After Dean's departure, AEC's relationships with the press suffered along with its relationships with the Congress as a result of the Dixon-Yates affair. A part of the problem was that Salisbury and his staff didn't know what was going on in the General Manager's office. One internal information service, a mimeographed periodical digest service distributed by the public information office of the AEC staff, was stopped after a national magazine story viciously critical of Strauss had been carried in full by the digest. The public information office became—with a vengeance—what Salisbury had said it should be, a strictly programmatic reporting center. Eventually, Strauss came to value Salisbury's judgment and the latter was able as the responsible public information head to serve the other function he considered his proper role, that of adviser on public affairs to the head of the agency. For the most part, the public information people in AEC have been effectively and properly used as before-the-fact advisers on management actions. Most of the agency's public relations troubles have come from actions taken without first notifying the public information people. The problems arising from the environmental impact of nuclear power and the criticism of AEC stemming from its dual role of promoter and regulator had been foreseen for a long time, but such matters were not among the responsibilities of the information staff.

When John A. McCone succeeded Strauss as Chairman in 1958, it was widely rumored in Washington that President Eisenhower had impressed upon the wealthy shipbuilder and construction contractor the importance of improving relations with the

Joint Committee and the Congress. McCone made Salisbury a special assistant to the General Manager in order to take full advantage of his long experience in Washington, which, in addition to his information work, included handling the complicated congressional relations in the field of agriculture. Salisbury retired in 1961 and died a year later. The top information job had been taken over by Duncan Clark, an 8-year veteran of the office, who served until his death in 1966. He was succeeded by John Harris, former Washington AP reporter who had joined the AEC information staff at Oak Ridge.

The Technical and Public Information Services were recombined under Schlesinger, and Harris supervises both. One of his program changes has been to expand AEC's film operations along lines urged for years by Edwin L. Wilber, head of film activities since the beginning. The library of footage available and finished films are distributed through ten film distribution points. Wilber estimates that about five million people see these films yearly, but the program is now being reoriented toward TV. No films for public showing have yet been produced that meet the standards of technical reporting on film—a technique both government and industry are beginning to use more and more—set by an imaginative Air Force moviemaker, Colonel James L. Gaylord, onetime head of the AEC-financed Lookout Mountain Laboratory, where top secret film reports were made to explain to the military the intricacies of new weapon designs. A representative of the Joint Chiefs of Staff once said that the admirals and generals and staff got more out of a four-hour film report than they could have gotten out of weeks of reading of written reports that would have taken months to produce. As of 1972, AEC and National Science Foundation were planning cooperative TV film shorts, explaining things of interest to both agencies, such as control of the fusion reaction.

The speeches of AEC Commissioners are no less a vehicle of public education today than they were under Lilienthal. There is a steady flow of them, and newsmen—as well as the Washington people who watch every AEC move for their own (not the public's) interest—have learned to read them carefully. A good deal of planning goes into the speaking program, deciding who will say what and where, and it may be this fact that gives the appearance of functional division of work among the five Commissioners. Each of the Commissioners has a personal assistant who does the research, if not the writing, for the speeches, and these aides tend to concentrate on areas of greatest interest to their bosses. Then too, the public information people get some of their own guidance this way, and so do the field offices of the Commission—to an even greater extent because they don't have direct contact with the top-side.

The licensing and regulatory activities, applications for construction permits, notices of hearings, findings of review panels, and actions by the Commission on power projects account for a substantial part of the flow of public information materials from AEC. The public document room, maintained as part of the Secretariat at the AEC H Street office in Washington, is a unique public information function and is, of course, indispensable to lawyers and others directly involved in the regulatory and licensing work. It is one of the best run services of its kind in Washington and is an important factor in AEC's response to its obligation to the public. Despite the aura of secrecy surrounding AEC, you can find out here more about what that agency is doing in less time than you can in most any other part of the government, big or little.

An outstanding example of availability of information about AEC is the annual AEC financial report, which is unlike any other in government. It provides a quick and sound perspective on the atomic energy program. John Abbadessa, who watched over AEC from the General Accounting Office for many years, has continued and improved on the practice of his predecessors as AEC Controller by publishing an annual financial report that makes it easy for any intelligent taxpayer to tell where his money has been going. It is well written and aimed at the layman, not the government accountant or economist.

The outflow of public information materials from AEC is greater than ever envisioned even in Lilienthal's day. Trying to keep up, as student-officers attending wartime compacted courses at the Army's Command and General Staff School used to say, is like trying to get a drink from a fire hose.

VII

Congress and AEC

When the atomic bomb first burst upon the consciousness of the U.S. citizenry, it seemed more to stultify than to stimulate that historic political awareness that has steered the republic away from authoritarianism and kept it on a course of citizen control and participation. The "light of a thousand suns" must have dazzled the war-weary Americans so much that, if they didn't actually deem it prudent, they were at least content for the time being to have the awful power of the atom under the control of those who had developed it.

Perhaps they weren't quite ready to think about it, concerned as they were about postwar demobilization, relief and rehabilitation in Europe, finding jobs for returning servicemen, and getting on with building America. As we learned in the debate on civilian vs. military control, they reckoned without the alert conscience of the young scientists who had helped to develop the bomb, or at least understood it, and without the latent concern of the Congress for its legislative prerogatives and its late-blooming eagerness to get into an act from which it had been excluded during the war.

Both research scientists and administrators of science had been too busy for months before the atom came along to bother the public. At least a year before either Congress or the public was aware of any problem, the Chicago scientists on the Manhattan Project had begun to worry about postwar control of the atom. In Washington, Vannevar Bush and his deputy, Irvin Stewart, had

163

put on paper their own ideas of an administrative structure that would keep nuclear research free of political interference. Their ideas called for a governing board for federally sponsored research with the balance of power in the hands of civilian scientists nominated by the National Academy of Sciences. The plan apparently had the approval of the Secretaries of War and Navy—Henry Stimson and James Forrestal, both businessmen serving government for the duration—but not of such an experienced administrator as Budget Director Harold D. Smith, who knew that the government was going to have to continue heavy investments in research but felt they should be made through the normal machinery of government.

Throughout the late spring and early summer of 1945, intensive debate and administrative jockeying went on over the issues of postwar control of the sizable bureaucracy that would clearly be needed to carry on atomic development, with the roles of science and the military as the critical points at issue. The Chicago scientists, with an articulate and bureaucratically—if not also politically—savvy Dr. Norman Hilberry as their scribe and spokesman, showed an acumen that many politicians wished they had been aware of when the debate on control of the atom became public. Within the executive branch of the government, there was equally intensive consideration of the question of international control of the atom and how to enlist the cooperation of the Russians. The debate was not confined to the halls of government. Congress, ever conscious of its responsibilities, had to play catch-up ball when it reconvened in September of 1945.

The experience left its mark. Congress was never again to be caught so off base. Young Senator Brien McMahon of Connecticut introduced the first bill on atomic energy, a hastily drawn piece of legislation that would have failed to pass but served to establish his claim to a role in the Senate's consideration of atomic energy. He subsequently introduced a resolution to create a special committee and, with the critical backing of Senator Arthur Vandenberg, the towering Republican leader of the Foreign Affairs Committee, was made its chairman. No one knew what the mechanism would be, but the die was surely cast for some kind of instrument that would give both houses of Congress a hand in whatever machinery might be designed for control and management of the atom. The mechanism that was eventually developed to ensure continuing broad-gauge congressional review of the national atomic energy program was the Joint Committee on Atomic Energy.

AN EXTRAORDINARY INSTITUTION

There is nothing quite like the Joint Committee on Atomic Energy—JCAE in the shorthand of the atomic energy community —in the American system of government. One can make a reasonable case that its existence and operations over the years have constituted a continuing violation of the separation of powers principle of the Constitution. In the preface of *Government of the Atom: The Integration of Powers,* an analysis of JCAE operations, Harold P. Green and Alan Rosenthal observed that the "Joint Committee's behavior uniquely resembles that of the higher echelons of the Executive Branch," and that it represents a "significant innovation" in a governmental system of separated powers.

Students of government, members of the Joint Committee, other congressmen, and officials of the executive branch, wrote Green and Rosenthal, "have long recognized the JCAE as an extraordinary Congressional institution." Despite its unique character as the only joint committee with legislative powers, its special statutory assignments, and its unprecedented role in the formulation of national policy, Green and Rosenthal are the only scholars to have given these operations any thorough study. Their *Government of the Atom,* published in 1963, was financed by a grant from the Edgar Stern Family Fund to the National Law Center of the George Washington University. It is recommended reading for any student of the control and development of atomic energy.

To understand the basis for the Green-Rosenthal estimate of the innovative and extraordinary character of the JCAE, one need only examine the Joint Committee's own published description of its "Organization and Functions," which has been abbreviated and paraphrased in the next few pages.

Although the JCAE was first organized on August 2, 1946 (charter memberships were prized), it didn't begin operations until the 80th Congress was organized in 1947, when the Republicans took over as the majority party. The first active chairman was Senator Bourke

B. Hickenlooper of Iowa. The Committee has nine members from each house with no more than five members from either being of the same party. The Senate held on to the chairmanship until 1953 when Congressman Sterling Cole, a Republican of New York, was elected chairman. The 1954 Act made rotation of the chairmanship between the two chambers a matter of statute, so that it changes with each Congress, with the vice-chairman coming from the other house.

WHY THE JCAE?

The JCAE is one of the few committees established by statute instead of by rule of each house. Few committees of the Congress conduct as much business in executive session, reflecting the security requirements of the Atomic Energy Act, and few committees have conducted more hours of open hearings, reflecting the fact that the civil side of the atom and the nuclear power business have gained momentum. In its own words: "The Joint Committee was established as an agent of the Congress and the American people, and is charged with the responsibility of making 'continuing studies of the activities of the Atomic Energy Commission and of problems relating to the development, use, and control of atomic energy.' " The functions of the committee include:

1. The legislative function, which covers all phases of the legislative process. The jurisdiction of the Joint Committee is complete, a factor that some observers say may be the source of the jaundiced view some JCAE members have of various proposals to break up the Atomic Energy Commission, lest the role of the committee be diluted and its policy influence reduced. The committee's Senate section handles the confirmation of Presidential appointees provided for in the Act.

2. The "watchdog" function, which the committee describes as a "necessary part of the operation of a government of separated powers and a vital legislative responsibility." This function was of prime importance when the AEC was first established and most activities were of a secret nature. The JCAE maintains surveillance of the work of the AEC and the related programs of the Department of Defense:

The AEC is required by law to keep the Joint Committee fully and currently informed with respect to all of the Commission's activities. The Department of Defense is required to keep the committee fully and currently informed with respect to all matters within the Department relating to the development, utilization, or application of atomic energy. All other Government agencies are required to furnish any information requested by the committee with respect to the activities or responsibilities of those agencies in the field of atomic energy. In accordance with the latter requirement the Joint Committee receives briefings from other agencies and departments of the Government, including the Department of State and the Central Intelligence Agency.

3. The policy and review function, whereby the JCAE proposes policy changes or other innovations in atomic energy programs. The Joint Committee, in its own words, has "expedited and supported the naval nuclear propulsion program" and (in the authors' words) has willingly, if not knowingly, cooperated in the remarkably successful manipulative bureaucratactics of Admiral Rickover. The JCAE has also "expedited the hydrogen bomb project, an expanded atomic power program, the preservation of food through irradiation, and the utilization of atomic energy for space applications" and (the committee might have added) the insurance provisions for the nuclear power industry and the establishment of the International Atomic Energy Agency.

4. The information function, in which the committee has played an unusual role. The records of its hearings have in many cases provided information of critical importance to the public, and the Joint Committee has made AEC operating divisions respond to many inquiries from various segments of the public in situations where the AEC did not feel itself obliged to divulge as much as some of those segments wanted. The JCAE has itself been a fruitful source of information for reporters and others. It provides universities, libraries, and industrial, religious, and private organizations with many different types of information materials. Speeches of members of the committee have been important sources of information for the power industry.

In addition to these four general functions, the JCAE has a number of statutory duties specifically assigned in legislation. It must authorize all appropriations for AEC. The 1954 Act provided for JCAE authorization of capital expenditures; a 1958 amendment provided for authorization of cooperative programs with industry or with other nations; and in 1963 all AEC operations were placed under the committee's authorization procedures.

COMMUNICATION AND COOPERATION

The 1963 amendment, according to the Joint Committee, "was enacted in order to further ensure adequate Congressional control over the atomic energy program." Under section 261, Congress's specialized arm—the Joint Committee on Atomic Energy—reviews and recommends authorization for the AEC's entire budget, thereby permitting the Joint Committee to deal effectively with the critical problems in the atomic energy field.

One cannot fault the committee as to the clarity of its intentions. The effect is to give full legal or statutory impact to the pattern of relationship that had been building over the years. In the early days, the JCAE had to depend heavily upon the energetic probing and technical-managerial competence of its staff. In those days, there was considerable cooperation between the staff members of the Commission and the committee, strained during the Lilienthal "incredible mismanagement" period, but relaxed and effective during the tenure of Gordon Dean as Chairman of the AEC and three-fourths of the way through the committee chairmanship of Sterling Cole—until the injection of the Dixon-Yates issue.

Chairman Cole departed from the traditional pattern of congressional committee chairmen when he found a gimmick to lure scores of members of Congress into the bailiwick of the Joint Atomic Energy Committee. That gimmick—Cole said he got the idea from his staff director, Allardice—was to invite his colleagues to witness the testing of small-yield nuclear weapon devices at the AEC's Nevada Proving Ground. During the test series in 1953 and 1954, planeloads of congressmen were ferried to Las Vegas to see the shots. It helped make friends for the JCAE, but a bonus Cole hadn't counted on was the greater understanding of things atomic on the part of those members of Congress who were exposed to the charming pedagogy of Dr. Alvin C. Graves of Los Alamos Scientific Laboratory, the test director. More often than not, a shot would be delayed a day or two for weather, and AEC and Los Alamos representatives took advantage of the time to do their congressional relations work. Graves was the star performer. During the decade and a half he was in charge of the test programs at Nevada and Eniwetok, he directed the release of more explosive energy than the planet earth has ever experienced except through its own convulsions by earthquakes and volcanic eruptions.

Equally important from tne standpoint of congressional relations and legislative understanding of the nuclear weapons business was the communication between the national legislators and quiet-spoken Norris Bradbury, director of the Los Alamos Scientific Laboratory for more than twenty-five years and one of the most important men in the nation's history in the realm of military preparedness.

All of the tests witnessed by the senators and representatives went off as planned, but not always on the day announced. In one test of a prior series, however, when the computerized control sequencer that set all the test instrumentation into operation came to the last step of detonating the nuclear charge, there was no explosion. The test device was atop the 300-foot tower in Yucca Flat, one of the test areas of the proving ground. Circuits were checked and a fault was found—within about five minutes. Continued rechecking for hours confirmed the point of signal failure. Later, Jack Clarke, Graves's predecessor, climbed the tower alone and disarmed the nuclear detonating mechanism.

On another occasion, when a planeload of congressmen and senators landed at Indian Springs Air Force Base, forty miles from the test site, the AEC congressional tour conductor was pulled off the plane early and told that the FBI had informed the Commission that the Bureau's files indicated that one congressman was very probably an active Communist Party member and should not be allowed to witness the test. The suspect legislator was quietly told. A telephone call from his district was arranged to provide an excuse for his emergency departure, and the congressman calmly said good-bye to his colleagues at the messhall table. An Air Force plane whisked him off before dinner was over that evening. Months later, the New York *Herald Tribune* reported that a member of the House of Representatives from California had been barred from a nuclear test. When the facts were presented in testimony before the

Joint Committee, even the members who had been on the trip were surprised—as was Wayne Brobeck, the JCAE staff member, to whom no degree of apology could make up for his having been kept in the dark.

Despite the security policy that kept a member of the House of Representatives from seeing a test shot, barring the press while admitting the legislators was galling to reporters trying to cover the series. It made life miserable for Richard G. Elliott, the experienced newsman who was the AEC public information officer on the spot. He did a quiet bit of lobbying on his own during visits of members of the Joint Committee to the test site. When Salisbury, AEC director of information in Washington, proposed admitting the reporters to witness specific shots, the Joint Committee, primed in advance, approved the suggestion so timidly put forth by the Commission.

Cole was succeeded by Senator Clinton Anderson of New Mexico as chairman of the committee, and for two years, the publicly visible taut relationship between Anderson and Chairman Strauss of the AEC made any kind of cooperation difficult. When President Eisenhower appointed John A. McCone as Chairman at the expiration of Strauss's term in 1958, his instructions were to get along with the Joint Committee. It was no secret in Washington that Commissioner John S. Graham had been put on the Commission by Eisenhower the year before "as the Joint Committee's man." Graham, an affable North Carolinian with a typical taste and technique for temperate politics and a respectable Washington law practice, remained on the Commission until 1962, when his place was taken by Commissioner James T. Ramey, who had been executive director of the JCAE for six years.

Ramey has maintained his communication lines with Capitol Hill and hasn't been known to oppose the JCAE on any public issue, but his knowledge of the Hill and his standing with some of the members of Congress has enabled him to facilitate much of the work of the Commission. During the Administration of President Johnson, there was talk in Washington that, if and when the promotion-production functions of AEC were separated from the regulatory function, Ramey was slated for the single administrator job for the former function, and the remaining five Commissioners for the latter. (The same kind of talk, for whatever it is worth, has also held that the Joint Committee was less than enthusiastic about any such separation of functions lest its own control be diluted.)

The paternalism of the Joint Committee—its fatherly concern for the atomic energy program—has never been more clearly revealed than in the committee's response to criticism from environmentalists. Witnesses who appeared before the Joint Committee during hearings on the issues of thermal pollution and the hazards of power plant radiation were heard to complain that some JCAE members were unabashed advocates of nuclear power, whereas the witnesses had expected legislative objectivity.

In large part because of the way in which the JCAE has guarded its bailiwick and control over the atom, few other members of either chamber have bothered to delve into atomic energy matters. The massive barrage of expertise and information that the Joint Committee with AEC help can mount at any time is pretty discouraging to the congressman or senator who takes on the powerful atomic energy legislative group. There have been no such testings worthy of note, possibly because the Joint Committee has zealously looked after the prerogatives of the legislative branch. The only non-JCAE senator who has made much impression on the atomic body politic is Senator Edmund Muskie, who is too wise to make a frontal attack but by skill and persuasion has been able to get both the AEC and the Joint Committee to respond constructively to his efforts to strengthen environmental safeguards.

The AEC Congressional Relations Office—headed since 1967 by Robert D. O'Neill, who, after ten years in AEC's Division of Biology and Medicine, is program-oriented but politically wise— doesn't have to pay as much attention to the rest of Congress as does its counterpart in other agencies.

As a matter of fact, the Joint Committee even helps out with the Appropriations Committees. In the committee's words: "The requirement for authorizing legislation has proven of value in many ways. The Joint Committee receives testimony in both executive and open hearings. The hearings give a meaningful story of the Commission's program needs, and furnish needed information to Members of Congress for their consideration of the appropriation bills."

The Appropriations Committees over the years have learned that the Joint Committee gives AEC a pretty good going over in the authorization process, and it is rare that the money step is very far out of phase with the authorization step. There is another factor involved, however, probably as important as the effective work of the JCAE. That is the caliber of the AEC men with direct responsibility for budgets and continuous communication with the staffs of the Appropriations Committees.

Special mention should be made of Francis J. McCarthy, Jr., who was in charge of AEC budgets from day one until his death in the mid-1960's. He was known on Capitol Hill as "an honest budget man," an accolade reserved for those whom both the General Accounting Office sleuths and Appropriations Committee staff members have learned are competent and can be trusted completely to respond to any query "with the straight dope." One of those who worked with McCarthy and knew him "from the Hill side" was John P. Abbadassa, who has been Controller of AEC since 1962, when he was recruited from the General Accounting Office, where he was deputy director of the Civil Division. He made McCarthy his deputy, and to this day credits McCarthy for AEC's status with the appropriations staffs. AEC has had a remarkably smooth money path, and these two men share much of the credit.

INTERNATIONAL COOPERATION

The foreign relations aspect of the atom has always been one of the nuggets that Congress eyed greedily despite the Constitutional prerogatives of the President. The statutory secrecy built into the McMahon Act effectively severed the arrangements the Manhattan Project had made to mobilize the brains of physicists remaining in the countries from which had come much of the raw data and polished talent required to build the bomb in the first place. When the 1954 Act was written and industrial participation was equated with international cooperation, the Joint Committee on Atomic Energy was endowed with the power to exercise the safeguards.

The Cole-Hickenlooper Act, as the 1954 legislation was known until the Democrats regained control of Congress in 1957, was drafted during a period when the atom's political earth still showed the scorching effects of the spotlight Senator Joseph R. McCarthy turned on security. By replacing the McMahon Act's built-in prohibitions with congressionally monitored agreements for cooperation, the drafters of the legislation were able to give the Atomic Energy Commission the authority it needed in a manner that gave progressive legislators something they could defend against the super-security patriots.

Section 11b of the Act defines "agreement for cooperation" as any "agreement with another nation or regional defense organization (NATO) authorized or permitted by" a half dozen sections of the Act specifying what AEC might do in cooperation with other nations in both the military and civilian applications of atomic energy. Section 123 provides certain procedural checks.

With respect to agreements for cooperation concerning the civil uses of atomic energy, Section 123 provides that no such agreement may become effective until the proposed agreement document, together with the approval of the President and his written determination "that performance of the agreement will promote and will not constitute an unreasonable risk to the common defense and security, has been submitted to the Joint Committee and a period of thirty days has elapsed while Congress is in session." The section provides, however, that the JCAE can waive the conditions of the waiting period by resolution in writing.

A 1958 amendment permits, subject to certain limitations, conditions, and procedures, greater exchanges of specifically defined types of military information and materials with military allies. Such agreements for cooperation in the uses of atomic energy for mutual defense purposes, together with the approval and determination of the President, must be submitted to the Congress and referred to the JCAE, where they "must lie for a period of 60 days while Congress is in session before becoming effective." An agreement can't become effective if, within the 60-day period, Congress passes a concurrent resolution stating in substance that it does not favor the proposed agreement.

The Joint Committee exercises other restraints over the authority of the Commission. Section 51 of the Atomic Energy Act of 1954 authorizes the AEC to determine materials other than those specifically defined in the act to be special nuclear materials. The "definitions" section of the Act defines these as plutonium and uranium enriched in the isotopes 233 or 235. When the Commission wants to add another nuclear material, its findings have to lie before the JCAE for 30 days while Congress is in session. A similar check is provided for findings by the Commission as to source materials. The waiting period is 30 days for the extension or modification of long-term electric utility service contracts, but 45 days for determinations by the Commission of the guaranteed purchase price—or purchase price period of guarantee—and 45 days on contracts to perform enrichment services for foreign customers, including the establishing of criteria for the performance of such services, and 45 days on any arrangement under the cooperative power reactor demonstration program not specifically authorized.

When a matter has been submitted to the Joint Committee for review as required by the statute, the committee as a general rule promptly schedules a hearing to consider it. The JCAE has frequently waived the waiting period.

THE PERSONALITIES

It is difficult to write about Congress and the AEC without some unavoidably subjective references to some of the veteran members of the Joint Committee on Atomic Energy.

The first Joint Committee on Atomic Energy was formed on August 2, 1946, with Senator Brien McMahon as chairman. Two of the House members on that first committee, who had previously served on the House Military Affairs Committee, which considered the May-Johnson military control bill, are still serving. One is Melvin Price of Illinois. The other is Chet Holifield of California, who has been alternating as chairman with Senator John O. Pastore of Rhode Island ever since 1961. Whenever the chairman is a senator, the vice-chairman is the senior House member or the member next in line, and vice versa. When Representative Holifield relinquished his JCAE chairmanship to become chairman of the House Committee on Government Operations, he designated Representative Price as vice-chairman of the Joint Committee on

Atomic Energy. As chairman of the JCAE Research and Development Subcommittee, Price has probably conducted more hours of hearings than any other member of the House. Having started life as a newspaper reporter, he believes in getting the facts into the record.

Because the Democrats have had a congressional majority consistently since 1956, when Sterling Cole was chairman, they have naturally been more in the spotlight of public activities. Senator Pastore, serving as chairman in the 1971–72 period, first went on the Committee in 1953, when the Republicans had the majority. Even as a "rookie," however, he was one of the strongest supporters of Chairman Cole in getting the international cooperation provisions into the Atomic Energy Act of 1954 and ever since has taken special interest in international affairs.

Generally speaking, the House members are more active on the JCAE than the senators. One exception, among those still serving, is Senator Henry M. Jackson of Washington, who has always concerned himself with the defense aspects of the nation's nuclear program and was singularly instrumental in getting acceptance of the test ban treaty in return for the commitment that the U.S. would always maintain a readiness for testing and carry on with an intensive weapon development and improvement program.

Senator Albert Gore of Tennessee, who served on the Joint Committee from 1953 through 1970, was usually teamed with Chet Holifield in defense of public power interests whenever the issue appeared in any AEC proposals. Senator Gore was as indefatigable in his defense of TVA's interests as Senator Jackson has been in protecting the waters of the Columbia River. Senator Howard H. Baker of Tennessee has picked up the baton from Gore and is a very active member of the Joint Committee. The senior Republican, Senator George D. Aiken of Vermont, is a very interested and active member of the committee and has taken a special interest in environmental problems.

Representative Craig Hosmer of California is now the senior Republican House member and by far the most active Republican on the House side. He got started in atomic energy as an AEC attorney at Los Alamos shortly after the war, then returned to his native California to run for Congress.

The senior Democrat on the Senate side, Senator Clinton P.

Anderson of New Mexico, served twice as chairman and retired in 1972. He kept an eagle eye on many aspects of the atomic energy program, particularly raw materials, weapon research, and insurance. He was cosponsor, with Mel Price, of the basic government insurance backup (Price-Anderson Act) in case of extraordinary damage from a nuclear reactor accident.

It was during Senator Anderson's 1955–56 chairmanship that JCAE-AEC relations became so strained that both bodies suffered loss of prestige. It was a personal struggle. No such stress between their two chairmen has built up since. The Strauss-Anderson conflict was no backdoor ancient-grudge affair like Senator McKellar's opposition to Lilienthal, but an open no-quarter-given struggle between two strong men who believed they were right and that their good names were at stake.

Future AEC chairmen will find plenty of support at the Joint Committee for the AEC program of intensive promotion of nuclear power. They will doubtless be reminded that the Joint Committee as far back as 1961 began to worry about future power needs and even a possible shortage in the 1970's unless nuclear power developments were pushed. They will find that some members of the Joint Committee are a bit short of patience with the environmentalists. Chet Holifield, for one, feels that in raising a fuss about nuclear plants, they are barking up the wrong tree. He has been pushing nuclear power for a quarter of a century and feels it is the least insulting to the environment of all the ways of meeting the nation's growing demands for more and more power.

NEW WATCHDOG ROLE

Television sportscasters use the expression "get the offense untracked" when they really mean "get it on the track." Journalists in the political area misuse the term "watchdog" in the same way when they apply it to the Joint Committee vis-à-vis the Atomic Energy Commission, forgetting that the traditional role of the watchdog is to protect its own family and watch everybody else. The Joint Committee has fulfilled the journalists' watchdog role very well over the years but has recently taken on the traditional watchdog role by snapping at anybody who threatens the property it is watching.

Make no mistake, the JCAE has always considered the Commission its property, and has zealously guarded its legislative territory against invasion by any other committee of either house of Congress. But that is very traditional, a strict norm of congressional behavior. What is not a norm of congressional behavior is for a committee to take on vociferous taxpayers and voters in defense of the executive branch agency it is "watchdogging." Some environmental activists who have testified at JCAE hearings on the potential impact of nuclear power plants on the ecology have complained of their reception on the grounds that the presumably impartial and voter-oriented legislators were on the side of the atom.

A book, *The Atomic Establishment,* by the prominent environmental protectionist Peter Metzger (with the help of newsman Anthony Ripley) was published in 1972. It actually lumped the congressional Joint Committee on Atomic Energy with the atomic energy community, which is composed of AEC staff, the engineering and manufacturing firms designing and building nuclear power plants, the power companies, the contract operators of AEC facilities, and the broad-based trade association called the Atomic Industrial Forum. Probably the book's most telling point is its criticism of AEC for lack of candor and withholding of information about the hazards of certain AEC activities and about the means of protection against hazards. A costly fire at the Rocky Flats, Colorado, plutonium processing plant and the handling of the aborted plan to bury radioactive wastes in a Kansas salt mine were cited as examples. These critics acknowledge the possibilities of the nation's future dependence on nuclear fuel as a source of electrical energy, but they fear a "blunder" of some kind will result in a power plant accident with serious radioactive danger to the public. The way to avoid such a blunder, they contend, is to dismantle AEC in a way that would permit greater public participation in the making of policy decisions affecting utilization of nuclear energy.

Another book endorses the "establishment" theme in its subtitle—*The Nuclear Power Rebellion: Citizens vs. the Atomic Industrial Establishment.* The author, Richard S. Lewis, editor of the *Bulletin of the Atomic Scientists,* tellingly makes the point that the environmental barriers that have caused a lot of rethinking of plans for nuclear plants (including the requirement that full "environmental impact statements" be prepared for every proposed power plant) resulted largely from the failure of the power industry and its industrial suppliers to appreciate the seriousness of the public concern about the environment.

There is no question about the seriousness of that concern, nor is the concern totally without justification in view of the difficulties the Commission has had in setting standards for emergency core cooling and stability under thermal stress of fuel elements. The Joint Committee thinks of its role in this controversy more as referee and moderator, apparently sharing the views of John Maddox, editor of the British science magazine *Nature,* that extremists among the defenders of the environment are part of the problem.

Public health and safety has been an area of most aggressive "watchdogging" by the Joint Committee, which has consistently provided a forum for dissemination to the public of information about radiation hazards. This is one reason some antinuclear witnesses at JCAE hearings have not been received with open arms. Their testimony is felt by the members to be a reflection on the work of the committee as well as upon AEC.

Probably the most vigorous defender of the committee's work has been Representative Holifield, a staunch and effective advocate of the public's right to know about the hazards of all kinds of nuclear activities. He has maintained a consistent surveillance of the Commission's radiation protective measures. Holifield comes about as close to being the conscience of the nation as any legislator we know, a motivation that led to his giving up the chairmanship of the Joint Committee in favor of the broader field of Government Operations. That committee has jurisdiction over government reorganization.

The House Democrat in line for the chairmanship of JCAE is Representative Melvin Price of Illinois. He has a sound grasp of nuclear technology and commands the respect of the science community as well as the whole "atomic establishment." The fact that he also commands the respect of members of the House of Representatives may be important for the future of AEC.

The senior Republican on the House side of the Joint Committee, Representative Craig Hosmer, has a background of loyalty to the program, knowledge of the workings of the Commission, and an understanding of the nuclear business acquired by doing his homework. He qualifies willingly as a member of the atomic establishment and has no interest in its dismantling. A solid line-backer for Hosmer is the second-ranking Republican, Representative John B. Anderson of Illinois, who also sits on the powerful House Rules Committee and whose home state boasts two major AEC installations, the Argonne National Laboratory and the National Accelerator Laboratory.

The most stalwart "watchdogs" of the atom on the Senate side are John O. Pastore and Henry M. Jackson. Jackson is next in line among the Democrats. Pastore has had a continuing interest in international cooperation as well as in the health and safety of atomic workers and of the public. Senator Jackson is the recognized authority in the Senate on nuclear weapons and the role of nuclear armament in the defense posture of the country. His special interest in nuclear power is based on its importance to the continuation of the hydroenergy-based economy of the Northwest. Partly because he is sensitive to any charge of regionalism, but mainly because he has done his homework on U.S. energy requirements, Jackson has consistently supported aggressive nuclear power development by AEC.

The senior Republican on the Senate side, the venerable George D. Aiken, is a traditionalist in the context of American politics but a convinced progressive in the context of the nation's need for nuclear fuels as a clean source of electrical energy.

The personal convictions of these seven men—Senators Pastore, Jackson, and Aiken, and Representatives Holifield, Price, Hosmer, and Anderson—and their stature in the Congress mean that efforts to reorganize the federal atomic energy program by dividing it among a number of other agencies will experience rough sledding. The committee has made clear its readiness to have the regulatory and the production-development functions of AEC separated, and then to broaden the development responsibilities of AEC in the energy field. The committee is determined to continue to be the watchdog against any slowdown in the work of bringing about environmentally and economically viable systems for generating electric power, first by fission breeders and then by fusion reactors.

VIII

In the Matter of
J. Robert Oppenheimer

One of the important wartime decisions of General Groves was his selection of a relatively unknown young physicist, Dr. J. Robert Oppenheimer of the University of California at Berkeley, to head the weapons laboratory in New Mexico where all the knowledge of the fission process could be brought together. Oppenheimer had suggested the laboratory in the first place and had helped select its site. When the use of the bomb designed and built under his direction at Los Alamos abruptly signaled the end of the war, even Groves's severest critics lauded his selection of the brilliant young Oppenheimer.

Some of Groves's critics hadn't quite understood the choice, because young Oppenheimer was known to have free-wheeling political views, leftish friends, and no prior administrative experience. He was relatively unknown outside the circles of the world's top theoretical physicists. As a child, he had been identified as a potential genius, and his entire education and training, particularly during the formative years of his life, had been carefully managed after the manner of, say, a great pianist, so that the normal exposures of a growing boy would not be permitted to interfere with his development. He was graduated from Harvard in 1925, spent a year at Cambridge, and was awarded a Ph.D. at the University of Göttingen in 1927. He did additional work at Leyden and Zurich, and in the United States earned a reputation as an inspiring and brilliant teacher at the California Institute of Technology at Pasadena and at the University at Berkeley, holding professorships in physics at both institutions. In the early days of the planning of the atomic development effort, he was brought into the deliberative councils at the insistence of Dr. Ernest O. Lawrence. Oppenheimer was apparently the first man to determine or predict the amount of fissionable material that would be needed for an atomic bomb.

In the official announcement of the development and use of an atomic weapon on August 6, 1945, Secretary of War Henry Stimson said of Oppenheimer: "The development of the bomb itself has been largely due to his genius and the inspiration and leadership he has given to his associates." That accolade was to be cruelly scarred within nine years when the scene and the actors changed. The national mood of victory and confidence was to give way to frustration and fear. Oppenheimer's advice was to be rejected, perhaps because he hated war more than he feared Communism. Old complaints were to be re-evaluated under different rules. Humiliation was to be his reward from a government which, in a lapse of memory of its onetime gratitude, reconsidered its exculpation for unconventional behavior. Violation of the rules of the security system was to prove weightier than Oppenheimer's contribution to national security. Officially imposed exile from public service was eventually to be lifted, but no one really knows how much it did to relieve the hurt that he carried to the grave.

Little wonder that after the war Oppenheimer came to symbolize the scientist. He was appointed to the top posts, or selected for them, by both politicians and peers. He was scientific adviser to the Acheson-Lilienthal Study, and when the Atomic Energy Act of 1946 was passed, President Truman made him chairman of the super-prestigious General Advisory Committee. Words of derogation of Oppenheimer were not heard during those days of the second half of the 1940's, but there was a small company whose admiration was heavily damped by memories of the lash of his cryptic but soft-voiced disapproval of their inputs to sessions with "Oppie," as he was commonly referred to by many who worked with him and under him. If Dr. Oppenheimer felt that any contribution to the discussion was based on other than demonstrably sound knowledge or experimental data, whether the subject was physics or national policy, he had a way of making the contributor feel that his offering was simply unworthy of the company. On one occasion, however, he reportedly left both the victim and the company puzzled when he responded to one discussant, "I could hardly disagree with you less." On another occasion, he humiliated—in a way that was painfully embarrassing for those present—a prominent industrialist who ventured too far in expressing views based on a newfound knowledge of nuclear power economics. One of the principal contributors to the success of the wartime project once observed of Oppie, "He's so much smarter than I am, I'm afraid of him." Oppenheimer could humiliate a prominent figure by demolishing his argument with a scalpel of calm speech, but he could give the little people the patient and instructive attention of a kindergarten teacher.

OPPOSING VIEWPOINTS

During the early years of AEC, before the smugness of A-bomb monopoly was rudely shattered by President Truman's announcement of the U.S.S.R. atomic explosion of August, 1949, Oppie was above criticism. He didn't seek glory, it was thrust upon him. But he was human, and some observers felt he began to enjoy the role and to expect deference to his views. The Soviet blast set in motion a series of events that were to bring his views into question. He was to face opposition and a punishing attempt at discreditation.

The first, and obvious, response of the Atomic Energy Commission to the Soviet achievement had the full endorsement of the General Advisory Committee and its articulate and persuasive chairman, Oppenheimer. AEC began at once to expand the manufacture of fission weapons and improve them in every possible way. The Joint Committee on Atomic Energy and its chairman, Senator Brien McMahon, approved wholeheartedly, as did the military community. Commissioner Lewis L. Strauss went farther. He urged reviving work on the thermonuclear bomb, which had been de-emphasized in the last year of the wartime work on the A-bomb because success seemed too remote and some of General Groves's advisers feared it would distract from the all-out effort on the fission weapon. Strauss not only urged reviving work on the thermonuclear weapon but recommended putting the work on a high-priority, crash basis.

Our purpose is not to retrace the steps which led to the decision on the H-bomb but only to point out that the issue divided the innermost councils of the atomic family in a manner not previously experienced. Three of the AEC Commissioners opposed Strauss, but President Truman, with the support of the Secretaries of State and Defense and the next Chairman of the AEC, Gordon Dean, ordered full speed ahead on the H-bomb. Throughout this period, the AEC sought guidance from the General Advisory Committee, as envisioned in the McMahon Act. Committee chairman Oppenheimer, with impressive, technically based arguments, advised against a massive, high-pressure effort.

But his ill-concealed doubts as to the wisdom of having an H-bomb at all inevitably resulted in his taking the lead in polarizing positions on the issue and articulating opposition to the H-bomb. Public discussion of the issue, which followed President Truman's order of January 31, 1950, made it clear that Oppenheimer and his followers based their reservations on grounds more moral than technical, but it was a morality rooted deeply in considerations of political and military efficacy. Few of them would agree that their doubts were necessarily resolved by the fact that the U.S. achieved a fusion reaction within three years and the Soviets within four.

With all arguments before him, President Truman made the decision to pursue the fusion objective. The President seemed to share the views of some of the topside staff of AEC who were privy to the Commission's arguments, if not its deliberations and, even though torn between the deeply felt positions of respected colleagues and friends, had come to the conclusion that there was really no choice. "We have to find out whether it can be done" was justification enough. The righteousness with which each side claimed to be endowed applied to both.

Righteousness entwined with patriotism is a kind of sinew, but a sinew that doesn't heal easily when it is bruised and cut in an engagement of such intensity. The scar tissue, even that of the victor, remained sensitive. One of the things that makes the atomic energy program what it is, and makes the AEC different as a government agency, is that such gut issues force everyone in the organization to search both mind and soul for an answer to the question.

It is not possible in this brief chapter to give the reader a basis for deciding who was right in the matter of J. Robert Oppenheimer, but we believe it necessary to try to report how the case came about. It is a significant case in the annals of American government as well as in the history of the American people. Five books on the case were on the bookstands two decades later, reflecting the wide range of opinions regarding the government's use and abuse of this brilliant physicist.

The human side of the story and the interplay of temperaments of the everything-but-dull personalities involved has proved tempting to writers. Philip M. Stern, in his book *The Oppenheimer Case,* treats the dilemma and the difficulty of free people in trying to buttress the bureaucracy of their government against espionage and subversion. The book highlights the hazards inherent in any system installed for such a purpose. Stern was stirred to write his book from reading an exhaustive analysis of the procedural complexities and nuances of the case prepared by Harold P. Green,* who, as AEC Assistant General Counsel, had drafted the charges against Oppenheimer. The analysis by Green, now professor of law at George Washington University, has never been published. It is described as a legal-technical study-in-depth of the case. Stern's flowing account of the roles and responses of the amazing number of people involved in this strange tragedy makes it seem almost inevitable that the scientist who drew the accolade of the Secretary of War at the end of World War II would eventually be found unworthy of his country's trust. Not even the President of the United States could have saved Oppenheimer from some kind of retribution, but a politically more confident President could have put an end to the bizarre proceedings set in motion by the letter of a troubled former executive director of the Joint Committee on Atomic Energy. Some observers at the time felt that a bit more of a "the-buck-stops-here" willingness to make tough decisions at the White House could have cut off the proceedings—and Oppenheimer's role as a high level government consultant at the same time.

* Green is author of *Government of the Atom.* See Chapter VII.

Perhaps the White House response could have been predicted. During the period of preparation for the cross-channel invasion of World War II, General Eisenhower drew the approval of his peers and public when he promptly sent home from England a senior officer who, the invasion commander felt, had carelessly breached security. Had "Ike" treated the Oppenheimer case with the same dispatch, that would have been the end of the matter, as it had been for the luckless officer. Oppie suffered because President Eisenhower's political behavior lacked the decorum of his military behavior, as forecast by the failure of candidate Eisenhower to stand up for his former chief and longtime friend and patron, General George C. Marshall, when the latter was attacked during the 1952 Presidential campaign.

Busy Years

The AEC was preoccupied and busy in the years between President Truman's decision to build the H-bomb in January, 1950, and William L. Borden's decision in November, 1953, months after his resignation from the staff of the Joint Committee on Atomic Energy, to flag anew for government officials the difficulties J. Robert Oppenheimer had given the security people, reporting by letter his conclusion that Oppenheimer was "more probably than not" a Soviet agent. Shortly after the go-ahead order from Truman to build the hydrogen bomb, Chairman Lilienthal resigned from the AEC to be succeeded by Gordon Dean. Strauss, feeling his mission accomplished, resigned in April, 1950.

The scene changed in many ways during those busy years. It was a period of expansion for the production of both fissionable and thermonuclear materials. Fission weapon testing increased. The first crude thermonuclear device was designed and tested. And the first atomic-powered submarine was launched. They were also busy years for the Russians, who set off their first H-bomb a scant 10 months after the November, 1952, U.S. test. Senator McMahon died in the summer of 1952. The Eisenhower election of the same year brought a Republican majority to Congress. Oppenheimer completed his term on the General Advisory Committee in December. When Congress convened in January, 1953, it was decided to rotate the chairmanship of the Joint Committee and Representative Sterling Cole, Republican of New York, took over as first chairman from the House. Senator Hickenlooper became vice-chairman. Borden left the post of executive director in June, 1953, and was succeeded by Corbin Allardice.

By midsummer of 1953, many changes had taken place at the AEC. Gordon Dean completed his term as chairman on June 30 and was succeeded three days later by Strauss, who had spent the first half of the year as special adviser on atomic energy to President Eisenhower. Only Smyth remained of those who had been there when the H-bomb debate took place. Thomas E. Murray had been there since May of 1950 and Eugene M. Zuckert since February of 1952. T. Keith Glennan had resigned in November, 1952, and his place was not filled until late July, 1953, when Joseph Campbell was appointed to give Strauss a full Commission. In the meantime, the AEC had begun to relieve Oppenheimer of the control and custody of much of his secret data by consolidating all of the classified files at Princeton into one installation in order to reduce the number of guards required. Because of the time required for such a move, the action was largely symbolic. It came at a time when Oppenheimer's usefulness as a consultant to any part of the government was on the downgrade, perhaps because his advice was predictable, but also because the knowledge was so widespread—among the Departments of State, Defense, and Justice, the CIA, the FBI, the AEC, the Joint Committee, and the ranks of the wartime scientists—of Oppie's curious security file. No agency wanted to be caught using him as a consultant in case Senator McCarthy should decide to put the finger on the by-this-time vulnerable architect of the A-bomb.

It is important to recall the dark atmosphere (in retrospect it seems like a nightmare) of the period when Senator Joseph McCarthy of Wisconsin was riding the broomstick of Communist espionage. He took off from the documented runway of postwar exposure and trials of espionage agents like Klaus Fuchs, who had really penetrated atomic security. The beetle-browed junior senator from Wisconsin, who had been elected in the 1946 sweep of the red-hunters, kept hammering away—and hammered on many luckless witnesses, who couldn't quite extricate themselves from alleged associations with people McCarthy labeled as Communists—to such an extent that he convinced many Americans of the prevalency of a vast plot to subvert every institution of the nation. He concentrated on the government but aimed at the churches, the labor unions, the schools, and any organization of citizens that harbored a political view that the senator thought was liberal. Many of these organizations, said the senator, had already been taken over and were active in the conspiracy. For the disgruntled, the envious, and the lunatic fringe, McCarthy was a rallying point, and the cruel way his Senate Subcommittee treated witnesses, even obviously innocent ones, struck fear into the hearts of many thinking citizens and career public servants. It became so bad that claiming the protection of the Fifth Amendment to the Constitution—which states that a man may not be compelled to testify against himself—was to all intents and purposes interpreted by the McCarthy committee and staff as an admission of guilt. Far worse, much of the nation's press gave currency to such misinterpretation of one of the fundamental principles of our system of government.

McCarthy gained a large part of his notoriety from the prosecution of security cases considered inconsequential by the executive branch, or already resolved there through adequate, professionally manned federal investigative and adjudicative processes. Sober and responsible officials in both the Truman and Eisenhower administrations feared that somehow McCarthy would get his hands on a complex, ambigous case, involving a prominent personage, thereby justifying his witch hunt and perhaps launching a twentieth-century Know-Nothing Party.

The voluminous dossier on J. Robert Oppenheimer—much of it based on wartime reports and investigations of uncertain reliability and only in part on FBI investigation—was known to be full of ambiguous material well suited to McCarthy's purposes and methods. A clever selection of material from this file, it was justifiably feared, could publicly crucify Oppenheimer, cast doubt on the atomic energy security system, and polish McCarthy's image of himself as a crusading patriot. After Oppenheimer left the General Advisory Committee, his duties as director of the Institute for Advanced Studies at Princeton, of which Strauss was a trustee, took up more and more of his time. He had not been called to Washington—for reasons best known to the people who in the early months of the Eisenhower Administration had moved into the spots where Oppenheimer's advice had once counted so heavily. Some didn't want the advice, some didn't want the association. As a result, Oppenheimer's value to McCarthy (as a victim) dwindled, as did worry about the possibilities that the case might be used to pillory the Eisenhower Administration as well as its predecessor.

THE MACHINERY GRINDS

But in the meantime, away from Washington and its constant political churning, a former key congressional staff member who had been identified with the preceding administration had begun to brood. After leaving the staff of the Joint Committee on Atomic Energy, William L. Borden was working in Pittsburgh when he decided to write to the director of the Federal Bureau of Investigation about his conclusions regarding a case with which he had been thoroughly familiar during his four and a half years as executive director of the Joint Committee. Throughout most of 1953 the new Administration was preoccupied with review and revision of the security system, although AEC procedures were not changed. Significantly, AEC, on November 1, had acquired a new General Manager, Major General K. D. Nichols, who resigned from the Army to take the job. Nichols had been General Groves's second in command in the Manhattan Project and should have been thoroughly familiar with the Oppenheimer case.

Borden applied his training and skill as a lawyer and his knowledge of the workings of government to the task of constructing a letter that would focus on his conviction that Oppenheimer

> more probably than not . . . was a sufficiently hardened Communist [and] that he either volunteered espionage information to the Soviets or complied with a request for such information. (This includes the possibility that when he singled out the weapons aspect of atomic development as his personal specialty, he was acting under Soviet instructions.) [Borden's parens.] . . . more probably than not . . . has since [the 1939–42] period been functioning as an espionage agent; and . . . more probably than not . . . has since acted under a Soviet directive in influencing United States military, atomic energy, intelligence and diplomatic policy.

Borden drew from the voluminous files, or from his memory of them, assumptions or conclusions that had been effectively resolved in other ways by professional security reviewers and the people who had the ultimate responsibilities in the areas of Oppenheimer's advice. The file entries included references to Oppenheimer's contributions to the Communist Party before the war, to Communist affiliations of his wife and younger brother, to a Communist mistress, and to allegations that he had brought Communists into the atomic project, had recruited for the Communist Party, had given false information to the Manhattan Project security representatives regarding his association with a suspected Communist, Haakon Chevalier, had used Communists in nontechnical work at Los Alamos (including the writing of the history), and had advocated the disbanding of the Los Alamos group at the end of the war.

Borden sent his letter to FBI Director J. Edgar Hoover, whose long career at the topmost level of civil service had given him skills in handling politicians and manipulating the machinery of bureaucracy. Hoover immediately put the FBI to work, setting Oppenheimer's file in order and clarifying as many unclear aspects of the case as possible. On the last day of November, 1953, Hoover sent the Borden letter with the reworked file to the White House. We do not know what the director of the Federal Bureau of Investigation wrote or told the President, but he is bound to have made the point one way or another that Borden could not be dismissed as a crackpot. Copies of a new FBI report on Oppenheimer were also sent to the AEC, the Department of Defense, and probably other sensitive agencies.

But what probably jelled President Eisenhower's response and put it into the only mold he knew for the handling of such difficult decisions (the bureaucracy itself with all its built-in protective machinery) was the linking of all the file material to the policy positions Oppenheimer had taken since the war against the H-bomb and related matters.

Philip Stern, in his account of the affair, makes the point that the discomfiture of the Administration over the Borden letter was aggravated by the fact that, during the month of November, Attorney General Herbert Brownell had been severely and widely criticized for his charges in a luncheon speech that President

Truman had appointed a known Soviet spy to high office despite an FBI report that should at least have aroused his suspicions. Brownell was not referring to Oppenheimer, but it may well have been this allegation that kept President Eisenhower, whose forte was dealing with people on a face-to-face basis, from taking the direct step of calling Oppenheimer in and lecturing him as he had probably lectured the officer who, shortly before the invasion of the Continent in 1944, committed the security indiscretion described above. Had he followed that procedure, he would merely have sent the luckless physicist home after a dressing down and cut off his access to classified data and forbidden his participation in any kind of national security policy formation in the future.

Instead of attacking the problem as a Commander in Chief invested with the necessary authority and responsibility, however, Eisenhower chose to play the role of the isolated Chief Executive. He acted quickly but not conclusively. He may have acted from fear that McCarthy might get hold of the new FBI dossier on Oppenheimer—or, worse yet, the Borden letter—and use it to brand the Administration as soft on Communism, or he may have acted out of deep personal concern. In any event, he ordered that a "blank wall" be erected between Oppenheimer and all government security information and that the entire case be restudied and recommendations made as to his own next step.

Chairman Strauss of the AEC directed General Manager Nichols to carry out the President's orders. Under AEC procedures this meant formally rescinding Oppenheimer's clearance and presenting him with written charges so that he could be given a hearing before a board, with right of counsel, the right to cross-examine witnesses, and the right of appeal to the AEC's Personnel Security Review Board.

Nichols undertook the task with zest and zeal. On December 23, 1953, he sent Oppenheimer a letter—although the scientist had been told about the charges two days before, apparently to give him an opportunity to resign without a hearing—rescinding his security clearance and listing twenty-four charges as the reasons. The first twenty-three dealt with character and associations and all the messy security reports and allegations covered in the dossier. The twenty-fourth dealt with Oppenheimer's opposition to the H-bomb. Most of Borden's complaints were covered in the charges. Except for some clarification, there were few items that General Groves hadn't known about when he ordered Nichols, as District Engineer of the Manhattan Engineer District, to clear Oppenheimer and put him in charge of the Los Alamos weapons center. Mainly what was different was the 1953 climate of suspicion and the public's fear of a possible Communist conspiracy—as well as the growing number of people who had been stung or rebuffed by Oppenheimer (Nichols was reportedly one) and the fact that the government had not taken Oppenheimer's advice on a major policy matter. The twenty-fourth charge referred to his continued opposition to the development of the H-bomb after his advice had been rejected. It was not a charge in the same sense as the first twenty-three, since it depended too much on speculation and interpretation.

Oppenheimer requested a hearing. It was Hobson's choice. He could resign and leave the charges standing and subject to exploitation by McCarthy, or he could gamble on their being cleared up via the AEC hearing process, which he believed to be thorough and fair. As many times as those charges had been evaluated up to then, Oppenheimer could hardly lose, it seemed to many, by simply walking away from his consultant's job, where many did not want him anyway. Speculative hindsight would indicate that, had the Borden charges been leaked to McCarthy and had the latter taken his usual tack, the Administration would have had to come to Oppenheimer's defense, along with enough of the scientific brains of the country to put the senator in the position of himself being the one who was endangering the national defense and security. Borden may have thought to ward off a possible attempt by McCarthy to invade the Joint Committee's jurisdiction, of which Borden had been a zealous guardian. Borden may even have thought it better for Oppenheimer to have the case formally and properly heard on the initiative of the Administration rather than to have it publicly aired by McCarthy. Either a resignation, in effect forced by the Administration, or a full hearing initiated by the Administration would have stymied McCarthy. In the light of subsequent events, resignation would have brought a strange kind of support to Oppenheimer's side, had McCarthy attacked him. At any rate, after considering advice favoring both courses, Oppenheimer chose the hearing route.

Then the machinery started grinding. A special Personnel Security Board, with no experienced reviewers, was appointed by AEC. Its chairman was Gordon Gray, former Secretary of the Army and then President of the University of North Carolina. The other members were Thomas A. Morgan, an industrialist who had come up the hard way without any of the advantages enjoyed by Oppenheimer in his youth, and Dr. Ward V. Evans, a chemistry professor and expert on explosives. The board met for nearly a month, starting in mid-April, 1954. The transcript of its hearings covered more than 3,000 typed pages. The board heard 30 witnesses. The members made their report to the General Manager late in May. It was clear from their report that they had trouble with some of the evidence of Oppenheimer's behavior, associates, and the degree of his cooperation with the security investigators. The matter of his communications to his friend Haakon Chevalier was never cleared up to anybody's satisfaction. It was this more than anything else that caused one observer to remark, "Oppie was his own worst witness." The Gray Board was unanimous in finding Oppenheimer loyal, but by a vote of 2 to 1, Dr. Evans dissenting, the Board recommended against reinstatement of his clearance.

Oppenheimer's attorneys decided to skip the next step—review by the standing AEC Personnel Security Review Board—and appealed directly to the Commissioners. With the appeal went the recommendation of the General Manager against Oppenheimer on grounds not entirely covered, said some lawyers, in the original charges.

On the June 29, 1954, the day before Oppenheimer's consultant contract with the AEC would expire anyway, the Atomic Energy Commission by a vote of 4 to 1 officially and finally removed his security clearance, thereby canceling the contract and severing J. Robert Oppenheimer from his twelve-year key role in the conduct of national security affairs.

WHAT THE MACHINERY GROUND OUT

The Oppenheimer hearings didn't settle anything, with the possible exception of Borden's charge of disloyalty. Nobody gave that any credence.

The proceedings didn't expose any basic deficiency in the AEC security system, which, in the opinion of the authors, was then and is now the best in the U.S. in terms of protection for the employee. It has worked well in the situations for which it was designed. Its most common application is in the case of a candidate for a job who might find his eligibility for clearance questioned, providing an opportunity for him to confront his accusers and enabling the employing agency to resolve questions of the reliability or dependability of a would-be employee in a manner fair to the candidate. After two years of experience with personnel security operations, AEC had established the Personnel Security Review Board in order to provide for appeal in cases of decisions adverse to employees or applicants. It reports to the General Manager. The first permanent chairman of the board served for eighteen years and made as great a contribution to the worthiness of the AEC personnel security system an anybody who ever had anything to do with it, but his name seldom, if ever, appeared in the newspapers in that connection—Ganson Purcell, a Washington lawyer who until his death in 1967 advised the Commission on all aspects of the personnel security system.

Perhaps the AEC procedures just did not fit the Oppenheimer case. The Personnel Security Review Board was not used. The wise, trusted, and experienced "reviewer" who usually acted for the General Manager in such cases was not consulted. It was a different kind of case from the normal flow. Here was a situation, not of a new job applicant but of a key wartime executive-scientist who had been cleared several times, a world-renowned statesman of science currently employed as a consultant and scientific adviser at the pleasure of the Commission and therefore subject to being dismissed at any time, or just not being called upon for advice. It seemed to the authors that Oppenheimer's status and stature were doubly jeopardized by retrial, in effect, of charges reinstated in a way that called for prior clearances to be declared invalid.

The Oppenheimer case was a procedural anomaly. It was actually handled outside the established procedures and practice. Hearings were usually granted an employee or applicant to provide an opportunity for him to clear himself. The people who heard the cases were trained for the purpose and sought constructive resolutions. The findings of these hearings were reviewed by a responsible representative of the General Manager. At the time of the Oppenheimer hearings, the reviewer was Deputy General Manager Walter Williams, whose rough-hewn features and quiet speech reinforced the confidence that his straightforward manner and insights engendered in his subordinates, his managerial peers, and his superiors on the Commission. Many a case was fairly and soundly resolved because of Walt Williams's judicial temperament and firmness. Harold Green, when he turned in the statement of charges to General Counsel William Mitchell, had recommended that the normal procedures be followed. But Oppenheimer's case was handled by a board completely unfamiliar with the process, and the review at the General Manager's level was by Nichols himself, who had nothing like the experience of Williams in the area. The appeal—Oppenheimer's choice—was made directly to the Commission instead of to the Personnel Security Review Board, headed by Ganson Purcell, who had all of Williams's qualifications plus a fine legal mind. To the knowledge of the authors, Oppenheimer's was the only case in which there was, in effect, a prosecutor assigned to substantiate the indictment. He was Roger Robb, a former U.S. Assistant District Attorney and an experienced Washington trial lawyer.

The Commission's 4 to 1 decision reflected all of the ambiguities and anomalies of the case. Commissioner Thomas E. Murray, in an independent opinion in support of the General Manager's order to withdraw the security clearance of the scientific architect of the atomic bomb, developed the proposition, which remains uniquely his, that Oppenheimer's being a security risk who, over the years, had showed disregard for the rules made him in fact disloyal. The separate supporting opinion of Commissioner Joseph Campbell, in essence, was that the AEC was in the position of an appellate court and that he could see no errors in procedure or substance that would constitute grounds for reversing the action of the General Manager based on the findings and recommendation of the Gray Board. Commissioner Eugene M. Zuckert also joined in the majority decision but submitted a separate opinion to the effect that, while none of the twenty-three charges was sufficient justification by itself to warrant denial of clearance, the cumulative effect showed Oppenheimer to be enough of a security risk to justify the General Manager's action. The majority opinion, signed by Chairman Lewis L. Strauss and by Campbell and Zuckert, confirmed the Gray Board's decision by finding the twenty-three charges essentially proved. Special significance was placed on about a half dozen charges relating to Oppenheimer's responses to security investigators involving his friend Chevalier and an alleged Communist named Eltenton, about whom Chevalier said he had warned Oppenheimer. Oppenheimer was able to explain these things to the wartime security people and to the AEC security staff in 1949 in order to obtain clearance but not to the Gray Board under cross-examination by a determined prosecutor in the role of examiner in what amounted to an adversary proceeding.

Commissioner Henry D. Smyth, in a legally sound and sharply reasoned dissent, differed head-on with all of the varied findings of the majority. He considered that all twenty-three charges had been adequately dealt with in prior proceedings and were inconsequential or understandable in the light of the times in which the events themselves occurred. With the help of Clark Vogel, an AEC attorney, he found there was no evidence Oppenheimer had ever divulged any security information and that "for much of the last 11 years he has been under actual surveillance, his movements watched, his conversations noted, his mail and telephone calls checked." Smyth said that the purpose of the security system is to prevent sabotage and protect secrets, and that if a man "protects the secrets he has in his hand and in his head, he has shown essential regard for the security system." He concluded that Oppenheimer's continued employment would not endanger the common defense and security, but "will continue to strengthen the United States." Had he been a sports commissioner, he might have added there's a difference between breaking the training rules and throwing the game. Smyth's dissenting opinion is a bench mark in the ongoing struggle of individual rights vs. bureaucracy.

Chairman Strauss, in signing the majority opinion, stated that Oppenheimer had "placed himself outside the rules which govern others," and had "exhibited a willful disregard of the normal and proper obligations of security." He found that Oppenheimer was "not entitled to the continued confidence of the government and of the Atomic Energy Commission because of the fundamental defects in his 'character.' " Shortly afterwards, Strauss, acting in his capacity as trustee of the Institute for Advanced Study and making a distinction between working for the government and the private Institute, voted to continue Oppenheimer as director.

Dr. Oppenheimer accepted the Commission's verdict with dignity and without rancor. He carried on his work at the Institute at Princeton until 1966 when he was stricken with throat cancer. His counsel continued to be sought by organizations abroad, including the International Atomic Energy Agency. President Johnson, on December 2, 1963, acting on the approval given by President Kennedy, presented Oppenheimer with the AEC's Enrico Fermi Award. The reception that followed at the National Academy of Sciences seemed to complete Oppenheimer's rehabilitation. He was very much in demand as a lecturer until his death in 1967.

Earlier in this chapter it was stated that the Oppenheimer security dossier was full of ambiguities and contradictions. They were never resolved. The question remains, how did the case come about? The answer is that the case must be interpreted in the context of its time. In 1943, General Groves was willing to take chances in order to develop an atomic weapon before the Nazis did. Against the background of the 1930's, Oppenheimer's associates posed no threat to national security, and interpretation of the regulations was favorable to Oppenheimer. In 1947, any other interpretation would have denied the new Commission the services of one of wartime's greatest scientists and brought down on its head the wrath of General Groves. But in 1954 the McCarthy hysteria was at its height, and in the context of a narrower and more structured review, the outcome was unfavorable to Oppenheimer.

In some ways, the men who made the final decision were in a trap. In the McCarthy era, the stakes were high, and demagogues could make capital out of almost any course of action—or so the people on both sides feared—and that is why the course was plotted as it was.

IX

Pax Atomica

On September 25, 1945, the last day of his public service and his seventy-eighth birthday, Henry L. Stimson was awarded the Distinguished Service Medal by President Truman. He told the assembled Cabinet group that if the destructive atom were to be controlled, the U.S. should seek cooperation with the Soviets in the peaceful uses of atomic energy because the real future of the atom lay in its research applications and the development of power.

Realism was on the side of this wise and experienced statesman—a prominent and progressive Republican—whom Roosevelt had called back to duty at the approach of war in 1940. Stimson had served as President Herbert Hoover's Secretary of State and throughout a long and distinguished career had carried out many public service assignments in the defense and foreign relations fields. He had been General Groves's impersonal backer and confidant throughout the period of the building of the atomic weapon. His wisdom and stature were influential in the negotiations of 1946 and 1947, and national atomic energy policy has continued on a course lighted by his understanding and vision. Stimson may not have foreseen in 1945 that neither the Americans nor the Russians were prepared for the kind of denationalization necessary for effective control of the military atom, but he seemed to sense that cooperative development of the peaceful atom might pave the way to control of the war atom, a concept that remains valid today.

Cooperation among the nations of the world in developing and sharing the benefits of the peaceful atom has been proudly proclaimed but practiced with such diplomatic reticence as to dim its promise for the technologically dependent nations. Progress has been slow, partly because of the realities of the nuclear energy business and partly because of timid leadership, but progress has been made. To use a mechanical analogy, the machinery has been assembled, even though the speed control devices get more attention than the fuel injection system. Member governments of international organizations seem to worry lest the machinery move too fast.

Progress toward effective control of the military atom has alternately dragged and surged ahead. It has been sustained by the thrusts of piecework agreements, the most recent—and possibly most significant—of which was the 1972 accord on nuclear weapons systems that President Nixon went to Moscow to sign. U.S. policies over the years have not been consistent with respect to either direction or motive, but AEC, in furtherance of its own interests and in response to the wishes of its scientific constituency, has always sought stronger international arrangements. Its role in policy-making has been growing in recent years, but AEC has had an up-and-down part in the pulsing drama of weapons control.

From the autumn of 1945 until the spring of 1947, efforts to obtain international agreement on control of atomic energy to prevent its use in war occupied the attention of the foreign affairs and defense elements of government. The effort was concentrated on an historic attempt to establish an international development and control authority under the aegis of the United Nations. A rigid treaty statute was to have provided for inspection of national programs to guard against clandestine weapons work, with violators subject to punishment. The basic idea, modified for purposes of negotiation, had been proposed in the fall of 1945 by J. Robert Oppenheimer and David Lilienthal, serving as consultants to a State Department Committee on Atomic Energy, chaired by then Under Secretary of State Dean Acheson. The so-called Acheson-Lilienthal Report formed the basis for the U.S. proposal for a United Nations Atomic Energy Commission. It was presented June 14, 1946, by Bernard M. Baruch—adviser to presidents and

senior even to Stimson in tenure of public service—and fruitlessly
pursued by him at the U.N. until January, 1947. The idea came
to naught within a few months due to Soviet insistence that
punishment for violations be subject to veto in the Security Council.
But behind this formal policy position of the Soviets was something
else that deepened the disappointment and left a nagging concern with the all-out supporters of the U.S. proposal—the obvious
unwillingness on either side to lower any of the barriers to communication and understanding, not just those involved in atomic
secrecy.

SEVEN LEAN YEARS

During its early years, AEC efforts in international cooperation
were limited to meeting the demand for raw materials, which
were shared with the British under wartime agreements. Those agreements had been rendered invalid by the McMahon Act. In the
delicate job of extricating the U.S. from these agreements, the
Commissioners ran into another policy issue that many feared
might plague the atom, a possible new version of the historic issue
of free trade vs. protectionism—whether to distribute radioisotopes
abroad. In their first split vote, the Commissioners favored the idea
4 to 1, with Strauss as the lone dissenter. His position was no
precursor of his future action, since he was later to lead Eisenhower's unprecedented atomic export program, covering far more
than isotopes.

President Truman launched the first export program with a
message to the Fourth International Cancer Congress at St. Louis
announcing the availability of radioisotopes for medical research
throughout the free world. Presiding over the congress of medical
researchers was Truman's old friend, Dr. E. V. Cowdray, a world-
renowned leader in the cancer field. The action gave a boost to
the isotope distribution program, which had been started domestically by General Groves in 1946. The X-10 Pile, as the Oak
Ridge reactor was called, had been built as a prototype for the
Hanford production reactors. It became the chief radioisotope
production facility of the world and continues to supply the first
great, widely distributable benefit of atomic energy.

Most of the AEC international involvement for the first seven years had to do with arrangements for obtaining raw materials, primarily uranium concentrates from the Belgian Congo, Canada, and the Union of South Africa, where uranium was extracted from the gold mine tailings. Despite the fact that the wartime agreements made by Roosevelt and Churchill at Quebec and Hyde Park had been effectively abrogated by the McMahon Act, cooperation with the British and Canadians continued under an informal agreement known as the *Modus Vivendi*. Under it, the British permitted the continuing flow of raw materials to U.S. plants, pending the buildup of their own requirements. Close working liaison was maintained in the area of declassification policy so that the two countries and the Canadians were able to keep in step in controlling technical data.

The foreign distribution of isotopes grew rapidly as more and more countries acquired the skills and facilities for their use. By 1953, the number of shipments was more than 2,000 annually to nearly fifty countries, which had entered into agreements with the U.S. not to permit the use of these valuable new research tools for other than peaceful purposes.

In the meantime, foreign hopes and expectations for low-cost electric power from the atom mounted, unaffected by the rugged experience the U.S. was having with the difficult job of developing materials for reactor construction and designing and building the complex machines for generating power from fissionable material.

ATOMS FOR PEACE

President Eisenhower himself must have shared some of the unfulfilled hopes of the European countries. He had come back from his heroic victory in Europe in the fall of 1945 to find the country noisily preoccupied with the atomic bomb. Some of his officers took a dim view of the accolades conferred on General Groves. This was the attitude encountered when an emissary of Lilienthal attempted to stimulate the award of another decoration for Groves, to be presented as a part of a ceremony in turning over Manhattan Project activities to the civilian Atomic Energy Commission. During his tour as chairman of the Joint Chiefs of Staff, Eisenhower was known to be a stickler for security of any phase of the atomic program with any possible military application, but he believed in international cooperation. He had saved the United Nations Relief and Rehabilitation Administration from fiscal emasculation in the fall of 1945 in a dramatic Thanksgiving Day appearance before a House Appropriations subcommittee.

It was nevertheless a surprise to many when President Eisenhower, late in 1953, came up with the first positive and constructive idea for control of the atom since the abortive Acheson-Lilienthal-Baruch proposals. On December 8, 1953, the President appeared before the General Assembly of the United Nations in New York and came as close to electrifying that treadmilling diplomatic conclave as any man before or since. He proposed that the nations capable of producing fissionable material contribute to the United Nations a sufficient amount of fissionable material to create a pool from which all the nations could draw for peaceful purposes. He hoped that this would create a demand large enough to drain away material that might otherwise be used for weapons. To some extent, this concept was based on the faulty premise that there was a shortage of raw material. At any rate, his "Atoms For Peace Speech" at the U.N. in 1953 launched a program that continues to gain momentum and sustain hopes. Lewis Strauss, in his book *Men and Decisions,* credits Eisenhower with the idea, but it was Strauss, who had opposed isotopes for export lest they aid foreign military programs, that gave the multinational plan outlined by Eisenhower much of its impetus. The late McKay Donkin, then a special assistant to Strauss and later vice-president of Penn State University, and Trapnell spent many holiday hours that Christmas and New Year's attaching bones to the spine of the President's idea and putting meat on the ribs. These efforts turned out to be premature, and no trace of them is to be found in the treaty signed three years later. They dealt with the safeguard stage and concentrated on finding politically acceptable, realistically effective measures for the control and safe custody of materials to prevent their diversion from pooled international stores. Although the normal pattern of trade would be for material to move directly from producer to user, the idea of an international bank of nuclear fuels was a part of Eisenhower's proposal. The President allocated the first hundred kilograms of U-235 to the Atoms for Peace Program in November, 1954, followed six months later by a similar allocation for use under bilateral arrangements not utilizing the services nor subject to the safeguards of an inter-national body. The second allotment signaled U.S. intentions to use direct or bilateral, as well as multilateral, channels of atomic aid. For better or for worse, the dual-channel policy made Eisenhower's concept of a central international house for the peaceful atom into a kind of surburban duplex.

In October, 1956, in the midst of a Presidential election cam-paign, the unsuccessful Democratic candidate, Adlai Stevenson, argued bravely and futilely for a cessation of nuclear weapons testing but ignored the birth of a new international organism of comparable portent. The statute of the International Atomic Energy Agency came into effect that month with the completion of the signatory procedure by eighty nations. The painstaking drafting and negotiations had been conducted under the direction of an amiable and politically adept ex-congressman from New York, James W. Wadsworth, whose disarming manner belied a rare diplomatic skill. A staunch Republican, he commanded re-spect on both sides of the aisle in Congress. His service to his country was never adequately recognized during his lifetime. His efforts had been given a boost the year before by the First Inter-national Congress on Peaceful Uses of Atomic Energy. It was the greatest international gathering of scientists up to that time and brought 3,600 scientists, engineers, political leaders, and equip-ment salesmen from eighty nations together for a constructive exchange of technical ideas as well as for a sharing of hopes for peace and the opportunity to use atomic energy for peaceful purposes. The 1955 Conference served to divert criticism and relieve the impatience created during the near three years it had taken to negotiate the International Atomic Energy Agency treaty in response to Eisenhower's suggestions. An unexpectedly useful accomplishment of the 1955 Conference was to lure the Joint Committee on Atomic Energy (which sent a delegation of seven members as advisers to the U.S. delegation, headed by AEC Chairman Strauss) far enough into international waters to dampen any latent isolationist tendencies where the peaceful atom was concerned.

Geneva was the scene of similar conferences in 1958, 1964, and 1971. Off and on through these years, while cooperation in peace-ful uses expanded slowly but steadily, halting efforts at controlling the military uses of atomic energy were made. The most sustained and successful have been the so-called SALT (Strategic Arms Limitation Talks) conferences, alternating between Vienna and Helsinki. The nomenclature reflects the fact that, even though multiple warheads a thousand times more powerful than the Hiroshima-Nagasaki bombs are the instrument of destruction, the delivery system is of more topical and military significance than the nuclear explosive. The course of events has confirmed Stimson's intuitive estimate that cooperative international peaceful development held the most promise. At each Geneva Conference, the atomic powers have staged mammoth "Atoms For Peace" exhibits, and the American and Soviet scientists have eagerly and agreeably vied to demonstrate capabilities that will awe the representatives of the nations that seek only the peaceful uses of atomic energy and are not burdened with the continuing investment in explosives and delivery systems for nuclear arms. Most of these countries, however, are burdened with the fear that nuclear deterrence among the atomic powers might not work, or that some reckless possessor of a nuclear weapon might succeed—or fail—in some type of blackmail that ends both fears and hopes.

Much of the hopes that all nations now hold are centered in the International Atomic Energy Agency, which is growing slowly into the instrument of peaceful cooperation that Henry Stimson must have had in mind that day in the Cabinet Room when he urged cooperation in peacetime development as the surest road to control of the wartime atom.

THE PROMISE IS DILUTED

Despite the high hopes of many of the nonatomic countries— or perhaps because of them—the International Atomic Energy Agency did not at first "pay off." This was only partly due to the fact that the developing countries overestimated the payoff of atomic energy and underestimated the time it would take to get it. The U.S. underestimated the difficulty of starting up a new international agency. The structure of the agency had clearly been designed to protect the interests of the atomic powers: a carefully balanced Board of Governors and carefully limited authority for the chief executive, the Director General. In the final treaty-negotiating stages, it was tacitly agreed that the Director General would come from a neutral country, thus avoiding an East-West confrontation over his election. It was assumed, and not so tacitly according to some of the negotiators, that both the Soviets and the U.S. would advance names of candidates of sufficient prominence to indicate their high regard for the role and then withdraw their candidates in favor of the candidate from Sweden, Harry Brynielson. At the last minute, after the U.S. delegation had arrived in Vienna for the First General Conference of all the members of the International Atomic Energy Agency (IAEA) in the fall of 1957, the U.S. changed its mind and insisted upon the election of its certainly worthy candidate, Representative Sterling Cole, the 1953–55 Republican Chairman of the congressional Joint Committee on Atomic Energy. His was a name of sufficient prominence in the atomic world to demonstrate the seriousness of U.S. intentions. Unfortunately for Cole, those intentions did not extend to the period after the election for the U.S. failed to provide the kind of administrative and diplomatic backup that the American Director General of IAEA was going to need. The eleventh-hour switch was a surprise to both East and West and, in the view of some of the United Nations professionals on hand, could not have been carried through successfully without the midnight efforts of the universally respected U.N. Assistant Secretary General, Ralph Bunche.

It was not an auspicious start for a new international body so heavily loaded with hope. It carried U.S. colors on the flagstaff of Eisenhower's initiative, but some of the neutral countries wondered about their own roles if the atomic powers insisted on running the show. The response of the Soviets was to place their candidate, the venerable Vladimir Emelyanov, one of the world's leading atomic scientists, on the Board of Governors and to insist upon the election to the powerful chairmanship of the Board of Governors a skilled Czech lawyer-diplomat, Gerhart Winkler, who was a stickler for form and effectively tied the hands of both the Director General and the U.S. in the start-up year.

In a memorandum prepared for the Chairman of the Joint Committee and the Chairman of the Atomic Energy Commission in 1960, dealing with the lack of U.S. support for IAEA, Trapnell, who had served as Special Assistant to Cole for the first year and a half of his term as Director General, said the Soviets had "tolerated the agency." They had avoided a visibly obstructionist role but had withheld support, "content with the continuing existence of an international bureaucracy whose shortcomings can be laid to the United States." The memo also claimed that there were other nations assuming a substantive role in IAEA that were unsympathetic for fear the work of the agency might benefit U.S. industry as atomic trade expanded. It mentioned the disillusionment of the smaller nations, which had embraced the too hasty generalizations regarding the benefits of the atom, and pointed out that some of the participants quarreled with the very idea of IAEA, which they regarded as an "instrument for the maintenance of the exclusivity of the 'atomic bomb club.' " The diplomatic problem of dealing with these attitudes was further complicated by the unwieldy management structure of the IAEA. Cole had been an unusually effective congressman but not even 22 years in Congress could endow a man with experience as a manager, the techniques of the diplomat, and the prestige of a scientist, to the degree called for by his position in this new, technologically oriented international agency.

Cole felt his own government did not adequately back him up. The first U.S. Governor, Robert McKinney, the New Mexico publisher who had headed an atomic industry survey for Senator Clinton Anderson, Chairman of the Joint Committee, was no match for the professionals on the Board of Governors from countries like South Africa, Britain, France, and even some of the smaller countries whose representatives made up in diplomatic skill what they lacked in atomic sophistication. But worse, the U.S. carried on a competing foreign atomic aid program, bypassing IAEA with bilateral agreements (for which President Eisenhower had provided an allotment of nuclear materials) carrying direct cash gifts of $350,000 for the construction of research reactors, all at a time when the IAEA was unable to provide anywhere near similar assistance.

President Eisenhower's skilled ambassador in negotiating these agreements was a broad-gauged industrialist-turned-diplomat, Morehead Patterson, chairman of the American Machine and Foundry Company (now AMF, Inc.). Patterson believed the IAEA had a critically important role to play, but he had more to offer to signers of U.S. bilateral agreements. Cole's problems were further complicated by the fact that McKinney resigned from the Board of Governors in September, 1958, and the U.S. didn't bother to replace him until the following spring. During the long interim, his chair was filled by the U.S. deputy chief of mission, Harold Vedler, a Foreign Service officer who did a superb job under the handicap of substituting for an ambassador without an ambassador's credentials. Cole's experience on the Joint Committee had given him a broad acquaintanceship among the technical leaders of atomic development in the United States, but when he sought to make selections on his own and deal directly with the specialists he wanted to come to Vienna, he met resistance from both the State Department and AEC. He was able to get competent technical people, however, as the Agency has been able to do ever since. At the same time, he learned how the specialized agencies of the U.N. suffer because Foreign Service personnel policies put a career penalty instead of a premium upon tours of duty in international organizations. Many other nations, however, try to put their best people into the administrative ranks of international organizations. The way the professionals in the U.S. Foreign Service avoid duty in the international bureaucracies leads one to question the adequacy if not the sincerity of our government's commitment to the multinational approach to the solution of world problems.

Cole also suffered from difficult office relationships with some of the senior staff members skilled in the ways of international bureaucracy. Because he was used to the independence of the legislator, he did not fully realize the importance of support and backup by the State Department. The cumulative effect of all this was when his term was up in the fall of 1961, Cole had no constituency to back him for a second term. Largely on the basis of the advice of the continuing specialists in both AEC and the State Department, the Kennedy Administration, which had taken office in January of that year, went back to the original plan (some of these specialists had helped work it out) and, in order to avoid a continuing East-West tug of war in administering the Agency, supported Sigvard Eklund of Sweden as the second Director. General.

After giving up a safe seat in the Congress to go to Vienna, the sudden loss of support from his government was a traumatic experience for the sensitive Cole. Whatever his problems with the Eisenhower Administration and lack of communication with the Kennedy Administration, no one ever questioned Cole's devotion to the cause of the Agency and his belief in its ultimate contribution to peace and the atomic bond among the nations. Even the cynics who disdained his spirited and (to hardened international bureaucrats) amateurish enthusiasm for the idea of IAEA said he should have had some honorary withdrawal assignment to his home country.

Cole's friends wondered why he ever took the job in the first place, but his presence at the helm of the newest international ship of state assured a safe launching as far as the U.S. Congress was concerned. There was never a word of complaint, although the support formula committed the U.S. to something like 30 per cent of the operating cost of the Agency, and the U.S. kept right on with its competing bilateral program with generous gifts of money and equipment. The Argonne National Laboratory training school for students from abroad, known as the International Institute of Nuclear Science and Engineering, was a technical manpower source for IAEA, thanks in part to the fact that the laboratory's director, Norman Hilberry, was as enthusiastic about the IAEA as was Cole. Similar support came from the Oak Ridge Institute of Nuclear Studies (now the Association of Oak Ridge Universities), which sent W. W. Gregorieff to Vienna to manage the sizable IAEA scholarship program.

During the 1961 IAEA Fifth General Conference, at which he was replaced, Cole had the satisfaction of witnessing the approval and adoption of the first international statute providing for a system of safeguards against diversion of nuclear materials. Two years later, the first trilateral agreement was signed providing for IAEA safeguards and inspection of Japanese facilities utilizing U.S.-supplied fuel. The U.S. put several of its research reactors under IAEA safeguards, and in 1964 the Yankee Atomic Power Plant at Rowe, Massachusetts, became the first commercial power plant in the world subject to international inspection.

However sluggish the start-up of the International Atomic Energy Agency, Cole's single term seems to have provided a sound foundation for the future. Sigvard Eklund, his successor, has not entirely pleased the few activists in the atomic foreign affairs community of the U.S., but neither has he offended those of any country who worry about the IAEA's moving too fast or becoming too strong. After Cole's unhappy experience, the U.S. began to do better by the Agency in terms of the men appointed to the Board of Governors. President Kennedy in 1961 sent Dr. Henry D. Smyth, who commanded respect as a scientist and who had administrative experience both through his service as a member of the first Atomic Energy Commission and later as vice-president for research at Princeton. President Nixon in 1969 sent T. Keith Glennan, onetime member of the Atomic Energy Commission, first Administrator of the National Aeronautics and Space Administration, and former President of Case Western Reserve University. Support for the Agency at the Atomic Energy Commission was strengthened in 1971–72 with the appointments to AEC of James Schlesinger as Chairman (who had a background of study of how the atomic bomb had affected the real relationships among the nations), of Commissioner William O. Doub, who had a lawyer's interest in the international atom, and of Commissioner Dixy Lee Ray, a life scientist with strong convictions as to the importance of public understanding of the atom and international cooperation in general.

UMBRELLA FOR VIOLENCE

In the early days after World War II, David Lilienthal said on a number of occasions and in a number of ways that fear of nuclear war was not a dependable basis for peace. Little did anyone realize how right he was. The atomic powers have been wary enough of nuclear war but seemingly content to conduct or nourish what euphemistically has been called conventional warfare under an umbrella of fear-inspired assurance that the ultimate weapon—nuclear explosives—would not be used.

The theory of "massive retaliation" propounded by Secretary of State John Foster Dulles in the mid-1950's meant that U.S. defense investment in ground forces in those years went down relative to the investment in strategic missile and bomber forces—the effective instrument of which, the nuclear warhead, is not a precision battlefield weapon. Massive retaliation with nuclear weapons was hardly a viable form of response to the tough and determined action sustained for so long by the North Vietnamese in the Indochina War.

By the early 1960's, the U.S. investment in military support of the South Vietnamese government set up after the defeat of the French at Dien Bien Phu in 1954 had reached a billion dollars with little effect on the conflict. As a result, our involvement began to go up. We forgot the solemn declarations at the end of World War II—punctuated by atomic explosions—that military violence was not an effective instrument of national purpose. Somehow, we assumed the lesson applied only to the atom bomb. Military men argued convincingly that the Vietnam War demonstrated the need for modernized ground and air forces that could handle conflicts of unprecedented ferocity, as in Vietnam, but of lesser dimensions than nuclear warfare. Even had there been no prospect of public revulsion to use of nuclear weapons, the military situation in Southeast Asia offered little opportunity for application of the awesome force of the atomic explosion. The specter of the mushroom cloud characteristic of the atomic bomb thus became a sort of umbrella under which one of history's most violent conflicts took place. The true costs and consequences for the U.S. of the Vietnam War will take a long time to assess. Aside from the human costs, the diversion of human and material resources from pressing domestic needs, the long-term economic effects, the detrimental impact on the military profession, and the divisions among our people over a war they still wonder how they got into, the image of America in Asia may have been damaged more by the thousands of tons of conventional bombs rained on a small piece of Southeast Asian real estate than by the two atomic bombs dropped on Japan.

Since fear of the atom, as Lilienthal predicted, has provided no basis for peace, preparations for atomic warfare have continued. The original four nuclear powers—U.S., U.K., U.S.S.R., and France—were joined by a fifth—Communist China—which the U.S., as a matter of misguided policy, had been stiff-arming economically, diplomatically, and culturally since the early 1950's. All five powers have continued to strengthen their nuclear capabilities in a race for ephemeral nuclear security. They may have been diverted, but hardly slowed, by the U.S.-U.K.-U.S.S.R.

Limited Test Ban Treaty of 1963, which prohibits nuclear testing in the atmosphere. France and China have kept right on testing in the atmosphere. In the ten years following the treaty, the AEC tested nearly 250 nuclear devices underground, the Soviets less than a third as many. The developing, testing, manufacturing (from acquisition of raw materials to finished product), and storing of nuclear warheads is big business, yet AEC has seldom been cited in published references to the "military-industrial complex," which had been identified by President Eisenhower as something a democratic society should be concerned about.

NEW REALISM AND NEW HOPE

The opening of the atom by the physicists, who had to think up strange new names for the particles that came out, changed life for everybody. Sometimes our response to that change has not been very realistic. Sometimes despair seems about to take over. As with Pandora's box, the particles can't be put back—but hope remains. To be sure, there are benefits galore. There are radiation hazards, of course, but there is reason to believe they can be dealt with adequately. There is energy to sustain for centuries the complex life system of societies whose work needs have long outrun their muscle power. Democracy's constructive response to the challenge of managing the atom within the framework of a free society has been sustained for more than a quarter of a century, and the people who have served in the nation's nuclear energy program can be proud of the manner in which they have discharged their heavy responsibilities.

Even so, throughout this time, we as a nation may have been kidding ourselves when we thought we were being realistic. Bombs, missiles, nuclear submarines, secrecy, hardline diplomacy—these have been the stuff of realism. Dependence on military hardware is only half realistic. The hope that remains amidst the particles let out of Pandora's nuclear box depends on something more. There are signs—communication with China, cooperation with the Soviets, the SALT (Strategic Arms Limitation Talks) agreement—that awareness of the world-shattering potential of the nuclear blast is beginning to take root in our national consciousness. Lilienthal may yet be proved wrong

about the war-deterring effect of fear of the atom. There are in-
dications that such fears may not be wholly without influence for
peace. At least, we may be about to stop kidding ourselves.

As 1972 drew to a close (together with this book) the nation
appeared to be facing reality instead of kidding itself that tough
talk and more missiles assured "the common defense and security," in the words of the Atomic Energy Act. We seemed to be
moving toward disposal of that rigidity in America's policy that
served for two decades as a strategic deterrent to the type of
communication and cooperation that Henry Stimson suggested the
day President Truman presented him with the nation's highest
civilian award. Perhaps the decks were being cleared for a strategic advance toward peace through a broader and more intensive
pooling of brains and resources than envisioned in the International Atomic Energy Agency—and all the other U.N. agencies
—in order to reduce the stress rooted in disparities in well-being
among the nations. The nuclear and space decades of the 1950's
and 1960's generated fantastic technological capabilities. Howard
Kurtz, through his proposal for War Control Planning, suggests
that such capabilities can be used for worldwide surveillance and
communication to control war. He says the military-industrial
complex should be converted to making the hardware needed to
police wars, not peace. Under Kurtz's War Control system, all
results of electronic and space surveillance would be public.

Some of the political ironies in the international phase of the
atom's development and control are significant enough to cite
here. The Republican President under whom the most recent international advances have taken place was once a most ardent
advocate—and one of the architects—of the stiff-arm policy. As
Vice-President in the campaign of 1956, Richard Nixon was the
bitterest critic of Adlai Stevenson's idea for a moratorium on
atmospheric weapon testing. International concerns have traditionally been the sphere of the Democratic Party in the U.S., but the
internationalizing of the atom took place under the Republicans.
The Act that made possible our participation in the International
Atomic Energy Agency was passed by the only Republican Congress in nearly a quarter of a century. The conclusion the authors
draw from their inside and outside observation of the events is that
right-wing Republicans would never have let a Democratic ad-

ministration take such steps but were unable to restrain the progressive leaders of their own party.

But the new approach by the White House toward the problem
of the nuclear weapon in world affairs is more than an irony. It
is a milestone along the path to realism. The destructive potential
of the atomic bomb is a fact of life, and its role in world affairs is
no longer subject to being played for domestic political advantage
any more than it is for international advantage. The lesson was
clearly stated by Presidential Adviser Henry Kissinger when he
briefed congressional leaders—including members of the committees on foreign affairs, armed services, and atomic energy—on
the Strategic Arms Limitation Talks agreement on June 17, 1972,
at the White House. He said the historic concept of balance of
power among the nations no longer applies "to the extent that
balance of power means jockeying for marginal advantages over
an opponent," and that "both we and the Soviet Union have begun
to find that each increment of power does not necessarily represent an increment of usable political strength."

According to the record of Kissinger's briefing, the President
decided at the beginning of the negotiations (and so instructed his
representatives) that the U.S. should avoid direct confrontation
in the hope that "the Soviet Union would acquire a stake in a wide
spectrum of negotiations."

The man who had led the arms negotiations for three years up
to the payoff point accomplished by Kissinger was a former AEC
staff member, Gerard Smith, Director of the Arms Control and
Disarmament Agency. He had been brought into AEC as an adviser to Commissioner Thomas E. Murray but remained to assist
Chairman Strauss through the period when Strauss was a principal architect of hardline dealing with the Soviets. Close observers
thought Smith was short-changed in the publicity payoff of the
SALT agreement, but Smith doubtless figured his purposes were
better served that way. Smith's predecessors, William C. Foster
and his deputy, Adrian Fisher, General Counsel of AEC under
Lilienthal, never had the type of instruction that Kissinger said
President Nixon had given him. The reason: Under a Democratic
administration, such rapprochement with the Soviets could never
have obtained bipartisan blessing.

But Stimson, Baruch, Acheson, Lilienthal, and Adlai Stevenson (whose arguments, unlike the wartime line of "too little and too late," were too early and too much) could all have stood with Kissinger when he said, from the safety and solidity of a White House podium, that most of the world's hopes for stability and peace depended upon the ability to "reduce tensions between the United States and the Soviet Union."

Much of the public acceptance and support—including the bipartisan blessing—of Kissinger's report on SALT rested upon the fact that he did not try to talk away the tensions. He acknowledged them realistically, saying:

> We are ideological adversaries, and we will in all likelihood remain so for the foreseeable future. . . .
>
> We are political and military competitors, and neither can be indifferent to advances by the other in either of these fields. . . .
>
> We each have allies whose association we value and whose interests and activities of each impinge on those of the other at numerous points. . . .
>
> We each possess an awesome nuclear force created and designed to meet the threat implicit in the other's strength and aims. . . .
>
> Each of us has thus come into possession of power single-handedly capable of exterminating the human race.

The challenge to survival remains.

Appendix A
Careers in Atomic Energy

In the early days of AEC, a leading scientist told a group of deans of engineering schools that the country didn't need nuclear engineers, it just needed good engineers. There are many nuclear engineers in the world today but the real point of the advice still holds. The demands of the nuclear field are such that better trained people are needed in every field, including the crafts. Even before the scientist's remark about good engineers, the director of education for the boilermakers union told his colleagues not to worry about loss of jobs due to the new way of generating energy. His advice was that nuclear power would require more and better boilermakers.

What both the scientist and the union educator were saying was that the impact of nuclear progress on education and training would result in new dimensions being added to traditional fields rather than in the creation of new fields. Of course, there are wholly new opportunities in atomic energy, but there are far more jobs to be had in traditional areas of employment.

AEC issues a brochure, *Employment with the United States Atomic Energy Commission,* which deals with employment in the federal service (not in the state, local, or private employment sectors). States and cities, however, are now looking for people with nuclear training because of site-planning problems, health and safety, and regulatory activities. The brochure lists federal jobs in four principal categories: accounting, law, management, and science and engineering. In all four categories, a bachelor's degree is a minimum requirement. Almost the entire range of specialization is covered in each field. Management disciplines, for example, include business administration, computer science, economics, finance, labor relations, personnel management, public administration, and—when combined with management courses— political science, liberal arts, and scientific disciplines. The AEC *Employment* brochure includes the following paragraph, under the heading "The AEC—Future Outlook":

> Filling the rapidly expanding need for energy for home and industry and for special needs such as power for spacecraft, developing artificial hearts and desalting seawater while at the same time protecting and preserving man's environment is our exciting assignment for the future. Those interested in dedicating themselves to advanced science geared to both preserving and improving man's way of life and locale are invited to come work with us.

Employment areas outside of government service are covered in a booklet in AEC's "Understanding the Atom" series: *Careers in Atomic Energy*. (Single copies are available free from USAEC, P.O. Box 62, Oak Ridge, Tennessee, 37830.) The current version, written by an English major, Loyce J. McIlhenny, who worked for several years in editorial capacities at Oak Ridge, makes the point that students can find careers in atomic energy in any field of science they choose, because "atomics" is not a field unto itself, divorced from the rest of the scientific world. The broad categories of employment opportunities (opportunity increases with degree of education) are the physical and biological sciences, engineering, medicine, veterinary science, and a host of supporting categories, starting with technical writing and editing and including nursing, instrument design and maintenance, librarianship, translating, glassblowing, and accounting.

Another useful way of categorizing atomic energy employment opportunities is by type of activity—research and development, exploration and mining, manufacturing, power generation and distribution, design and engineering, health and safety, fuel management and control, and the wide range of applications of nuclear techniques and materials in agriculture, medicine, public health, industry, the environmental sciences, materials development, and the life sciences.

Appendix B
AEC Commissioners
and General Managers

COMMISSIONERS

	From	To
Sumner T. Pike	Oct. 31, 1946	Dec. 15, 1951
David E. Lilienthal, Chairman	Nov. 1, 1946	Feb. 15, 1950
Robert F. Bacher	Nov. 1, 1946	May 10, 1949
William W. Waymack	Nov. 5, 1946	Dec. 21, 1948
Lewis L. Strauss	Nov. 12, 1946	Apr. 15, 1950
Chairman	July 2, 1953	June 30, 1958
Gordon Dean	May 24, 1949	June 30, 1953
Chairman	July 11, 1950	June 30, 1953
Henry DeWolf Smyth	May 30, 1949	Sept. 30, 1954
Thomas E. Murray	May 9, 1950	June 30, 1957
Thomas Keith Glennan	Oct. 2, 1950	Nov. 1, 1952
Eugene M. Zuckert	Feb. 25, 1952	June 30, 1954
Joseph Campbell	July 27, 1953	Nov. 30, 1954
Willard F. Libby	Oct. 5, 1954	June 30, 1959
John Von Neumann	Mar. 15, 1955	Feb. 8, 1957
Harold S. Vance	Oct. 31, 1955	Aug. 31, 1959
John S. Graham	Sept. 12, 1957	June 30, 1962
John Forrest Floberg	Oct. 1, 1957	June 23, 1960
John A. McCone, Chairman	July 14, 1958	Jan. 20, 1961

217

	From	*To*
John H. Williams	Aug. 13, 1959	June 30, 1960
Robert E. Wilson	Mar. 22, 1960	Jan. 31, 1964
Loren K. Olson	June 23, 1960	June 30, 1962
Glenn T. Seaborg, Chairman	Mar. 1, 1961	Aug. 16, 1971
Leland J. Haworth	Apr. 17, 1961	June 30, 1963
John G. Palfrey	Aug. 31, 1962	June 30, 1966
James T. Ramey	Aug. 31, 1962	June 30, 1973
Gerald F. Tape	July 15, 1963	Apr. 30, 1969
Mary I. Bunting	June 29, 1964	June 30, 1965
Wilfred E. Johnson	Aug. 1, 1966	June 30, 1972
Samuel M. Nabrit	Aug. 1, 1966	Aug. 1, 1967
Francesco Costagliola	Oct. 1, 1968	June 30, 1969
Theos J. Thompson	June 12, 1969	Nov. 25, 1970
Clarence E. Larson	Sept. 2, 1969	June 30, 1974
James R. Schlesinger, Chairman	Aug. 17, 1971	Jan. 26, 1973
William O. Doub	Aug. 17, 1971	June 30, 1976*
Dixy Lee Ray	Aug. 8, 1972	June 30, 1977*
Chairman	Feb. 6, 1973	

* Date term expires.

GENERAL MANAGERS

Carroll L. Wilson	Dec. 31, 1946	Aug. 15, 1950
Marion Boyer	Nov. 1, 1950	Oct. 31, 1953
Kenneth D. Nichols	Nov. 1, 1953	Apr. 30, 1955
Kenneth E. Fields	May 1, 1955	June 30, 1958
Paul F. Foster	July 1, 1958	Nov. 30, 1958
A. R. Luedecke	Dec. 1, 1958	July 31, 1964
R. E. Hollingsworth	Aug. 11, 1964	

Appendix C
Members of Congressional Committees Concerned with Atomic Energy

SENATE SPECIAL COMMITTEE ON ATOMIC ENERGY
79th Congress, 1945–46

Brien McMahon, Connecticut, *Chairman*

Richard B. Russell, Georgia
Edwin C. Johnson, Colorado
Tom Connally, Texas
Harry Flood Byrd, Virginia
Millard E. Tydings, Maryland

Arthur H. Vandenberg, Michigan
Warren R. Austin, Vermont
Eugene D. Millikin, Colorado
Bourke B. Hickenlooper, Iowa
Thomas C. Hart, Connecticut

HOUSE COMMITTEE ON MILITARY AFFAIRS
79th Congress, 1945–46

Andrew J. May, Kentucky, *Chairman*

R. Ewing Thomason, Texas
Overton Brooks, Louisiana
John J. Sparkman, Alabama
Paul J. Kilday, Texas
Carl T. Durham, North Carolina
John Edward Sheridan,
    Pennsylvania
Robert L. F. Sikes, Florida

Philip J. Philbin, Massachusetts
Paul Stewart, Oklahoma
Arthur Winstead, Mississippi
Chet Holifield, California
James A. Roe, New York
Melvin Price, Illinois
J. Lindsay Almond, Virginia
Walter G. Andrews, New York

219

Dewey Short, Missouri
Leslie C. Arends, Illinois
Charles E. Clason, Massachusetts
J. Parnell Thomas, New Jersey
Paul W. Shafer, Michigan
Thomas E. Martin, Iowa
Charles H. Elston, Ohio
Forest A. Harness, Indiana

Ivor D. Fenton, Pennsylvania
J. Leroy Johnson, California
Clare Boothe Luce, Connecticut

Joseph R. Farrington, Hawaii
E. L. Bartlett, Alaska
Jesus Piñero, Puerto Rico

JOINT COMMITTEE ON ATOMIC ENERGY
In approximate chronological order

Member	Congress
Sen. Brien McMahon, Connecticut	79–82 (*Chairman:* 79, 81, 82)
Rep. R. Ewing Thomason, Texas	79 (*Vice-Chairman:* 79)
Sen. Richard B. Russell, Georgia	79–91
Sen. Edwin C. Johnson, Colorado	79–82
Sen. Tom Connally, Texas	79–81
Sen. Harry Flood Byrd, Virginia	79
Sen. Arthur Vandenberg, Michigan	79–80
Sen. Eugene D. Millikin, Colorado	79–84
Sen. Bourke B. Hickenlooper, Iowa	79–90
Sen. William F. Knowland, California	79–85
Rep. Carl T. Durham, North Carolina	79–86 (*Chairman:* 85; *Vice-Chairman:* 81, 82, 84, 86)
Rep. Aime Forrand, Rhode Island	79
Rep. Chet Holifield, California	79–92 (*Chairman:* 87, 89, 91; *Vice-Chairman:* 88, 90)
Rep. Melvin Price, Illinois	79–92 (*Vice-Chairman:* 92)
Rep. Charles H. Elston, Ohio	79–82
Rep. J. Parnell Thomas, New Jersey	79
Rep. Clare Boothe Luce, Connecticut	79
Rep. Sterling Cole, New York	80–85 (*Chairman:* 83; *Vice-Chairman:* 80)
Sen. John W. Bricker, Ohio	80–85
Rep. James E. Van Zandt, Pennsylvania	80–87
Rep. James T. Patterson, Connecticut	80, 83–85
Rep. Lyndon B. Johnson, Texas	80, *Senate Member:* 82
Sen. Millard E. Tydings, Maryland	81

Rep. Paul J. Kilday, Texas	81–85
Rep. Henry M. Jackson, Washington	81–82, *Senate Member:* 84–92
Sen. Clinton P. Anderson, New Mexico	82–92 (*Chairman:* 84, 86; *Vice-Chairman:* 85)
Rep. Thomas A. Jenkins, Ohio	83, 85
Sen. Guy R. Cordon, Oregon	83
Sen. John O. Pastore, Rhode Island	83–92 (*Chairman:* 88, 90, 92; *Vice-Chairman:* 87, 89, 91)
Sen. Albert Gore, Tennessee	83–91
Rep. John J. Dempsey, New Mexico	84
Rep. Wayne N. Aspinall, Colorado	85–92
Rep. Craig Hosmer, California	85–92
Sen. Henry Dworshak, Idaho	85–87
Sen. George D. Aiken, Vermont	86–92
Sen. Wallace F. Bennett, Utah	86–92
Rep. Albert Thomas, Texas	86–89
Rep. William H. Bates, Massachusetts	86–90
Rep. Jack Westland, Washington	86–88
Rep. Thomas G. Morris, New Mexico	87–90
Sen. Carl T. Curtis, Nebraska	88–91
Rep. John B. Anderson, Illinois	88–92
Rep. William M. McCullough, Ohio	89–92
Rep. John Young, Texas	90–92
Rep. Ed Edmondson, Oklahoma	91–92
Rep. Catherine May, Washington	91
Sen. Norris Cotton, New Hampshire	91
Sen. Stuart Symington, Missouri	92
Sen. Alan Bible, Nevada	92
Sen. Peter H. Dominick, Colorado	92
Sen. Howard H. Baker, Jr., Tennessee	92
Rep. Orval Hansen, Idaho	92

EXECUTIVE DIRECTORS OF THE
JOINT COMMITTEE ON ATOMIC ENERGY

*Executive Director**	*From*	*To*
Fred B. Rhodes, Jr.	Feb. 13, 1947	Jan. 27, 1949
William L. Borden	Jan. 28, 1949	Sept. 30, 1953

* Christopher T. Boland was staff director of the Senate Special Committee on Atomic Energy, November 15, 1945, and served on the Joint Committee as staff director until January 9, 1947.

Corbin A. Allardice	Oct. 1, 1953	Sept. 30, 1955
James T. Ramey	Apr. 1, 1956	Aug. 30, 1962
John T. Conway	Sept. 19, 1962	Oct. 31, 1968
Edward J. Bauser	Nov. 1, 1968	

Appendix D
Nuclear Power Reactors
in the United States

A map showing locations of U.S. nuclear power reactors will be found on pages 118–19. The following three pages list nuclear power reactors by states, giving the site of each reactor, the plant name, the capacity in net kilowatts, the utility, and the year in which power was first (or will first be) made available.

SITE	PLANT NAME	CAPACITY (Net Kilowatts)	UTILITY	INITIAL DESIGN POWER
ALABAMA				
Decatur	Browns Ferry Nuclear Power Plant: Unit 1	1,065,000	Tennessee Valley Authority	1973
Decatur	Browns Ferry Nuclear Power Plant: Unit 2	1,065,000	Tennessee Valley Authority	1974
Decatur	Browns Ferry Nuclear Power Plant: Unit 3	1,065,000	Tennessee Valley Authority	1974
Dothan	Joseph M. Farley Nuclear Plant: Unit 1	829,000	Alabama Power Co.	1975
Dothan	Joseph M. Farley Nuclear Plant: Unit 2	829,000	Alabama Power Co.	1977
Selma	Orville: Unit 1	1,100,000	Alabama Power Co.	1981
Selma	Orville: Unit 2	1,100,000	Alabama Power Co.	1982
ARKANSAS				
Russellville	Arkansas Nuclear One: Unit 1	820,000	Arkansas Power & Light Co.	1973
Russellville	Arkansas Nuclear One: Unit 2	920,000	Arkansas Power & Light Co.	1976
CALIFORNIA				
Humboldt Bay	Humboldt Bay Power Plant: Unit 3	68,500	Pacific Gas and Electric Co.	1963
San Clemente	San Onofre Nuclear Generating Station: Unit 1	430,000	So. Calif. Ed. & San Diego Gas & El. Co.	1967
San Clemente	San Onofre Nuclear Generating Station: Unit 2	1,140,000	So. Calif. Ed. & San Diego Gas & El. Co.	–
San Clemente	San Onofre Nuclear Generating Station: Unit 3	1,140,000	So. Calif. Ed. & San Diego Gas & El. Co.	–
Diablo Canyon	Diablo Canyon Nuclear Power Plant: Unit 1	1,060,000	Pacific Gas and Electric Co.	1974
Diablo Canyon	Diablo Canyon Nuclear Power Plant: Unit 2	1,060,000	Pacific Gas and Electric Co.	1975
Clay Station	Rancho Seco Nuclear Generating Station	804,000	Sacramento Municipal Utility District	1974
Pt. Arena	Mendocino Power Plant: Unit 1	1,128,000	Pacific Gas & Electric Co.	1978
Pt. Arena	Mendocino Power Plant: Unit 2	1,128,000	Pacific Gas & Electric Co.	1979
*	–	770,000	Southern California Edison Co.	1981
*	–	770,000	Southern California Edison Co.	1982
COLORADO				
Platteville	Ft. St. Vrain Nuclear Generating Station	330,000	Public Service Co. of Colorado	1973
CONNECTICUT				
Haddam Neck	Haddam Neck Plant	575,000	Conn. Yankee Atomic Power Co.	1967
Waterford	Millstone Nuclear Power Station: Unit 1	652,100	Northeast Utilities	1970
Waterford	Millstone Nuclear Power Station: Unit 2	828,000	Northeast Utilities	1974
DELAWARE				
Middletown	Delmarva Unit 1	770,000	Delmarva Power & Light Co.	1978
Middletown	Delmarva Unit 2	770,000	Delmarva Power & Light Co.	1981
FLORIDA				
Turkey Point	Turkey Point Station: Unit 3	693,000	Florida Power & Light Co.	1972
Turkey Point	Turkey Point Station: Unit 4	693,000	Florida Power & Light Co.	1973
Red Level	Crystal River Plant: Unit 3	825,000	Florida Power Corp.	1973
Ft. Pierce	St. Lucie Plant: Unit 1	800,000	Florida Power & Light Co.	1975
Ft. Pierce	St. Lucie Plant: Unit 2	890,000	Florida Power & Light Co.	1979
GEORGIA				
Baxley	Edwin I. Hatch Nuclear Plant: Unit 1	786,000	Georgia Power Co.	1973
Baxley	Edwin I. Hatch Nuclear Plant: Unit 2	786,000	Georgia Power Co.	1976
Waynesboro	Alvin W. Vogtle, Jr. Plant: Unit 1	1,105,000	Georgia Power Co.	1978
Waynesboro	Alvin W. Vogtle, Jr. Plant: Unit 2	1,105,000	Georgia Power Co.	1979
ILLINOIS				
Morris	Dresden Nuclear Power Station: Unit 1	200,000	Commonwealth Edison Co.	1960
Morris	Dresden Nuclear Power Station: Unit 2	800,000	Commonwealth Edison Co.	1970
Morris	Dresden Nuclear Power Station: Unit 3	800,000	Commonwealth Edison Co.	1972
Zion	Zion Nuclear Plant: Unit 1	1,050,000	Commonwealth Edison Co.	1972
Zion	Zion Nuclear Plant: Unit 2	1,050,000	Commonwealth Edison Co.	1973
Cordova	Quad-Cities Station: Unit 1	800,000	Comm. Ed. Co.-Ia.-Ill. Gas & Elec. Co.	1972
Cordova	Quad-Cities Station: Unit 2	800,000	Comm. Ed. Co.-Ia.-Ill. Gas & Elec. Co.	1972
Seneca	LaSalle Co. Nuclear Station: Unit 1	1,078,000	Comm. Ed. Co.-Ia.	1977
Seneca	LaSalle Co. Nuclear Station: Unit 2	1,078,000	Comm. Ed. Co.-Ia.	1978
Byron	Byron Station: Unit 1	1,120,000	Comm. Edison Co.	1979
Byron	Byron Station: Unit 2	1,120,000	Comm. Edison Co.	1980
Braidwood	Braidwood: Unit 1	1,100,000		1980
Braidwood	Braidwood: Unit 2	1,100,000		1981
INDIANA				
Dune Acres	Bailly Generating Station	660,000	Northern Indiana Public Service Co.	1977
IOWA				
Palo	Duane Arnold Energy Center: Unit 1	529,700	Iowa Electric Light and Power Co.	1973
LOUISIANA				
Taft	Waterford Generating Station	1,165,000	Louisiana Power & Light Co.	1976
St. Francisville	River Bend Station	940,000	Gulf States Utilities Co.	1979

SITE	PLANT NAME	CAPACITY (Net Kilowatts)	UTILITY	INITIAL DESIGN POWER
MAINE				
Wiscasset	Maine Yankee Atomic Power Plant	790,000	Maine Yankee Atomic Power Co.	1972
MARYLAND				
Lusby	Calvert Cliffs Nuclear Power Plant: Unit 1	845,000	Baltimore Gas and Electric Co.	1974
Lusby	Calvert Cliffs Nuclear Power Plant: Unit 2	845,000	Baltimore Gas and Electric Co.	1974
Douglas Point	Douglas Point Project: Unit 1	1,100,000	Potomac Electric Power Co.	1980
Douglas Point	Douglas Point Project: Unit 2	1,100,000	Potomac Electric Power Co.	1981
MASSACHUSETTS				
Rowe	Yankee Nuclear Power Station	175,000	Yankee Atomic Electric Co.	1961
Plymouth	Pilgrim Station: Unit 1	655,000	Boston Edison Co.	1972
Plymouth	Pilgrim Station: Unit 2	1,180,000	Boston Edison Co.	1978
MICHIGAN				
Big Rock Point	Big Rock Point Nuclear Plant	70,300	Consumers Power Co.	1963
South Haven	Palisades Nuclear Power Station	700,000	Consumers Power Co.	1971
Lagoona Beach	Enrico Fermi Atomic Power Plant: Unit 2	1,123,000	Detroit Edison Co.	1976
Lagoona Beach	Enrico Fermi Atomic Power Plant: Unit 3	1,124,000	Detroit Edison Co.	1980
Bridgman	Donald C. Cook Plant: Unit 1	1,060,000	Indiana & Michigan Electric Co.	1973
Bridgman	Donald C. Cook Plant: Unit 2	1,060,000	Indiana & Michigan Electric Co.	1974
Midland	Midland Nuclear Power Plant: Unit 1	492,000	Consumers Power Co.	1977
Midland	Midland Nuclear Power Plant: Unit 2	818,000	Consumers Power Co.	1978
St. Clair County	Greenwood: Unit 2	1,240,000	Detroit Edison Co.	1979
St. Clair County	Greenwood: Unit 3	1,240,000	Detroit Edison Co.	1981
Quanicassee	Quanicassee: Unit 1	1,150,000	Consumers Power Co.	1981
Quanicassee	Quanicassee: Unit 2	1,150,000	Consumers Power Co.	1981
MINNESOTA				
Monticello	Monticello Nuclear Generating Plant	545,000	Northern States Power Co.	1971
Red Wing	Prairie Island Nuclear Generating Plant: Unit 1	530,000	Northern States Power Co.	1973
Red Wing	Prairie Island Nuclear Generating Plant: Unit 2	530,000	Northern States Power Co.	1974
MISSISSIPPI				
Port Gibson	Grand Gulf Nuclear Station	1,275,000	Mississippi Power & Light Co.	1978
NEBRASKA				
Fort Calhoun	Ft. Calhoun Station: Unit 1	457,400	Omaha Public Power District	1973
Brownville	Cooper Nuclear Station	778,000	Nebraska Public Power District and Iowa Power and Light Co.	1973
NEW HAMPSHIRE				
Seabrook	–	1,100,000	Public Service of N.H.	1979
Seabrook	–	1,100,000	Public Service of N.H.	1981
NEW JERSEY				
Toms River	Oyster Creek Nuclear Power Plant: Unit 1	640,000	Jersey Central Power & Light Co.	1969
Forked River	Forked River Generating Station: Unit 1	1,070,000	Jersey Central Power & Light Co.	1978
Salem	Salem Nuclear Generating Station: Unit 1	1,090,000	Public Service Electric and Gas, N.J.	1974
Salem	Salem Nuclear Generating Station: Unit 2	1,115,000	Public Service Electric and Gas, N.J.	1975
Bordentown	Newbold Nuclear Generating Station: Unit 1	1,067,000	Public Service Electric and Gas, N.J.	1978
Bordentown	Newbold Nuclear Generating Station: Unit 2	1,067,000	Public Service Electric and Gas, N.J.	1979
Little Egg Inlet	Atlantic Generating Station: Unit 1	1,150,000	Public Service Electric and Gas, N.J.	1980
Little Egg Inlet	Atlantic Generating Station: Unit 2	1,150,000	Public Service Electric and Gas, N.J.	1981
NEW YORK				
Indian Point	Indian Point Station: Unit 1	265,000	Consolidated Edison Co.	1963
Indian Point	Indian Point Station: Unit 2	873,000	Consolidated Edison Co.	1973
Indian Point	Indian Point Station: Unit 3	965,000	Consolidated Edison Co.	1974
Scriba	Nine Mile Point Nuclear Station: Unit 1	625,000	Niagara Mohawk Power Co.	1970
Scriba	Nine Mile Point Nuclear Station: Unit 2	1,080,000	Niagara Mohawk Power Co.	1978
Ontario	R. E. Ginna Nuclear Power Plant: Unit 1	420,000	Rochester Gas & Electric Co.	1970
Brookhaven	Shoreham Nuclear Power Station	819,000	Long Island Lighting Co.	1977
Scriba	James A. Fitzpatrick Nuclear Power Plant	821,000	Power Authority of State of N.Y.	1973
NORTH CAROLINA				
Southport	Brunswick Steam Electric Plant: Unit 1	821,000	Carolina Power and Light Co.	1975
Southport	Brunswick Steam Electric Plant: Unit 2	821,000	Carolina Power and Light Co.	1974
Cowans Ford Dam	Wm. B. McGuire Nuclear Station: Unit 1	1,180,000	Duke Power Co.	1975
Cowans Ford Dam	Wm. B. McGuire Nuclear Station: Unit 2	1,180,000	Duke Power Co.	1977
Bonsal	Shearun Harris Plant: Unit 1	915,000	Carolina Power & Light Co.	1977
Bonsal	Shearun Harris Plant: Unit 2	915,000	Carolina Power & Light Co.	1978
Bonsal	Shearun Harris Plant: Unit 3	915,000	Carolina Power & Light Co.	1979
Bonsal	Shearun Harris Plant: Unit 4	915,000	Carolina Power & Light Co.	1980

225

SITE	PLANT NAME	CAPACITY (Net Kilowatts)	UTILITY	INITIAL DESIGN POWER
OHIO				
Oak Harbor	Davis-Besse Nuclear Power Station	872,000	Toledo Edison-Cleveland Electric Illuminating Co.	1974
Painesville	Perry Nuclear Power Plant: Unit 1	1,100,000	Cleveland Electric Illuminating Co.	1979
Painesville	Perry Nuclear Power Plant: Unit 2	1,100,000	Cleveland Electric Illuminating Co.	1980
Moscow	Wm. H. Zimmer Nuclear Power Station: Unit 1	810,000	Cincinnati Gas & Electric Co.	1976
OREGON				
Prescott	Trojan Nuclear Plant: Unit 1	1,130,000	Portland General Electric Co.	1975
PENNSYLVANIA				
Peach Bottom	Peach Bottom Atomic Power Station: Unit 1	40,000	Philadelphia Electric Co.	1967
Peach Bottom	Peach Bottom Atomic Power Station: Unit 2	1,065,000	Philadelphia Electric Co.	1973
Peach Bottom	Peach Bottom Atomic Power Station: Unit 3	1,065,000	Philadelphia Electric Co.	1974
Pottstown	Limerick Generating Station: Unit 1	1,065,000	Philadelphia Electric Co.	1978
Pottstown	Limerick Generating Station: Unit 2	1,065,000	Philadelphia Electric Co.	1979
Shippingport	Shippingport Atomic Power Station: Unit 1	90,000	Duquesne Light Co.	1957
Shippingport	Beaver Valley Power Station: Unit 1	852,000	Duquesne Light Co.-Ohio Edison Co.	1974
Shippingport	Beaver Valley Power Station: Unit 2	852,000	Duquesne Light Co.-Ohio Edison Co.	1978
Goldsboro	Three Mile Island Nuclear Station: Unit 1	819,000	Metropolitan Edison Co.	1973
Goldsboro	Three Mile Island Nuclear Station: Unit 2	905,000	Jersey Central Power & Light Co.	1975
Berwick	Susquehanna Steam Electric Station: Unit 1	1,052,000	Pennsylvania Power and Light	1979
Berwick	Susquehanna Steam Electric Station: Unit 2	1,052,000	Pennsylvania Power and Light	1981
*	Philadelphia Electric Co.: HTGR No. 1	1,140,000	Philadelphia Electric Co.	1979
*	Philadelphia Electric Co.: HTGR No. 2	1,140,000	Philadelphia Electric Co.	1981
SOUTH CAROLINA				
Hartsville	H. B. Robinson S.E. Plant: Unit 2	700,000	Carolina Power & Light Co.	1971
Seneca	Oconee Nuclear Station: Unit 1	841,000	Duke Power Co.	1972
Seneca	Oconee Nuclear Station: Unit 2	886,000	Duke Power Co.	1973
Seneca	Oconee Nuclear Station: Unit 3	886,000	Duke Power Co.	1973
Broad River	Virgil C. Summer Nuclear Station: Unit 1	900,000	South Carolina Electric & Gas Co.	1977
Lake Wylie	Catawba Nuclear Station: Unit 1	1,180,000	Duke Power Co.	1979
Lake Wylie	Catawba Nuclear Station: Unit 2	1,180,000	Duke Power Co.	1980
TENNESSEE				
Daisy	Sequoyah Nuclear Power Plant: Unit 1	1,140,000	Tennessee Valley Authority	1974
Daisy	Sequoyah Nuclear Power Plant: Unit 2	1,140,000	Tennessee Valley Authority	1975
Spring City	Watts Bar Nuclear Plant: Unit 1	1,169,000	Tennessee Valley Authority	1977
Spring City	Watts Bar Nuclear Plant: Unit 2	1,169,000	Tennessee Valley Authority	1978
Oak Ridge	Fast Breeder Demonstration Plant	400,000	Tennessee Valley Authority	1980
TEXAS				
Glen Rose	Commanche Peak Steam Electric Station: Unit 1	1,150,000	Texas Power & Light	1980
Glen Rose	Commanche Peak Steam Electric Station: Unit 2	1,150,000	Texas Power & Light	1982
VERMONT				
Vernon	Vermont Yankee Generating Station	513,900	Vermont Yankee Nuclear Power Corp.	1972
VIRGINIA				
Gravel Neck	Surry Power Station: Unit 1	788,000	Virginia Electric & Power Co.	1972
Gravel Neck	Surry Power Station: Unit 2	788,000	Virginia Electric & Power Co.	1973
Mineral	North Anna Power Station: Unit 1	898,000	Virginia Electric & Power Co.	1974
Mineral	North Anna Power Station: Unit 2	898,000	Virginia Electric & Power Co.	1975
Mineral	North Anna Power Station: Unit 3	900,000	Virginia Electric & Power Co.	1977
Mineral	North Anna Power Station: Unit 4	900,000	Virginia Electric & Power Co.	1978
WASHINGTON				
Richland	N-Reactor/WPPSS Steam	800,000	Atomic Energy Commission	1966
Richland	Hanford No. 1	1,120,000	Washington Public Power Supply System	1980
Richland	Hanford No. 2	1,103,000	Washington Public Power Supply System	1977
WISCONSIN				
Genoa	Genoa Nuclear Generating Station	53,200	Dairyland Power Cooperative	1969
Two Creeks	Point Beach Nuclear Plant: Unit 1	497,000	Wisconsin Michigan Power Co.	1971
Two Creeks	Point Beach Nuclear Plant: Unit 2	497,000	Wisconsin Michigan Power Co.	1972
Carlton	Kewaunee Nuclear Power Plant: Unit 1	541,000	Wisconsin Michigan Power Co.	1972
PUERTO RICO				
Puerto De Jobas	Aguirre Nuclear Power Plant	583,000	Puerto Rico Water Resources Authority	1975

* Site not selected.

Bibliography

See also the section on "Technical Information"
in Chapter VI

COMPTON, ARTHUR H. *Atomic Quest*. New York: Oxford, 1956.

FERMI, LAURA. *Atoms in the Family: My Life with Enrico Fermi*. Chicago: University of Chicago Press, 1954.

The First Reactor (including "The First Pile," by Corbin Allardice and Edward R. Trapnell; "Fermi's Own Story," by Enrico Fermi; "Of Secrecy and the Pile," by Laura Fermi). Oak Ridge: USAEC Division of Technical Information Extension, 1967.

FOREMAN, HARRY, ed. *Nuclear Power and the Public*. Minneapolis: University of Minnesota Press, 1971.

GLASSTONE, SAMUEL. *Sourcebook on Atomic Energy*. 3rd ed. New York: Van Nostrand, 1967.

GROUEFF, STEPHANE. *Manhattan Project: The Untold Story of the Making of the Atomic Bomb*. Boston: Little, Brown, 1967.

GROVES, LESLIE R. *Now It Can Be Told: The Story of the Manhattan Project*. New York: Harper and Row, 1962.

HEWLETT, RICHARD G., and OSCAR E. ANDERSON, JR. *History of the United States Atomic Energy Commission*. Vol. I. *The New World, 1939/1946*. Vol. II. *Atomic Shield, 1947/1952*. University Park: Pennsylvania State University Press, 1962, 1969.

HOGERTON, JOHN F. *The Atomic Energy Deskbook*. New York: Van Nostrand, 1963.

LAWRENCE, WILLIAM. *Men and Atoms*. New York: Simon and Schuster, 1959.

Lewis, Richard S. *The Nuclear-Power Rebellion: Citizens vs. the Atomic Industrial Establishment.* New York: Viking, 1972.

Michelmore, Peter. *The Swift Years: The Robert Oppenheimer Story.* New York: Dodd, Mead, 1962.

Seaborg, Glenn T., and William R. Corliss. *Man and Atom: Shaping a New World Through Nuclear Technology.* New York: Dutton, 1971.

Seaborg, Glenn T., and Daniel M. Wilkes. *Education and the Atom.* New York: McGraw-Hill, 1964.

Serber, Robert G., Victor F. Weisskopf, Abraham Pais, and Glenn T. Seaborg. *Oppenheimer.* New York: Scribner's, 1969.

Smyth, Henry D. *Atomic Energy for Military Purposes.* Princeton: Princeton University Press, 1945.

Stern, Philip M. *The Oppenheimer Case: Security on Trial.* With the collaboration of Harold P. Green. New York: Harper and Row, 1969.

Woodbury, David O. *Atoms for Peace.* Rev. ed. New York: Dodd, Mead, 1965.

Zinn, Walter H., Frank K. Pittman, and John R. Hogerton. *Nuclear Power, U.S.A.* New York: McGraw-Hill, 1964.

Index